CULTURE AND TERROR

CULTURE AND TERROR

THE JACKAL AND THE PHOENIX IN AMERICA

7/04

To Coleen Rowley,

with my thanks

Karen A. Larson

KAREN A. LARSON

To order additional copies of this book, contact:
Xlibris Corporation
1-888-795-4274
www.Xlibris.com
Orders@Xlibris.com

22168

CONTENTS

FOREWORD 11

PREFACE 15

ACKNOWLEDGMENTS..19

INTRODUCTION: AMERICAN CONSCIOUSNESS 21

CHAPTER 1: PATTERNS OF TERROR 51

CHAPTER 2: CAN'T KEEP TRACK 86

CHAPTER 3: PSYCHOLOGICAL GROUND ZERO 115

CHAPTER 4: SYMBOL SHIFTS..................................... 141

CHAPTER 5: CONNECTING THE DOTS 177

CHAPTER 6: REFORGING COMMUNITY 192

CHAPTER 7: AMERICAN INTELLIGENCE 221

CONCLUSION: REGENERATION 265

NOTES 279

INDEX 293

To Joe Bluth, for reminding me how much this book needed to be written, and to Laura Larson-Cody, for reminding me why.

History is made by active, determined minorities, not by the majority, which seldom has a clear and consistent idea of what it really wants.

—Theodore Kaczynski

Never doubt that a small group of thoughtful committed citizens can change the world.

—Margaret Mead

We just want a better America
A place we feel good about
A place where our kids can grow up
With a government they don't have to doubt

—Matthew Hennek

FOREWORD

I wrote the words of inspiration that follow for *Newsday*'s young student readers. The goal was to provide a measure of comfort to junior high-aged readers who had been traumatized by the attacks on the World Trade Center and felt that there was little or nothing they could do to protect themselves from future attacks. My letter was entitled both "Step Up to the Plate," and "Honesty Makes America Strong." It appeared on *Newsday*'s June 2, 2003, "Student Briefing Page."

At the time, it was easy to see the havoc and senseless panic that had been engendered, not only in young people, but in average citizens, by the series of up-and-down "orange alerts" the government had issued in the wake of the horrible terrorist attacks on September 11. People were running to stores to stock up on duct tape, in a futile effort to gain some control over their fears. People were looking for easy answers, which made them more susceptible to the idea that launching a war against Iraq was the cure. To this day, one of the most frequent questions I am asked is: "What can I, as an ordinary citizen, do to combat terrorism?"

Unfortunately, duct tape and war are not the answer. The true answer is not that simple because defending and strengthening our country requires citizens on every level, from every profession and every walk of life, not only to remain vigilant, but also to take steps to reverse the internal decay that, despite the shock of 9/11, continues to plague our country in many forms—violent crime, drug abuse, corporate greed, dishonesty, and exploitation of the weak, including children. If we are truly patriotic, we must do more than just fly our flags. We must all look inwards, make healthy changes, and seek to reverse the internal rot that weakens us as a country.

It is obvious from reading her book that the author has devoted a great deal of personal and professional attention to these same issues, from her perspectives as a college professor and a cultural anthropologist. In this volume, she outlines ways in which Americans can think about their role as ordinary citizens in combating terror in America. There is horrible potential blowback to our society if we do not get our response to terrorism right. What does it mean that Tim McVeigh, sniper John Muhammad, and Robert Flores, who killed three University of Arizona nursing professors and then shot himself, were all products of the first Gulf War? What impact do the terrorists of one American generation have on the next generation? These are questions that Americans need to ask and answer—answer both in their minds and in their conduct as citizens.

Dr. Larson and I both believe that America's best hope for a strong response to terrorism lies in America's youth. Readers of this volume should understand the good news that we can and should scrap the duct tape, fear, and goofy conspiracy theories, and remain vigilant against all forms of crime and violence, by using the power we all have as ordinary citizens, old and young, rich and poor, to "fight terrorism" and make the world a better place:

Dear Students,

> *Our country needs you! We live in tense, dangerous times since terrorism has struck inside the United States, killing almost 3000 of our citizens and severely damaging our economy. It's easy to feel like a helpless victim or to allow senseless panic to take over, but there is something you can and must do. More than ever, our country, in order to rebuild itself, needs you to step up to the plate and be a person of integrity.*
>
> *Time magazine last year named WorldCom auditor Cynthia Cooper, former Enron executive Sherron Watkins and myself as their Persons of the Year for 2002. We were all surprised and shocked because none of us had discovered a new vaccine to cure an incurable disease; none of us had*

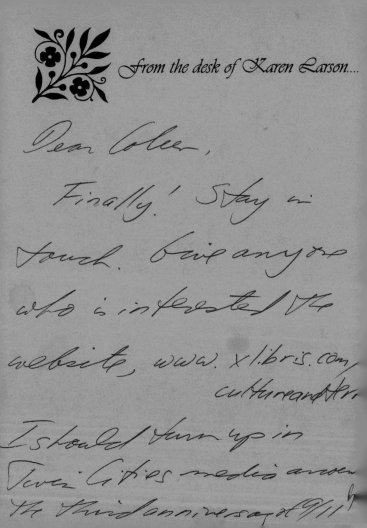

from the desk of Karen Larson....

Dear Colleen,

Finally! Stay in
touch. Give anyone
who is interested the
website, www.xlibris.com,
                    cultureandthe

I should turn up in
Twin Cities media around
the third anniversary of 9/11

produced a new strain of drought-resistant grain that could easily feed the world's people, and none of us had saved anyone from a burning building. We are just ordinary people, like you.

Then why were we chosen? I believe it was for having the guts to stand up and tell the truth as we saw it to powerful institutions. Telling the truth matters. Our country, as Time writes, "requires that people trust in the integrity of public and private institutions alike."

The primary element in trust is telling the truth. If government and private institutions lie or don't disclose the full truth, people will begin to distrust them even when they are telling the truth. Citizens need to know that companies aren't cheating their stockholders. They need to know that companies are playing fair and by the rules. Citizens need to know about mistakes in government so that those mistakes can be fixed. If citizens are deceived, they will begin to distrust the institutions they depend on. Or, worse, they will believe that because others are dishonest, they can be, too.

What can you do? And why does our country need you? Our institutions are only as good as the character of the people in them. You can grow up to be a person of integrity, knowing right from wrong and acting on it, telling the truth, accepting responsibility for your mistakes, learning from those mistakes, and treating others the way you would want to be treated. Good people trying to do the right thing is what makes our country great and, ultimately, less of a target for terrorism. Just as we have firmly shut our airplane cockpit doors in order to keep terrorists out, we must also shut the door on the greed, vice and dishonesty that weaken us as a nation.

A few months ago, a survey showed 70 percent of high school students admitted to cheating on tests and seeing nothing wrong with it! Additionally, many students—sometimes even athletes—are lured into using illegal and harmful drugs. Many young people are threatened by fellow students at school. If you cheat or hurt yourself by taking drugs or injure others now by fighting, what will you do as an adult?

You've probably heard adults tell you that the choices you make now will determine, in many ways, where you end up as an adult. You may even be tired of hearing this stuff. So tell them you don't need this lecture—that you are already working to make the right choices.

You can start—if you haven't already—by studying hard so you'll be qualified for a good job (and this way, you won't need to cheat on tests!); you can come to the aid of those who are being bullied; and you can take enough pride in yourself to resist those who would pressure you into doing alcohol and doing drugs. You'll already be well on your way to becoming a mature person of goodwill, compassion, and integrity—a role model to younger students and the kind of leader our country needs!

For as necessary as it may be to seal our borders from external threats, it will also be necessary for you, our new American leaders, to battle a major internal threat—the temptation each of us face to give in to our dark side. Failure to recognize and overcome this temptation will endanger America's security as much as—or maybe even more than—international terrorism.

Yours sincerely,
Coleen Rowley
Copyright © 2003, Newsday, Inc.

PREFACE

On September 11, 2001, at 1:30 p.m. (EST), after giving radio commentary on the cultural effects that the day's crisis had already begun to have on America, and in anticipation of a television crew, I stepped into my college classroom in cultural anthropology. Before talking about facts and impacts, I told the students a story. Immediately after the bombing of Hiroshima, anthropologist Margaret Mead had taken a book manuscript and torn it up. What she had intended to say about American culture no longer applied: "No sentence . . . could be meshed into any sentence written the week before."[1] Her manuscript was outdated. Into the trash it went, as humanity entered a new age. It took a few days, more media interviews, and the process of writing an opinion editorial piece for the *St. Paul Pioneer Press*, before I realized that the time was right for me not to tear up a book manuscript, but start one. More accurately, it was time to resurrect one.

My partial manuscript was from the days of my encounter with the Unabomber case, an experience that had reached deep into my cultural and personal roots, as well as my professional expertise as a cultural anthropologist. The Unabomber case invited me, while profiling the perpetrator for the FBI, to turn an analytical eye on American culture in a new way. The case swept me up into a question about whether a depressed man I had known when I was a graduate student in anthropology at the University of California at Berkeley at the beginning of the 1970s might also be the man the FBI wanted. My psychological and cultural profile of the man I knew caught the essence of an American subculture of that time and place, even though its subject did not turn out to be the Unabomber himself. Still, integrating personal experience and research on depression in America into my profiling work created a nexus of consciousness that tied together mental health, American culture, and terrorism. As I worked, a related drama, involving Tim McVeigh and Oklahoma City, unfolded and intertwined with the Unabomber story. Both were headline stories within a larger and emerging pattern of terror in American culture.

On September 11, several things came full circle. One of them was several years of teaching a seminar about how cultural evolution is coming full circle instead of describing a simple straight line. The relationship of terrorism to American mental health also closed into a pattern, which this time involved victims as well as perpetrators. American psychologists began to talk again about the "national psyche," rejoining the focus in psychological anthropology on the relationship between psychology and culture that the two disciplines had shared decades earlier. Psychological anthropology has its roots, in part, in Margaret Mead's work on American personality and culture, some of which was thrown in the trash after Hiroshima. Psychologists now used culture to help explain terrorism. The circle joining American national character and terrorism closed not just in my mind, but also in the academic culture around me. The direction of American culture and my relationship with the Unabomber also came together into a full circle.

A nagging voice gave me a growing sense of daring. The voice belonged to a colleague, who years previously had compared the breadth of the subject matter I studied in cultural anthropology with the topical breadth of the work of Margaret Mead herself. It is not the fashion in anthropology today to range that broadly. Specialization is the norm, and few tackle subjects as broad as American culture as a whole. Perhaps I had just come back into fashion, and could communicate with the public about American culture. The idea of culture in America became a growth concept after 9/11. One heard about the culture of the FBI, the culture of youth sports, and the culture of vigilance. One of the changes in post-9/11 American culture was that the concept of culture was back in American consciousness. People tried to understand ephemeral cultural shifts that were occurring, as the idea of culture itself floated around in a rapidly shifting American conceptual ether. People who tried to create cultural change did not always have a clear notion of what they were talking about. The whole business was a bit hazy. It might be a good time to be an anthropologist.

Karen A. Larson
September 13, 2003

ACKNOWLEDGMENTS

This writing is nuanced with the effects of many interactions with students, who have contributed to the text, both through intellectual ferment and editorial comments. American students of many national origins professed their conviction of the book's importance, fueling my will to write it. It is written, in turn, for them, and for the culture that they will soon direct. Of the many, the names of Amna Agha, Erik Dinsmore, Matthew Hennek, Carl Nelson, and Graziela Tanaka cannot be omitted. I am also indebted to many public servants for conversations concerning homeland security, including employees of the CIA, the Department of Defense, the Department of Homeland Security, the FBI, and the NSA.

Others who helped or inspired were Alan Bray, Mark Braun, Nancy Butler, Chris Cody, Deborah Downs-Miers, Barbara Fister, Beau Friedlander, Mark Gabriele, Patric Giesler, Steve Hogberg, Janet Dixon Keller, Eleanor Larson, Lou Marano, Julie Mayo, Marina Pisano, Leigh Pomeroy, Jeana Rogers, Sugo Satoshi, Darrell Shaffer, Barbara Simpson, Pete Steiner, Michelle Twait, and David Wellenbrock.

INTRODUCTION

AMERICAN CONSCIOUSNESS

TERROR AND TERRORISM

Terrorism in America is elusive. Difficult to prevent, or even understand, part of its power lies simply in the mystery of its existence. Its perpetrators are hard to find, and even the concepts of terror and terrorism are moving targets. Terrorism can overlap with war or with crime, but within America it is the boundary between terrorism and crime that has begun to blur. Americans are generating terror at the same time that they respond to its impact on their culture. Some think of terrorism as something that comes only from outside America, and is perpetrated only by groups. But whether the terror is generated by outsiders or insiders, it is unquestionably a growth sector in America's national consciousness. The enormity of America's problem with terror demands attention to both of its sources. Whether the "terrortory" in America grows or declines does not depend just on what perpetrators do. It also depends on the thinking and actions of everyone else.

Definitions of terrorism from academic sources and organizations like the United Nations, the U.S. Department of State, and the FBI, have four recurrent elements:

1. Terrorism is *political*, prompted by concerns such as religious, ethnic, and other forms of social identity or ideology.

2. Terrorism is *public*, aimed at an audience beyond its direct victims.
3. Terrorism is *violent*, physically and mentally, through intimidation and coercion.
4. Terrorism is *psychological*, intended to adversely affect the psyche of indirect victims by instilling fear.

America's post-9/11 forgetfulness about the tradition of terror in America emerged, even as the functional distinction between "international" and "domestic" terrorism eroded. America's domestic pattern of terror was already largely opaque to American consciousness before 9/11, because of the tendency for Americans to dismiss each of their own terrorists as a deviant individual. With that backdrop, the severity of the 9/11 blow to the national consciousness made blaming the problem of terror entirely on a non-American "them" easy. A culture enamored of convenience and ease turned its consciousness even further down the path of not perceiving terrorism as an American cultural problem.

Associating terrorism only with groups also enhanced America's denial of its own problems. A culture of individualism has produced a tradition of "lone" American terrorists, who act substantially alone, and are motivated to act partly because they feel isolated and alone in American society. The stereotypical image of the "lone" American terrorist is an antihero update of the icon of the lone American hero, and both have a basis in American patterns of social isolation. Associating terrorism only with groups diverts attention away from seeing it also as a pattern in an individualistic culture. Although some American terrorists function in groups, the accompanying trend to the "lone" end of the spectrum makes America's tradition of terrorism invisible, if terrorism is regarded only as a group phenomenon.

Other elements of the current American folk definition of terror also look aside from America as a source of terror. Some Americans classify Tim McVeigh as a terrorist, based not on whether or not he acted alone, but on the amount of damage he did. McVeigh's standing as a terrorist is assured because of the magnitude of his impact, but some do not regard his countryman, Ted Kaczynski, as a terrorist. Kaczynski's acts were public, political, psychological, and violent, but he did not kill as many people. McVeigh and Kaczynski do have one thing in common, if not universal agreement on their classification as terrorists. They did generate terror in America.

Determining whether the acts of current perpetrators of terrorist crime in America classify as terrorism is a more difficult exercise. As with much else in post-9/11 America, boundaries are blurred. Terrorism and crime have woven more closely together. Thinking on the subject is hazy. The relationship of terror and culture is evolving in America at the same time that definitions of terrorism are shifting. Even before 9/11, the relationship between acts of terror in America and formal definitions of terrorism was already in play. Some American terrorists have more than just "political" motivations. While "single-issue" forms of terrorism, such as anti-abortion bombing, animal rights activism, or environmental terrorism are clearly based in particular political stances, when perpetrators move beyond the realm of these three, or any single religious or ethnic grievance, and into a broader spectrum of motivation, the cultural plot thickens.[2]

When a bomber is anti-government, anti-technology, and protesting personal disempowerment in America all at once, something broader than a political statement is made. Both the pre-9/11 Unabomber and the post-9/11 "smiley-face" bomber had generalized complexes of motivations and complaints that could not be pinpointed to any specific political cause. In them, a different form of terrorism was afoot. The agenda, instead of being narrowly political, targeted an entire way of life. Their spectrum of concerns rendered their violent protest into a statement of opposition to American culture as a whole. The terror they promulgated went beyond politics, to something that could be called "cultural terrorism."

The mystery and grip of terror deepen when a perpetrator does not have a clearly identifiable cause. Fear multiplies forcefully when a perpetrator's intent is unclear. In the most terror-prone regions of the world, people know exactly who is supposed to be terrified by terrorism and why, but that is not true in America anymore. The inexplicability of terror in post-9/11 America intensified. The randomness in the beltway sniper's choice of victims was only half the horror connected with the campaign. The other half was the vague and hazy motivational structure behind it.

Even if sniper John Muhammad did chose targets based on hatred of people who were able to spend money, at malls, in restaurants, or at gas stations, or for the symbolic value those victims had as representatives of a money-oriented culture, the targeting was still a universalized mystery in the eyes of the beholders. The intended message, even with Muhammad's anti-American sympathies for Osama bin Laden taken into account, still was not clear. The demand for money provided Americans with some conceptual relief from chaos. Perhaps they were dealing with common, if grandiose, crime that simply borrowed from the tactics of terrorism. But the shootings went beyond anyone's interpretation of common crime. What had happened, at the very least, was uncommon crime in a terrorist key.[3]

Apparently random victims and an apparently random thought structure in the mind of the perpetrator combined to create the epitome of terror in an already traumatized post-9/11 American cultural consciousness. Everything was disjointed and disconnected, and that condition itself had the capacity to cause death. The pattern held up a mirror to a culturally chaotic nation, and the image horrified, as well as terrified. The rampage served to make the culture afraid, not just of terrorists, but also of itself. This was a frightening new form of terror that fit no previous categories, as unorthodox as crime as it was as terrorism. The crime was not just perpetrated against the individuals targeted, but also against the psyche of the nation. Whether the sniper perpetrated terrorism can be debated, but the impact the violence made in contributing to a culture of terror in America cannot.

When a pipe bomb went off in a Yale classroom in May of 2003, the news media reported that there was no terrorist connection, and no indication that the incident was terror-related. What that meant was that the perpetrator had most likely acted alone, and out of concert with any foreign interests. It was just a disgruntled American. Besides bomb damage, what was left in the wake of the bomb and the reporting was a semantic void. If the bomb did not generate terror, what did it generate? Students at Yale had to face the fear it provoked. So did their families, in resolving to attend commencement. Students vowed to reclaim the campus, and if not from terror, from what? Maybe the students were the only ones close enough to the subject to see it as terror. Maybe for the reporters the incident had become a normal part of American life. They invited their viewers to forget that terror has many faces.

Robert Bunker, writing about American street gangs, pinpointed aspects of domestic terror that are unrelated to stereotypical concepts of airline hijackers: "Today's terrorism . . . is based on social rather than political considerations. It represents a process by which the social fabric of a nation or other form of political community is gradually compromised by repeated trauma to the social psyche."[4] His point about trauma to the social psyche makes it much easier to understand after 9/11 than before that internal, display-oriented violent social statements by Americans, such as the Columbine high school massacre, cause trauma to an American social psyche also beleaguered by external attacks.

In the case of internal attacks, the resulting crisis of identity is also internal. Attacks make America unsure about itself. Columbine was not classic terrorism, but a crime with terrorist aspects. The national psyche took a hit either way. Bunker's concept of social terrorism is similar to cultural terrorism, but with more focus on the impact than on the targeting. Understanding that terrorism in America is a social and cultural, as well as a political, phenomenon is part of the key to understanding the growing domestic pattern of terror. The pattern is about more than just copycats. It is also about a culture increasingly disturbed within itself.

Private and public mix. Terror and terrorism mix. Even in a nation enamored of privacy, personal acts become public in nature when they are committed specifically with the intent of reaching the news. The suicide of American teenager Charles Bishop, who flew a Cessna into a Miami high-rise a few months after 9/11, was not just a personal act. It was also a terrorist act. His intent to make a public political statement by committing violence to others made his suicide more than the private act of a "crazy" kid. In this case, there was outside influence, with Bishop taking his inspiration in part from Osama bin Laden, but there are other cases demonstrating the effects of social terrorism in replicating terror strictly internally within America.

America is retraumatized by publicity about planned Columbine-stylized destruction plots among American high-school students, even when those plans are not carried out. Pipe bombs in California mailboxes in 2003 echo Luke Helder's alleged (but self-confessed) 2002 pipe-bombing spree. The tie between trauma from terror and the production of terror is only one of the reasons to reexamine post-9/11 America as a place where terror originates within, as well as from without.

When Americans perceive terror as only coming from without, they trick themselves into not strategizing against a force that also needs to be battled from within. Terror is in America's heart, socially, psychologically, and geographically. All Americans are now indirect, if not direct, victims of terrorism. Along with that victimization comes a challenge to understand that acts of domestic terror are an identifiable cultural pattern, with the deviant individual terrorists in America forming a parade that adds to the task of fighting terrorism from abroad. Statements of endorsement for Osama bin Laden made by Americans in conjunction with terrorist crime are only a recent plot twist. American terror was there before.

Among the generally hazy and unresolved understandings of post-9/11 American identity, some Americans do have a sense that part of the answer to the challenge of terrorism lies within, but turning that vague sense into clear thinking or action is another matter. Blaming the other guy is easy. Forgetting that fighting terror is also about transforming the American cultural self is convenient. But to make America into a society safer from terror, America will have to go beyond comfort and convenience, and take a hard look at itself.

TERROR IN THE HEART OF AMERICA

America is a superpower. While Americans do not like to think of themselves as vulnerable or weak, one of America's vulnerabilities lies in how it thinks about itself as a superpower. The idea almost always rests on a material view of economic strength and military might. The power of American consciousness, the state of mind of the American people and what they can do with it, is a largely neglected force. American consciousness has certain effects when focused on materialism, consumption, individualism, and entertainment. Focused on humanity, service, community, and social morality, it has others. Shifting the collective focus of American consciousness has the potential to change culture and mitigate the effects of terrorism.[5]

Terrorism has power. Terrorism attacks consciousness, and an effective response to terrorism will include adjusting consciousness both to meet the psychological threat of terror and to create a cultural world view with ongoing resilience, even in the face of renewed attacks. Two years after 9/11, the solutions under discussion on a public radio call-in show for how America should deal with terrorism were three in number; focusing on apprehending terrorists, improving homeland security, and making changes in U.S. foreign policy.[6] A fourth, and conspicuously missing option, was to strengthen more than security domestically. It was to pursue an America forever changed and strengthened internally, with a character more resilient in the face of possible future attacks.

Americans are plagued. The plague is paradoxical, given the tenets of the culture. Americans are plagued by the idea that individuals cannot make a difference in American society. They can. It is the idea that they cannot, and not the reality, that hobbles American consciousness and action. The heroes of 9/11 made a difference. So did Tim McVeigh. So did the American who phoned in a bomb threat in order to delay the plane he was trying to catch. The quality of American culture is generated by the behavior choices that Americans make. A consciousness of self-interest, social atomism, and individual isolation has come to characterize America, and create an atmosphere that robs Americans of a sense of personal effectiveness in society, even when they do act. In the process, an environment has emerged that helps to produce American terrorists.

The same compartmentalizing consciousness that leaves responsibility for fighting terrorism entirely to the government and views the government as categorically opposed to the individual, strips American individuals generally of their sense of social effectiveness.[7] A government, even one that is of, by, and for the people, cannot fight the roots of terror in the culture alone. The people have to fight, too. Since everyone, not just politicians, bureaucrats, and celebrities, creates culture, part of the power to demystify and combat terror in America's cultural soul lies in realizing again the universal involvement of all Americans in shaping their own culture. America needs curing from the plague of the free, affluent, and civically empowered American individual who feels that there is no possibility to have a positive impact on society.

The breakdown of social cohesion in America is a major problem in its own right, but it has also created the paradox underlying the plague of individual powerlessness. As the American individual has become more isolated, in a culture where everything "big" seems to rule, business, bureaucracy, and media, the theoretical empowerments of freedom and independence has developed instead in the opposite direction, into a distinct sense of individual powerlessness. A strange contradiction has emerged in the American cultural personality. Americans have a model of themselves, on the surface, as free and powerful, but underneath often feel as though they are not. America's unwritten cultural rule about serving one's own self-interest has backfired into a sense of powerlessness that boils beneath an American cultural surface with a received doctrine of individual power.

That sense of powerlessness creates a potent darker side to American identity. As long as the cultural contradiction between a philosophy of individual power and lived experience of personal and social ineffectiveness remains, frustration and anger in the culture will continue to grow. Americans did not lose their sense of their social power to coercion, a coup, or brainwashing. They took it away from themselves, freely. Living in a free society, they are free to take it back, starting in their minds.

The paradox of theoretical empowerment and felt powerlessness manifests itself in American conduct, and non-conduct. Politically free, materially affluent, and socially powerful American individuals largely do not use their assets to make a difference in society. They do not try. Why vote? What difference could a single vote make? Why try to make a difference in your neighborhood, in the local schools, at the office, or anywhere else, if you do not believe that you can have an impact? Why try to convince someone of a point of view in a small discussion, if you believe that what you have to say does not "count" unless you get it into the media?

People have adapted to the conundrum of feeling powerlessness by gearing their behavior ever more narrowly to serving themselves and their immediate families, because that is all that seems possible. Intensification of the American cultural rule of serving one's own self-interest does great damage, including the production of Americans who feel they must turn to terrorist violence as the only way they can recapture their ability to have an impact on society. American terrorism is a logical extension of contemporary American culture, and Americans other than the terrorists need to get out in front of the curve of cultural change created by terror with a better solution. Lip service to the concept of culture, flag waving, and unreflected reaffirmation of core values of freedom and independence will not get the job done. Americans have to think their way out of the huge cultural knot that they are in, and then do something to untie it.

As long as the American cultural script continues to read that individuals cannot do anything in the face of big bureaucracy, economic interests, or fame, nobody will know what to do with post-9/11 resolve to fight terrorism. There may be motivation, but there will be no way to translate it into a strategy for action. Stating rhetorically that everyone in America has a role to play in combating terrorism is easy. Figuring out the lines and enacting the role is much more difficult. To become serious about bettering American society, Americans will first have to go back to the social drawing board.

At the drawing board, the first question is how to understand American perpetrators of terror. Terrorism springs from a sense of disenfranchisement. Some of the Americans who feel most acutely disconnected, disempowered, and disenfranchised are America's terrorists. How do they come to feel that way? The second question is what to do about the problem. What can prevent the development of such acute feelings of disenfranchisement, here, in America, where people are free and privileged and brave? What needs adjusting? The third question is how to protect other Americans from the actions of those who cross into the realm of making terrorist plans. This third question is about vigilance as a community endeavor, not an individual one, as well as about where vigilance ends and intrusion into a neighbor's privacy begins. The alternative of neglecting the question of what everyday Americans can do to combat terror constitutes a serious tactical error. It leaves the paradoxical contradiction surrounding the America individual in place, and America at the mercy of its own terrorists.

Many Americans share domestic terrorists' frustrations about individual powerlessness. They just do not choose to try to bomb their way out of them. Mostly, they do nothing. American terrorists, on the other hand, do not concede the point that an individual can make a difference. They make a difference, but only after they have lost sight of how to do so positively. They choose to make a difference in a pathological way. Americans who neglect their positive potential to have an impact on the culture help to throw America toward its dark side. They pass up their chance to use their individual power constructively in order to counter the emerging destructive side of American character. They pass it up mostly because they cannot see it. In not fighting, they contribute to America's loss of a culture war far more fundamental than the one that rages between liberal and conservative commentators. America's war with itself is at the core not a battle about political perspectives, but a war for a positive sense of the American self.

The antidote for the dark destructive strain of American individualism is active resistance from a positive strain of American individualism, one that is rooted in Americans of all political and social stripes. Terrorism is an elusive and powerful adversary. It cannot be fought seriously without mustering all available forces and resources, especially when the terrorism lies at the heart of one's own culture. Improved security is a combat strategy, not a cure. America's internal battle with terror calls for coming to grips with how the core American values of freedom and independence have developed, through extreme individualism, to support American terror. America's concept of freedom has developed culturally in ways that have begun to rob Americans of their sense of freedom, and the interpretation of independence in America has become so individualized that it is beginning to constrict rather than liberate. Putting the situation right will take self-examination and work.

The need for revisionary thinking in America became immediately clear on 9/11, with the World Trade Center taken out, the Pentagon smoking, and the Executive Branch of the government on the run. The powerful symbolic strike at the core of America's image of itself demanded fundamental rethinking. But, partly because of the staggering immediate practical response needed to counter 9/11, broader questions of long-term adjustments to cultural identity went largely unreflected. Some people said everything about American culture had changed. Some said nothing had changed.

Neither view was correct, but without changes in American patterns of thought and action to go along with changes in security, post-9/11 "new normal" will blend back into problems from America's old normal, without creating new American strength. Added to the treacherous cultural mix in post-9/11 America are new toxic emotional residue and a cynical sense of America's inability, if it does not capitalize on 9/11, to change for the better. Americans can beat the negative effects of 9/11, or have those effects start beating them instead. There is no third choice. The problems producing domestic terror are still here, and if the body blow of 9/11 to American identity remains largely undeflected, those problems will be that much freer to grow. America was taken beyond belief on 9/11, but has yet to transform the experience into a clear plan for how to take terror out of its own heart.

Some commentators on American culture say that America needs another experience like 9/11 to remotivate it. The idea is not one that comes from a culture with a belief in the power of its own consciousness. It comes from a characterization of America as reactive, subordinate, and submissive to the experience that comes its way. It comes from a view that America needs to be hit more than once before it starts thinking seriously about how not to get hit. The idea says more about a lack of American cultural self-esteem than about America's adversaries. If America's affair with complacency, comfort, and forgetfulness is so extreme that it cannot muster itself to a mission broader than simply improving security and apprehending perpetrators—the mission of rooting terror out of America's cultural soul—its demoralization will continue. The opportunity to strengthen American character that was presented along with the pain of 9/11 can only be capitalized on by using American consciousness to fortify American culture. Americans just have to figure out how.

After 9/11, the word *culture* emerged everywhere. It was a word that was easier to use than to understand. Culture lived is not straightforward. The person on the street corner would be hard put to tell you what culture is, much less how it changes or evolves. They just know that they live immersed in it. While for a cultural anthropologist, culture is a technical term with a clear definition, most people do not think consciously about how their culture works, examine its internal contradictions, or set out consciously to change it. Steeped in it, they use its premises instead, without thinking about what they are, or how culture affects their thinking and behavior. Cultural knowledge is similar to grammatical knowledge. It is knowledge that everyone has, but seldom thinks about, and that would be hard to explain outright. Cultural knowledge is mostly rote. Living by the rules of a culture does not mean that you can state them, much less figure out how to go about changing them.

Most of the post-9/11 talk about culture change in America was not thought out. The concept was first a panacea and then a fetish. The term seemed to offer magical protection by its very invocation. American culture would change, and that would make everything all right. That American culture would change was an idea thrown at virtually every problem. An America that identifies itself with rationality failed to catch its own little magic trick. It tossed the concept of culture around as a trope for a social system, but made no rational plans for how to change it.

The mantra about America and its culture having changed forever soothed, but largely lacked actionable content. People assumed that culture would naturally change around them, and then derided both the culture and the prognosticators when it seemed not to. The concept of culture remains a fetish in post-9/11 America, albeit one with fewer worshipers as time goes by. Making culture into a buzzword and culture change a matter of faith in post-9/11 America was like eating comfort food. The practical problem was that making nebulous references to culture change does not change it. A more intentional approach is required, one that involves insight into the structure and nature of culture, conscious cultural self-examination, and action based on the knowledge gained. Culture as a fetish will not be effective in combating terrorism.

Another problem with applying the concept of culture in America is that, like so much else in America, the concept of culture has been commodified. In organizational management circles, culture is frequently rescripted into something that an organization "has," instead of something that permeates what it is. While the management of an organization can encourage a plan for cultural change, it cannot enforce it. Culture is not what one segment of a group does or promotes, not even management. Culture is what the entire group does. People at every desk may or may not conform to the cultural model coming from the top desks. What they do in response to a management plan for commodified culture will tell the story of the actual culture that is generated. Other elements of culture, such as opposition to management's commodified idea, may also be in operation.

Culture cannot profitably simply be made into a tool any more than it can be worshipped. Plans to engineer culture change can succeed, but culture itself is never separable from the thought and action of all the people who comprise it. While culture always seems just a bit bigger and more mobile than attempts to define or engineer it, that does not mean that nothing can be done intentionally to affect it.

Culture operates at more than one level. Contemporary political culture "wars" in America occur in a larger cultural context where "war" is a basic American cultural activity. Getting the whole picture of contemporary American culture means understanding why war is central, as well as what is going on in its battles. Culture subdivides into subcultures, which are smaller distinctive variations on the principles of the larger culture. The subcultures can in turn themselves subdivide. Still, an overarching issue now that applies to all of American culture is whether the paradox of American individualism, theoretical power together with felt powerlessness, will continue to turn American sensibilities of experiencing freedom and independence toward Americans wanting to be free from society and independent of one another. If it does, terror in America will continue to grow.

On the other hand, Americans can freely choose to generate a culture that is characterized by a greater sense of socially interconnected individual power and less terror. They can create more authentic social freedom by creating a pattern of more positive, effective, and constructive social connections. They can create an environment in which they feel like they can make a difference, simply by going out and making one. If America is serious about interrupting the increasingly intense connection between terror and its culture, it will have to come face-to-face, not only with perpetrators, but with the pathologies in its own cultural identity. Questions like "Freedom to what end?" and "Independence in whose service?" beg to be revisited in American cultural consciousness. In an America where many feel socially constrained to conform rather than free, or boxed in by society rather than independent, calls upon the individual to exercise patriotism and participate in democracy take on a new urgency.

Americans tend not to see the big picture. Thinking in terms of whole systems goes against their cultural grain. They are more likely to put parts of an overall pattern into separate conceptual boxes than to see the connections between the boxes. A customer service agent with a consciousness borrowed from channel surfing will produce "channel surfing culture," in which people receive the same depersonalized treatment as any quick stop on the remote. Social interaction begins to mimic channel flipping, but such a disconnected, piecemeal approach to solving America's problem with terrorism will not work.

Terrorism in America is a problem of the whole cloth, and the challenge of meeting it lies in coming to grips with the overall pattern of American culture. Thinking of each American perpetrator as an individual "nut case" leaves the pieces of the cultural puzzle scattered around, instead of assembling them into one place, much less putting them together. The story of terror in America is all one American cultural story. It has sociological subplots, subplots about the erosion of the American ability to create meaningful social bonds and the growing tendency in America to dehumanize, depersonalize, and drive people apart, and subplots about America's declining collective emotional health, but the outcome of the larger story is for every American to write.

The greatest unwritten and often overtly unacknowledged rule of American culture is that people should above all act in their own self-interest. The rule dovetails with more readily recognized and accepted rules about adversariality, ambition, and entrepreneurship. Cultural rules that limit the pursuit of self-interest have been steadily eroding in America in the face of a growing acceptance of extremes of self-interest, as any check into contemporary commentary on ethics in America will reveal.

Americans regularly work the seldom-stated but commonly practiced rule of extreme self-interest against the details of any other standard cultural rule book they face, whether that rule book is the law, the company's policies, or the rules of baseball. Witness American business, American sports, or American politics for examples of excessive individualism in accounting behavior, steroid use, and campaign contribution practices, and there are other fields in America where self-interest reigns. America's fixation on individual self-interest fuels the production of domestic terrorists, who, like other Americans, are people who have been schooled by the culture to disregard others in their own service. They just take that lesson to a violent extreme.

Extreme individualism also makes it harder for people in American intelligence agencies to catch terrorists. Americans employed in government, trained to serve organizational goals, are also trained by their culture to act first and foremost in their own perceived best interest. When the two sets of training conflict, it is most often the unwritten rule that prevails, producing American bureaucratic subcultures that are hobbled by individualism rather than served by it. The pattern reverberates in organizational cultures which themselves act in ways characterized by inwardly turned self-interest. Self-interested government employees cannot catch self-interested terrorists, or produce organizational cultures that can.

The problem is systemic in the culture. Extreme individualism in America also creates an environment in which terrorists can more easily conceal themselves. If Americans are concerned that spying on neighbors contravenes their privacy, they should simply, both on the basis of social principles and prophylactically, for self-defense, know their neighbors better in the first place. Unless something happens to change the direction of the story of the isolated and emotionally conflicted American individual, the culture is headed in the direction of more social fragmentation, chaos, terror, and pain.

While the huge scale of American society aids and abets the concealment of people with terror on their minds, the idea that scale is all there is to America's problems is a cultural comfort myth used to avoid facing hard questions about the quality of American culture. Terrorists of any stripe can conceal themselves easily, not just because of open borders or the size of American society, but also because of its generally disconnected quality, both in government and out. Keeping track of other people, even in the same American household, has become a chore. Excessive emphasis on individual independence and freedom have rendered even the core social building block of society, the family, into a structure as often characterized by isolated social "boxes" as by cohesion.

Americans, in general, have less to do with one another now than ever before, and more of the interaction they have is hostile. America is at a point in its cultural evolution where individuation is beginning to work against practical freedom and independence, instead of being the ultimate expression of them. Individualism has gone so far that opportunities for correction and connection are beginning to show themselves, one of them being the need to solve the cultural puzzle of domestic American terrorism. The walls of the individual American social box will not be "broken down," but do need to be redesigned and reconfigured, until American freedom and independence function again to create a strong American social fabric instead of working against it. If freedom from one another in America has become the freedom to terrorize one another, then freedom from terror will involve exercising the freedom to make positive social connections. In their freely chosen extremes of social fragmentation, Americans have become complicit in their own vulnerability to terror.

America saw the key to untying the knot created by the paradox of the American individual in its initial responses to 9/11. In the days that immediately followed, Americans understood that the core of their culture was American individuals who chose to support the human needs of people around them. Terrorism is about people. It hurts them. It dehumanizes them. The American individual was not disempowered on 9/11 by a stunning act of terrorism. It was reinvigorated in the sense that every American could make a difference. One of America's most painful days was also one of the best days in memory for American character.

The homage to those who sacrificed their lives, the gratitude for those who helped victims, and the realization that everyone could comfort and support someone near them, all belied the syndrome of the powerless self-interested American. The sense of social connectedness was in the power of the universally felt urge to do something to help, and the fact that people acted on it. The paradox of powerlessness went away briefly.

For a while, Americans retained their understanding that they could help and be helped by other Americans. The new heroes were right there to model on, with a heroism not related to politics or money, and which, for the most part, did not produce fame. American individualism was instantly rehumanized. It rediscovered its power in intense defiance of the dehumanization of terrorism. The terrorist strike at the core of America's humanity backfired over the short term, but for how long?

American memories are short. Collective consciousness of mutual support faded rapidly, and along with the fading consciousness, the sense of a long-term opportunity to improve American culture withered. It did not wither for a lack of voices urging that it not be allowed to pass by, or a lack of wherewithal to pursue the goal. It withered from the lack of an operating model of how to go about making it happen. Because it withered, Americans told themselves that they had no fortitude. They were angry with themselves for not having changed more. It was not true that Americans lacked fortitude, but thinking that they did became the latest form of cultural self-degradation. Little evidence was provided to refute the premise. Americans thought less of themselves for having done so little after 9/11, and their capacity for civil self-blame intensified exponentially.[8]

Without a clear new positive model for American culture out of the ashes of 9/11, fear and cultural self-hatred reasserted themselves with powerful post-traumatic force, and targets often in opposite political camps. Given that one of the goals of terrorism is to induce fear and tear apart the social constitution of the target, the terrorists appeared to be winning in America, at least to a degree. While the positive images created by the emergency responder heroes of 9/11 were extremely powerful, they remained mostly in the realm of short-term emergency consciousness, without the "legs" to translate back into powerful models for long-term non-crisis "normal" everyday American life.

Part of the problem with the post-9/11 claim that "everything" had changed was that the changes were more in psyche and mood than in the rational and material realms with which American culture tends to identify itself. The changes were hard to see. The American psyche might in fact never be the same again, but that effect was difficult to track.[9] Those who expected visible, physical effects on American daily life, such as an automatic disappearance of SUVs, were disappointed. Not seeing such changes, many came to the conclusion that there had been no change at all. Social passivity also played its role. Long-term changes in American culture are more to be engineered and less to be received, but culturally passive Americans were unable to understand that. Their sense of individual powerlessness helped them to miss the opportunity for long-term change.

Still, the brief glimpse of the largely forgotten power of American humanity had emblazoned itself in new American consciousness, perhaps almost as strongly as the traumatic image of collapsing towers. The image of the falling towers reminded that terrorism is the ultimate negative human connection, not just an attack, but an utter devaluation. The change in consciousness produced by the strike muted quickly, but was not forgotten. Encoded in that memory is the understanding that positive human connections do not just forestall terrorism. They negate it. The easiest thing to do in response to terrorism is to blame the terrorist. Terrorists are always blameworthy. The harder and more productive thing to do is to fight to enhance the place of humanity in America's cultural understanding of itself, a task that will require both mental and social work in a society accustomed to a consciousness of individual consumption. American resilience in the face of terrorism is not for consumption, but for creation. Conquering terror in America will take more than hating the nineteen men with box cutters who perpetrated 9/11. It will mean learning from them, however painfully, that if nineteen men with box cutters can change American culture, so can Americans.

TOTEMS

A totem is an animal, plant, or something else from the natural environment that is symbolically associated with a group of people. Sports teams use them. So do Boy Scouts, and family groups in many parts of the world. In Simon Reeve's 1999 volume, *The New Jackals*, he identifies his cast of characters and subject matter as Ramzi Yousef, Osama bin Laden, and the future of terrorism.[10] Reeve's title is a good totemic call. Yousef, mastermind of the 1993 World Trade Center attack, sits on the same cellblock at Colorado's Supermax federal prison with Unabomber Ted Kaczynski. While Reeve's updated jackal metaphor for terrorism is based on the original moniker for international terrorist "Carlos the Jackal," extending that symbolism to Ramzi Yousef and Osama bin Laden makes them, too, members of a symbolic jackal clan. Yousef's current neighbor, Kaczynski, and former neighbor, Tim McVeigh, are central figures in the American branch of the jackal clan. Globally, jackals promote a culture of terrorism, with identifiable and interacting regional subcultures in the Middle East, Europe, Asia, North America, and elsewhere.[11]

The attack of a real jackal is daring, deadly, often solitary, and difficult to prevent. Its cry reverberates, instilling fear in potential victims. It conceals itself, reproduces in seclusion, and feeds opportunistically. It can take down large prey by using speed and stealth to neutralize its size disadvantage. The ruthlessness of its killing is matched by its cowardice. The jackal is a well-chosen and widespread symbol for terrorists. The Egyptian death god takes the form of a jackal. FBI agents referred to the anthrax letter terrorist as a distant cousin of the jackal, a "lone wolf." Makers of the movie *Collateral Damage* also chose the wolf to symbolize the terrorist persona. When the jackal manifests in human form, everyone who is not a jackal becomes a potential victim. Unlike their animal counterparts, human jackals are fully aware of the suffering they inflict. The characterization is apt.

What symbolic totemic clan could counter the destructive force of the jackal? That symbol comes from beyond the objective world, out of the realm of myth, spirit, and dream. There, one finds a being that dies with a difference. It may be hit, crash, burn, and die, falling victim to the ever present attack of the jackal, but that is not the end of the story. The phoenix, while it dies in the flame and devolves into ash, rises right back through the same smoldering fire again to transformed life. No matter how many times it is hit, it will rise again, its demise only and always a temporary prelude to a stronger being on the other side of catastrophe. It can stand up to a persistent jackal clan.

If Americans reach beyond the realm of everyday reality, where the jackal seems to prevail, and into the realm of reimagining themselves, they can find a transcendent identity like that of the phoenix. The phoenix is a symbol to fight with, instead of conceding the territory of the American heart to the jackal. With a phoenix totem, America can fight both its own complacency and the capability of any terrorist to hit it again. The phoenix takes any hit knowing its power to regenerate, secure in the inevitability of its rebirth. Its sense of itself cannot be degraded by an attack. It can work to forestall being hit again, but does not have to tell itself that it will not be, or blame itself if it is. It is stronger than that. If it is hit again, it will become stronger yet in the aftermath. Its power is in the knowledge that it will not just survive, but thrive. If Americans nurture a clan with phoenix-like wings, they can counter the destructive cycle of the jackal. They can dread the possibility of another terrorist attack, but do so knowing that no attack can tear them apart.

Prevention is the toughest of antiterrorism goals. As difficult as response is, addressing the root causes that motivate terrorist acts is more difficult yet. A consciousness of cultural self-regeneration would work to counteract American-generated acts of terror at their source, by forestalling the formation of American intent to commit acts of terror and encouraging the social cohesion that makes vigilance social second nature. In a culture that fights for its character, the jackal may be able to take the phoenix down temporarily, but does not have the power to instill pessimism, despair, or apathy. It cannot get an upper hand borne of chaos and resignation. It cannot prevent rebirth.

A phoenix attacked, does not tear itself apart for having been victimized. It simply strengthens itself against the next attack, having learned from its pain. The phoenix wins, even if its campaign to eliminate the jackal is never perfected. It may go down, but it never goes out, and always flies knowing that it will rise again. Symbolic phoenix wings are as important to breaking the hold of terror on American culture as the physical wings on which post-9/11 Americans resumed flight.

While a phoenix is not an eagle, the two have been compared as similar in size and shape for millennia. Images of the American eagle rising from flames reinforce the comparison. The regenerative moral challenge set by terrorism is set broadly for humanity as a whole, but the human phoenix and the American eagle fly in formation to meet it. Jackal and phoenix totems are both universal, neither native to any one region of the world. The phoenix has mythical expressions east and west, from Arabia and China to an American game bird, the pheasant. It is a fighting cock and a creative hen. It is a creative cock and a fighting hen. It is all of the above, and the antiterrorist flight of the American phoenix is, at least in part, a domestic flight within America's own heart.

Shortly after 9/11, a network news logo, "America Rising" appeared. News commentators and Mayor Rudy Guiliani in New York City had a sense of something phoenix-like in the following month, as they made references to the fire under the World Trade Center as a living and breathing entity, from which a more unified country had emerged. The fire burned for months. November brought commentary about ceaseless work over a relentless fire, a fire that was in the totemic plus column if one thought in terms of a phoenix. *CBS Evening News* anchor Dan Rather was in the same symbolic territory in October, referring to anthrax scares as "brush fires of fear." They caused the phoenix to go down again, temporarily. Rather was still talking about coming up from the ashes at Ground Zero in 2003.

The flag-raising ceremonies before the first game of the 2001 World Series reenacted fire fighters raising the flag at the World Trade Center. The back of the T-shirt of the man taking the flag up for the national pastime in a burned but resurgent America read: "Phoenix Fire Dept." Point taken. Symbolic serendipity was back on the wing. Ironically, months later, the memo spearheading a flood of questions about the functioning of the FBI prior to 9/11 was the "Phoenix memo." Regeneration does not happen without going through a fire of pain first, and some of the transformation needed in America clearly went beyond the "Phoenix Project" of rebuilding the Pentagon.

When the phoenix rises, it does not care about tomorrow's adversary. Rebirth has integrity and its own promise, regardless of tomorrow. To overcome terror, Americans need to do more than just recover their sense of themselves before 9/11. They need to reshape themselves into a new and stronger state of being, into a culture with less anger and despair, and more cohesion and internal integrity. Those who sought comfort after 9/11 by modeling a return to an untransformed America were on the wrong track. Cultural change will happen. Post-9/11 American culture will not stand still. The question is just which direction the changes will take America— toward the jackal or toward the phoenix. September 11 can be yesterday's news, or a rallying point for America to actively recreate itself beyond the power of flames of terror to crush the national consciousness. America can keep walking a path of fear and destruction, and experience the worsening howl and bite of the jackal from within, or choose the transformative path of the phoenix, which sees death, but knows neither complacency nor fear.

ROOTS AND GRIT

To get to the root of the matter, America has to come to grips with itself, both as its own internal enemy and as a self-cure for domestic terror. Americans can help put the terror within into retreat by confronting the problems that create it. Terrorism confronted is already in retreat, since confrontation takes away its mystery. Choosing not to contemplate the cultural causes of American terrorism is easy. Leaving the fight against terrorism entirely to the American government is easy. Not fighting terrorism is tempting, not only because it is hard to figure out how, but also because fighting terrorism is always an energy-sapping enterprise against an elusive opponent. Terrorists are hard to find, and victory is never complete. There is, however, part of the ongoing challenge of terrorism that can be dealt with by Americans 24/7. They can answer the echo of the cry of the jackal within themselves, just by paying attention to themselves as members of American culture.

There were domestic acts of terror in America throughout the 1990s, including the Oklahoma City bombing, the Columbine high school massacre, and abortion clinic bombings. While the chances of any individual American becoming a direct victim of terrorism are still small, the level of victimization of the culture as a whole has grown with each instance. America has largely neglected its collective victimization in the aftermath of each new attack, because Americans tend not to think collectively. Instead, terror within has grown incrementally, with its cumulative effects on the national psyche largely unnoticed and uncombated. Fighting terror as an enemy within American culture will call for self-understanding, and a high level of fighting skill.

Chinese philosopher of war, Sun Tzu, emphasized the importance of will as an element in combat. Simply beating an opponent is a low-level goal. The highest skill is in finding the will and craft to subdue an enemy without fighting directly.[12] The approach is especially applicable when the enemy lies within. America needs to develop the level of combat skill that will transform the opponent within itself, in order to root terrorism out of its own heart. Since terrorists are so hard to find, preventing them is good strategy. The skill level necessary to do so goes well beyond gaining physical command over terrorist activity. It demands reclaiming ground from terrorism's will to strike. The greatest internal security against terror lies in changing the nature of America's cultural ground. While terrorist enemies may be hard to find, the effects of terror on one's own heart and mind are always there, and can always be set on the path of the phoenix.

The highest level of mastery of domestic terror in America would be to create a social environment in which Americans are less inclined to choose terrorist actions. That would take a highly concentrated force of will, a clear recognition of terror as an internal enemy, and a reshaping of the current effects of core American values on American culture. In an America where the martial arts related to Sun Tzu's philosophy are often erroneously interpreted as the mere acquisition of physical skill, achieving such a high level of mental and social mastery is difficult to envision. America's fascination with the martial artist on its movie screens tends to the glitzy effects of beating the opponent, rather than the hard work of self-mastery. But beating the internal opponent in the American cultural soul is now the goal. The jackal clan within will yield to nothing less. The challenge of this combat is first and foremost in reorienting American hearts and minds, not in toughness or muscle.

The phoenix will need to find unexpected fighting strategies to regenerate on the "home front" by adjusting American consciousness and character to produce less alienation, anger, and anxiety within. While coming to grips with yourself can be more difficult than facing any opponent, self-transformation is just the type of radical turn around that takes a disadvantage, like a hit from terrorism, and makes it into an advantage. In this case, self-examination for a "troubled" culture will be even tougher than for any one of its "troubled" citizens, because Americans tend not to think of themselves in collective terms. The same fractionated cultural identity that helps to spawn terrorism within has to be surmounted before Americans can even think about the problem. Finding the collective American self may be almost as tricky as finding the terrorists.

While digging to find the root of a conflict within can take as much or more grit as facing an opponent, knowing both the enemy and the self has advantages, especially in psychological warfare. Terrorism is psychological warfare, where the enemy makes a battleground of the mind. Witnesses to terrorism are not collateral damage. They are direct targets. Psychological damage from terror tests the power of an American character that is already challenged by high levels of fear, anger, and mistrust. Doing nothing to fight back allows the damage to fester. Anxiety about terrorism in the national consciousness is not just a healthy response to the possibility of more terrorism. Anxiety has also taken up space in American minds, and become part of its national character.

The American phoenix needs craft, will, and knowledge of both self and other to rise to and through the challenge of domestic terrorism. If

America is to dig within its cultural soul and find the grit to battle the enemy within, its first lesson is that the cast of characters in the story of American terrorism does not consist simply of "good guys" and "bad guys." They can be hard to tell apart, and often little separates them, but the story of terror in America is about good guys who choose to do bad things in a stressed social environment. It is also about bad guys who are generally good people, but choose in their daily lives to ridicule or ignore fellow Americans already at risk for becoming perpetrators of terror. Rooting out an understanding of why some Americans react to their own culture with catastrophic violence can help best, rather than just beat domestic terrorism, and that is good strategy, since terrorism by its nature is virtually impossible to completely beat.

While some foreign terrorists have been literally housed in caves, the isolated social boxes that many Americans live in create American caves of frustration and anger that contain America's potential terrorists. The only way Americans who choose terror know how to make connections in American society is by blowing things up. Blowing things up is sensational. It is easy. It makes headlines. It is the path of the jackal. America needs to pull itself off of this easy, sensationalistic high, by combating the culture of terror at home. The rhetoric that emerged after 9/11 about an unprecedented opportunity to reclaim basic values in American culture was about an opportunity that had always been there, and still is. September 11 just altered American minds briefly so that they perceived it. But the rhetoric and the perception both waned. References to America's collective determination and resoluteness to fight faded from 2002 to 2003 back into a consciousness of individualism, and a focus on fighting terrorism that was firmly anchored in thinking only about combating foreign adversaries.

Even some of the changes in thinking about American culture that occurred right after 9/11 were hard to catch. High-level military officials, and Director of Homeland Security Tom Ridge sounded strange, touting local and tribal social process both in America and in Afghanistan, in a culture more generally wedded to concepts of hierarchy. Ridge's longer-term track record in creating connections to local units of government would not be as bright, but in the short-term aftermath, people saw connections and perceived American culture as an integrated system. Then, even though the habit of thinking only about parts of the system at a time came back, the old habit had been modified. Thinking comprehensively, thinking deeply, and thinking about social connections were a larger sector of the new American mental landscape than before. That shift to systems-oriented thinking will not sustain over the long term, though, unless Americans consciously update their understanding of themselves to include it.

A drift back into the complacency that says it is the system that runs the people, and not the other way around will keep setting America up for unmanageable personal anger and feelings of personal disenfranchisement. The new megabureaucracy of the Department of Homeland Security serves an anxious public, touchy about terrorism and ambiguous about big government, even though it is more trustful at the same time. Simultaneously, the government struggles to work cultural transformation on itself. The post-9/11 upsurge in public trust in government could easily transform into an unforgiving attitude, if the government track record on the tough task of terrorism prevention is not a good one. Given terrorism's opportunism, another significant terrorist attack could easily become a recipe not for uniting American culture, but tearing it further apart.

We have met the enemy, and it is still an "us" steeped in adversarial and fragmented thinking. Tearing things apart is right up the jackal's alley. Those who contradicted Pogo after 9/11 by saying that the enemy was not us were factually correct in that case, but misdirected about the overall situation. Even though it was not us that time, the comforting but erroneous notion that it is not ever "us" led the culture the wrong way. Americans are no more directly responsible for attacks on the World Trade Center than they were for the Ryder truck that was detonated next to the Murrah Federal Building in Oklahoma City, but America's pitched battle with terrorism does require response from those involved indirectly, as well as directly. The enemy can be us, even when we are not the perpetrators.[13]

What is going on in the minds of America's least comfortable citizens is important. They are not "losers." They are potential criminals and terrorists. Like it or not, all Americans are linked to them. There are current perpetrators to be caught, and copycats and hoaxers to be forestalled. There are those who have Eric Harris, Tim McVeigh, or John Muhammad as role models to reeducate, before their emulation moves from consciousness into action. There is preventive social medicine to apply, to help redirect what could become the next high school shooting, or the next college student or professor who decides to build bombs. There are the negative effects of 9/11 on socially and psychologically vulnerable Americans to watch for, both in the sense of caring for them, and in the sense of staying alert for protection from them if they choose the way of the jackal. There is the idea that America has achieved closure on its experiences with terror to work against. Some violent responses to American victimization on 9/11 will happen later rather than sooner. They are likely to be directed at other Americans. America should be ready for them. There are also Americans who do not need 9/11 to help them produce violent responses to American culture.

Without countering domestic terror, each new hit America takes from within becomes like a fix for an addictive American psyche. Americans gobble up the news, and as they do, they become confirmed in a growing sense of instability in America's collective character. The next news story tells them that they were right. Even when the public does not get a hit over the short term, that does not mean that its growing expectation of terror has been reversed, just that it has not been reinforced lately. The cure will be when Americans do not find, or expect to find, their televisions reaffirming for them a declining sense of American character.

It is not just the FBI that needs a change in attitude and thinking. It is the entire culture. The home front on the war on terrorism is an old one. It did not start just after 9/11, and platitudes about culture change will not work to fight it by themselves. Phoenixes do not rise without going to the ground first, and they go to ground with themselves. American culture cannot change according to plan, unless it comes up with a plan. To reenvision itself, America will have to take more than a short-term intermission from seeing itself as composed of self-interested and socially isolated people. Its glimpse of an alternative image, out of the flames of 9/11, was a flash of insight that hyperindividualism, social fragmentation, and compartmentalized thinking work well together, and lead to destruction. That insight needs to be more than momentary.

If post-9/11 Americans remain vigilant to the increasing command of terror over the American heart, as well as to the prospect of the next attack, large or small, foreign or domestic, they can heal to a strengthened life. A momentary burst of consciousness about the untapped human power in American culture will not get to the root of the matter, and other American crises, of corporate and bureaucratic failure, and of stunningly savage, if not terror-related crime, all point in the direction of searching for the root causes of problems in American culture.

FINDING OURSELVES

As America drifts in a haze of victimization from 9/11, it also has a build up of psychological shrapnel from the pain inflicted by its own terrorist tradition. Clearing the haze from America's cultural air will demand getting the collective adrenaline flowing and using it to fuel action, instead of surrendering to collective anxiety. Since perpetrators of terror in America count on self-absorbed and socially fractionated adversaries, and terrorism can find Americans, Americans had better find themselves. Relentlessly individualistic thinking keeps Americans from seeing social patterns of terror at home. Quiet, bright, shy, and polite American students at high risk for producing violent behavior are not just individual anomalies. They are part of a cultural pattern. When an American terrorist is executed or imprisoned, a personal saga is laid to rest, but the terrorist's place as an actor in America's cultural story of terrorism is not. Overcoming the individual, and overcoming that place in the saga of American terrorism are two different things.

For example, with Tim McVeigh, America has only done the easier of the two. He found us, and we found him, but have we found ourselves? As long as America's perpetrators of terror, of any sociological profile, any occupational or mental health status, any age or former military status, are dismissed as "nuts," "wacko," "crazy," "sick," or "evil," America will not come to grips with the social forces that help to produce them. The next American terrorist could be almost anyone. It could be a female. It could be a government employee. It could be someone who is unemployed. It could be someone who is certifiably "crazy," or not.

Whoever it is, the cultural dynamics that undergird American terrorism will remain a puzzle as long as Americans persist in giving themselves collective absolution every time an individual American terrorist acts. Whatever advances profiling techniques make in helping to identify the individual trees, America will still have missed the cultural forest. Nor can Americans combat terror in their capacities as separate individuals. Most individual Americans are not "implicated" in terrorism, as Tim McVeigh's attorney argued, but they are involved in it—together. Complacency about violence and social disconnectedness help to regenerate it, and create complicity in America's victimization, driving the national psyche further into emotional ill health. An American public with confused thinking about how terror and culture are tied cannot produce an effective counteroffensive.

Long-term cooperative relations between the public and the government will be a centerpiece of an effective counteroffensive. Not only does the government have a long way to go in order to offer "seamless" protection to the public, the public also lacks a vision of its place in the process of fighting terror. American citizens are looking for cooperation within their government at a higher level than they are showing cooperation with it, so "seamlessness" is lacking at more than one level, and "disconnect" is not a term that can be reserved for the government alone.

The American cultural paradox of individualism helps to confound the overall situation. Many of the same American citizens who want perfect protection are also accustomed to being nonparticipatory "consumers" of a government that they view as an adversarial categorical threat to individual civil liberties. The social equation does not fit together. A cultural revolution transforming the American government could not possibly leave the populace untouched. Culture does not work that way. Americans working in "big" government with overly hierarchical models of social organization, for their part, may abet the ongoing "disconnect" in post-9/11 America, by discounting the role of the public, and even state and local authorities, in participating in protection from terror.

The currently needed collaboration within the government to combat terrorism is now at the vortex of the felt need for cultural change in America. Both terrorism itself and the paradox of American individualism stand in opposition to efforts to create that change. That paradox also works on the people who work in American government, and they must successfully resolve it in order to fight terrorism more effectively. A still-individualistic public, though, will continue to offer merciless critique, even to a government rapidly adapting toward collaborative culture, if that government does not also show practical success. "Accountability" has an upside, and the potential to divide in the face of a formidable opponent. The public's post-9/11 renaissance of good feelings about government will not last unless there is antiterrorist success, or the public comes to understand the difficulty of making cultural changes in government because it shares in the difficulty of making cultural changes itself.

The prospects for promoting positive cultural change in America now are unstable and unsure. Such change is event-dependent, and dependent on ongoing parallel commitments in the public and its government to create positive change. Without authentic cooperation in American culture, anything could happen, but one thing is clear. Ted Kaczynski and Tim McVeigh will have the last laugh if mistrust of a government that "fails" to protect the public from terrorism flowers again in America. To be like a phoenix, America will need adjusted models of culture that encompass the public and the government under one set of wings. The nation does not have it together yet, conceptually.

As America's initial post-9/11 galvanization began to fade, along with a clear sense of antiterrorist activism in the American public, what did not fade was the depth of reverence for the loss and sacrifices of that day. That reverence was profound and untouchable. What grew was a compromised sense of safety and security. While the sense of American invulnerability disappeared from American consciousness, it has yet to be replaced by a public that can state or remember its mission in fighting terror in America. The help that the government will need in forestalling terror in America goes far beyond assistance in apprehending perpetrators. That is only a small part of the overall mission of combating terror in America. To complete the mission, the profound sense of reverence for human life and human connection that arose from 9/11 will need to be translated into a changed American cultural context. American minds were altered by 9/11. The question over the long term is how, and in what direction, toward the jackal or the phoenix?

CHAPTER 1

PATTERNS OF TERROR

TERROR ON THE HOME FRONT

On 9/11, terrorism in America became a "war" on the home front. The terrorist opponent on 9/11 was an outsider. A foreign attack with a far greater impact than any domestic terrorist made it easy to define America in contrast to sources of terror, and people did. But America also changed because of 9/11. The blow had affected its victim. America was not responsible for this attack, but it still had to recover and defend. As America mobilized urgently into intense defense, the pattern tying terrorism to American culture drew closer. Terrorism was changing things at home. A TV news logo in mid-September 2001 appeared as though it had come from a home remodeling show. The schematic figure with the house labeled "Home Front" signified that home was on the front lines in the war on terrorism. What was tricky about an individualistic home front in the war on terrorism is that war is a collective challenge, met by a group. As comfort responses, including forgetting 9/11, kicked in almost immediately, fighting that war became trickier.

In the first days after 9/11, almost everyone said that their world had changed. But within a month, short-term consciousness staged a comeback. In October, students from Allegheny College fell into three categories; (1) the naive ("Why did they do that to us?"), (2) the jingoist ("Bomb the hell out of them!"), and (3) the ready-to-move-on. The feeling sequence in the third group had gone directly from shock to nothing. No emotion, no action, and no change intervened between those two levels of response. September 11 was no longer a concern. Dwelling on it was unnatural and unhealthy. Unless you knew someone directly involved, it was in the past. There could be no meaningful connection between the world of one month and that of the next, regardless of what had happened. No one event, not even 9/11, could knit time together. Some said that the same fragmentary mind-set robbed America of the vigilance that would have caused it to see the attack coming. Still, by October, those with disconnected mind-sets were ready to move on.

Between extremes of "dwelling on it forever" and "just going on and not worrying about it" were people with a mixed approach, but they did not know how to identify the nature of the mix. Some voices said America had "closure" by October, while others said the nation was still in shock in February. "New normal" was definitely not simple.

Extremist religious views, like short-term consciousness, invited inaction. For those who saw 9/11 as a glimpse of an end soon to come, a harbinger of Armageddon inexorably enveloping an evil society, no last ditch moral effort to dig America out could stop a final conflagration. There was little point in doing anything. Doomsday and the Apocalypse's horsemen loomed large, as end-day websites filled with debate and opinions that the wages of prophecy ignored and God's punishment were upon America. Separation of church and state had created the social degeneration that led to the attack. While these domestic myths of America as a nation of infidels simplistically consoled, they also produced a typical American behavioral response: do nothing, because there is nothing that you can do.

For doomsday prophesiers, everything had happened, or at least begun to. For those who wanted to move on, nothing had happened. What the extremes had in common was the idea that there was nothing to be done, no transformations of consciousness or action required. Both extremes encouraged continued passivity as an ongoing approach to 9/11 and to ongoing American cultural life. Some sought post-9/11 comfort in off-the-wall social philosophies and theories. Patriarchy would become matriarchy, as women took over the culture, or matriarchy would become patriarchy, as manly men reclaimed their proper position of supremacy. Speculation even emerged that America had perpetrated 9/11 on itself. People could pick whatever extreme view gave them psychological comfort, and believe in it.

A thoughtful and realistically complex response to America's updated cultural situation was harder to maintain, but moderate responses could also be found. From celebrities to custodial personnel in America, there was a broad-based perception that everyone was connected to and affected by what had happened. Tempered religious perspectives sought reconsideration and rebuilding of the America that God should bless. A sense of a revival of American citizenship was in the wind. Many watched to see how American culture would realign and reshape itself. Fewer set out to reshape it themselves.

People "cocooned" with their families with little thought that the metaphor implied later reemergence. Metamorphosis is an active process, even if you are hunkered down while you are doing it. During the holiday season 2001, America was in a state of cultural meditation, with Fireman Santas and Nutcracker Uncle Sams as its new ritual objects. The question that remained was whether the meditation would precede transformation, or the cocoon would quietly become a permanent fortress.

Emergence requires transformation. After 9/11 blew things apart, Americans used group consciousness, over the short term, to put them back together. Americans have trouble thinking of themselves as part of a group, but this time the tragedy was national and the bereavement was collective. In a culture of strong individualism, though, long-term maintenance of a sense of group identity in post-9/11 America was unlikely. The Americans who were ready within the first month to ignore the need for a collective American cultural response to 9/11 were few, but their ranks grew with time. People pushed briefly outside their individual social boxes had no map for navigating the territory between boxes. Going back inside the box became the default strategy. Those boxes continue to make it hard to see the ongoing breed of American terrorism for what it is. They hamper transformation.

ADDICTION, TERRORISM, AND THE AMERICAN SELF

A 1993 question about why abortion clinic bombings had emerged in America challenged me to explain what seemed to defy explanation. Making sense of why people killed in order to protect the sanctity of life called for a larger perspective. It took an understanding of increasing fragmentation in American culture, both social fragmentation and fragmentation in the way people think. Abortion clinic bombing was only one expression of the scattered tenor of America's culture. Bombing is a violent, but logical, extension of a pattern of cultural fragmentation into the physical realm. What is already torn apart, is torn apart some more.

When people in an already disjointed social environment separate out a single issue in their minds and put it categorically ahead of all others, the seeds of fanatic violence are sown. Their position becomes a sole driving force for action, taking on an importance greater than the sanctity of human life. In a fragmented culture, it is easy for issues to take on such virulent importance in people's minds. While the display of 9/11 stunned America with its perpetrators' ability to take human will out of human context, the seeds of that same ability had also been growing on the home front for some time.

How had American culture reached a point where Americans were bombing other Americans? The enemy was us, with American individualism helping to generate the acute form of personal indulgence in which people express their dissatisfaction with contemporary America in terrorist statements. A specific issue enflaming some Americans became an addictive single principle running life, and leading to death. The lives of other Americans could fuel the fire of the importance of the message by being forfeit to it.

It was not only single-issue terrorists, concerned with abortion, the environment, or animal rights, who lost the ability to focus on the larger human picture. It was also American terrorists who were concerned about a larger complex of interconnected issues in American culture. Either way, a given perspective exploded in importance in the terrorist's mind, and then justified, literally explosive, violent behavior. After 9/11, the history of American terrorism began to intertwine with 9/11 as well as fold in on itself. In 2001, Clayton Lee Waagner allegedly sent hundreds of anthrax hoax letters to abortion clinics, in an updated recipe for American terrorism that drew inspiration from several sources in the American cultural tradition of terror.

Whatever the addiction, to gambling, to alcohol, to profit, to status, or to drugs, an addiction drowns out the importance of everything else in life. Addiction in America is not reserved for the crack addict, the unscrupulous corporate executive, or the can't-stop shopper. The greatest addiction in America is pervasive, based on a burgeoning sense of the importance of the individual self. Addiction to the self, based in what sociologist Robert Bellah calls "radical individualism," helps to feed a myriad of other addictions in Americans.[1] The collective American focus on the self has reached a maladaptive extreme.

Walking on the same sidewalk with other people has become a complicated task for Americans, who are increasingly poorly trained or unwilling to even actively perceive and react to other people in the same public space. American roads tell a similar story. Hostile action can even represent an achievement of social relatedness in America, where for many relating to screens has become easier and more normative than relating to people. Americans have wrapped themselves in the idea that the individual self is the most important focal point in life, and then fed on that idea. Disconnected individualism permeates American society and thought. Ironically, the more intensive the focus on the atomistic American self, the less useful it becomes in building concepts of either individual identity or collective cultural identity.[2] The term "disconnect" has even entered contemporary American jargon.

"Thinking outside the box" is a catch phrase that acknowledges the myriad of conceptual and social boxes that Americans need to learn to think outside of. While any open and free society has predefined vulnerabilities to terrorism, a culture characterized by disconnected minds and social life, where people have to purposely think outside the box in order to make connections, helps to enhance that vulnerability. An America in which post-9/11 airport security personnel can watch football while they should be security screening has clear problems of social connection. What were they thinking? They weren't. They had a default cultural setting to self-oriented behavior in place.

Improving the connectedness of America's social and conceptual fabric does not have to cost money or have an impact on civil liberties. All Americans have to do is think and act differently. They are free to do so. Thinking of security as a zero-sum equation that can only be improved by sacrificing individual civil liberties is itself an artifact of a hyperindividualized model of society. From that no-win conceptual position, terrorism either erodes the culture's fundamental character, or strikes at it freely. The answer to finding a winning position is in thinking outside the strictly individualized American box.

Along with social fragmentation, mental fragmentation has become so typical of daily American life that it routinely defies attempts to see how people and things fit together into systems. A vignette from a plumbing supply store illustrates. After a history of failed connections between a contractor and subcontractors, a customer sought the third set of parts necessary to install one bathroom faucet. Three different people helped, shifting, as soon as any new piece of information became available, from one mental construct to another for what the parts were and how they might fit together. Concepts of social relationships behind and over the counter were just as instantly flexible as interpretations of the parts. "This part should have been in that box." "We have a kit in the back that will work." "No, guess not." "We can help you." "We can't help you." "We need a plumber." "We need the company representative." "We can't get him." Between multiple sets of parts and multiple models of social interaction, what went on was about as predictable as what was happening in the popcorn machine nearby.

The lack of conceptual, social, and technical coherence in the bathroom faucet microcosm is unfortunately representative of the larger cultural system that 9/11 terrorists successfully attacked. Similar dynamics apply at the INS and the FBI. The post-9/11 model for American security is "seamless" integration, but America has a long way to go to get from popcorn to integration. The metaphor in federal bureaucracy for restructuring and improving federal interagency relationships is, in fact, "plumbing." Effective coordination of the various subcultures of these agencies will demand a plumbing strategy based on something other than a culture of radical individualism. Improving patterns of human relationships will be as important to the effort as improving technology or reorganizing bureaucratic structure. There is a great deal of ground to cover before America can effectively offset Jessica Stern's observation in *The Ultimate Terrorists*, that "societies whose citizens feel alienated from the government and from one another are more vulnerable than more cohesive societies to terrorist violence and also provide more fertile ground for breeding of extremists."[3]

Conceptual fragmentation is endemic in American daily life. It is in how Americans package plumbing parts. It is in how they drive. It is in how they surf instantaneously from one focus of consciousness to the next. It is in how they conduct human interactions with the same mind frame. The sense that Americans are relating to other people who are whole human beings and not just obstructions, problems, market share, or the next client/customer/patient/student "unit" to be dealt with, is increasingly hard to find. Dehumanization in America helps feed the cultural tradition of American terrorism. People with a degraded sense of humanity find it easy to blow people up.

Confronted on 9/11 with a profound sense of the human victimization of terrorism, America's sense of humanity revived, but by and large has not remained revived. The sense that Americans understand how other people relate to them, to each other, or to a task at hand, is still hard to maintain. That difficulty is rooted in the American addiction to the American self. In the minds of American terrorists, that addiction justifies enacting hatred by sacrificing other humans whose humanity has been conceptually discounted. In the minds of most Americans, that addiction just causes them to disregard other people.

The walls of America's individual social and conceptual boxes have been thickening, but 9/11 perturbed them. Coordination became a sudden new expectation. There was post-9/11 fury, when decontamination of Washington office buildings for anthrax was not uniform and consistent. That anger went beyond just post-crisis sensitization. The intensity of emotion focused on a commitment to coordination also displayed an adjusted cultural norm. Before 9/11, similar anger about bureaucratic disconnection would have been clouded by resignation to entrenched disorganization. Now, fury about disorganization burned bright and demanded change. Enhanced coordination did emerge after 9/11 in some areas of American cultural life, including families. Then, expectations for a more cohesive America came to focus on the bureaucracies of American intelligence collection that are on the front lines against both foreign and American terror.

While the death tolls exacted by American terrorists range from 0 to 168 instead of being in the thousands, the dynamics of American terrorism are parallel to terrorism anywhere.[4] Everyone becomes both a potential victim and a combatant. Tim McVeigh tolerated civilian death as acceptable collateral damage in pressing his case against his own government. Had he known about the day care center in the Murrah Federal Building, he might have changed targets and produced collateral damage with a higher average age elsewhere, but his cause and his need for self-expression still ranked in his mind above the lives of others. If terror is to be rooted out of America, it will have to become harder for such conceptual fanaticism to survive. America's addiction to individualism will otherwise keep promoting the emergence of American terrorists who will tear apart not just their victims, but also America's sense of itself. So far, America has taken each of its internal hits from terror without doing anything to transform its cultural identity in defense.

Community and collaboration do not go together with addiction. A community consists of a complex balancing of relationships in a system. It counteracts the excesses of addiction by its own nature. America's sense of community came originally from its small town heritage. Small towns were, and are, social systems that are easy to comprehend. But as the importance of America's small town community history faded in relation to an urbanized, computerized, coast-hopping population, so did American metaphors for community—until 9/11. Then, suddenly, community, like culture, was on everyone's mind. New York City became "Main Street, USA," Washington was the national community's city hall, and the Internet its phone exchange, as America absorbed the impact.

What the new post-9/11 sense of national community did not have was an anchor in a longer-term sense of contemporary American community. Responses to 9/11 notwithstanding, Americans still have not quite wrapped their minds around the fact that communities do not have to be geographically-based, and they do not have to be small. Communities exist where people choose to make them. Contemporary American communities are sometimes geographical, sometimes virtual, and sometimes transitory, but all merit cultivation. The American concept of community, though, is still largely stuck in historic small town America. Community metaphors are sometimes applied where the effective bonds of community are needed, such as in "the intelligence community;" but without a vibrant and updated model for ongoing American community, post-9/11 sensibilities about its existence will fade. Ongoing cultural trauma and default individualism will help them fade. As America's post-9/11 sense of community fades, so does America's capacity to recover from terror.

Pathological as terrorism is, it is an intensive form of social engagement. Violent and self-serving, it is nevertheless a powerful form of social connection. Unfortunately, such a connection has its own logic in a culture low in social cohesion and high in alienation. Part of the cure for domestic terror is to pull away from America's collective addictive focus on the self. Culture does not just happen. It is made, and can be remade by the people who comprise it. Americans who think that culture is too big for them to change will find themselves changed by it instead. The question is simply "who is to be in charge," people or their cultural assumptions. The sense of a lack of control over the American environment that was part of the post-9/11 American experience will grow, unless Americans find a more socially constructive and less addictive sense of individual identity, and then do something with it to promote their long-term security as a culture as well as a nation.

OKLAHOMA AFTERMATH

From a cultural perspective, whether or not to execute Tim McVeigh was not the most important question at his sentencing in 1997. It was how to come to grips with him as a specimen of American culture. Executing him balanced his own account, but did not answer the questions left in his wake. The execution did not tell Americans what they needed to know in order to recover from what he had done. Labeling him a "monster" or "loser" did not heal America from victimization at his hands. Exacting retribution did not do it, either. None of that brought back the people he killed, or the sense of security that America had about itself before he struck. That sense of security cannot be reclaimed from him, or from any other perpetrator of terror. No matter how reprehensible their actions, the responsibility for resolving the experience they deal out lies with the victims. America has to deal with the experience that McVeigh perpetrated. His execution ended his ability to act or speak as an individual, but did not change the fact that there are others with complaints and disaffection similar to his, who could turn out like him. McVeigh's complaints about America remain concerns in America. In a 1992 letter, he criticized his homeland for extreme inequities of wealth, the loss of the American Dream, government mismanagement, and an escalating cycle of violence.[5] His methods for dealing with those problems were off, but his analysis was on. Executing him was only a short-term fix for domestic terrorism.

McVeigh's attorney, Stephen Jones, closed his defense by arguing that all Americans were implicated in McVeigh's crime. Perhaps Jones just could not let go of the mind-set of a conspiracy theory that he had pursued, over his client's objections, throughout the trial. Conspiracy or no, Jones's argument that all Americans were implicated in McVeigh's crime was not going to hold sway with an American jury. Still, there was a kernel of wisdom in it, and it was one that America needed to navigate its ongoing journey with terror. That journey would be longer on transformations than on closures.

As misapplied as Jones's argument was in the courtroom, it did pinpoint the complicity of Americans in the weakening of their own society. Those who do not perpetrate terrorism do not bear responsibility for it, but Americans do abet the production of domestic terrorists by tolerating a social environment that fosters it. Each internal attack then builds up more shrapnel in the nation's psyche, with little or no collective healing. America does not have to spare its perpetrators to find itself in their wake, but it does need to resist simplistically vilifying them. Doing that strikes another blow against an already endangered sense of national community. Americans already damaged by terror, damage themselves further by thoughtlessly demonizing their own terrorists. America's prodigals are still American.

Even if American terrorists are defeated as individuals, without America counteracting the cogency of their critiques and the weak social fabric that encourages their emergence, terrorists will become cultural leaders. America has to refute its prodigals, not just kill them. Other Americans may not be implicated in their crimes, but they are culturally connected to them. Until that is understood, it will not be possible to process the horror of the carnage created by McVeigh's disassociation with his own culture. Many Americans carry around bits of McVeigh's pathology of government hatred, or minor doses of Ted Kaczynski's pathologies of arrogance and social isolationism, or bits of Luke Helder's confused disorientation. All three native sons are more typical as Americans than most people think.

Tim McVeigh did not just damage Americans as individuals. He also damaged them as members of American culture. Without a sense of that cultural relationship to him, Americans will remain damaged by his act. Despite the temptation to focus only on his personal responsibility, McVeigh also has to be dealt with as one of America's own for America to heal. Nothing can make the problem of that response his. His trial took place in a courtroom, but the trial he created for the rest of America does not. Nor is it over. His loss in court and loss of life are not a win for America. The real loss comes in failing to take him seriously as an internal adversary of America's collective identity, rather than just a deranged individual.

America did not have a choice about whether to face McVeigh. That choice was his. America will not have a choice about whether to face the next one like him. What Americans can choose is whether to come to terms with the conduct of an internal war, by engaging him and other American jackals. That choice is theirs. American preparation for the next domestic attack can and should go beyond eliminating or dismissing the perpetrator du jour. Without addressing the underlying cultural problems, the alternative is to give in to the assumption that someone else will strike soon. Giving in would mean that the army winning in America is the jackal's.

The intelligent response to Tim McVeigh is to allow him to take American consciousness back to a long-standing and central question in American society of how best to choreograph the dance that relates the individual to the society. The question always has, and always will, demand periodic revisiting in this constructed culture. McVeigh was convinced, in an atmosphere of hyperindividualism, that the government had stolen his prerogatives as an individual. Government failings and misdeeds aside for a moment, what is part of the same truth is that Americans have freely given up a sense of a dynamic relationship with their government. McVeigh cared passionately about his relationship to his government, and did something about it. His response was chosen poorly, but Americans could borrow from that passion and commitment, and then get the relationship right instead of pathologically wrong. The pre-execution FBI document snafu ending the

McVeigh case threw the problems in the relationship between Americans and their government again into clear relief.

Ignoring McVeigh's story sets Americans up to lose a long-term war with themselves. Both his actions and the bureaucratic disorganization that delayed his execution are American systemic problems to solve. Even after McVeigh's death, additional questions arose about a lack of communication between federal agencies, and the case possibly having involved a domestic bombing conspiracy with white separatists of the Elohim City compound in Oklahoma. Studying the motivations of domestic terrorists, and the problems from which they spring, as well as the problems of disjointed American bureaucracy, could bring America a level of mastery over its own terrorist problem, instead of just short-term relief.

American responses to McVeigh varied tremendously, and processing that variation is an exercise in combating American conceptual fragmentation. If the white female from Oklahoma who was "glad" that McVeigh received the death penalty, and the black male from New York who thought that his death would not solve a lot are domestic soldiers in the same war on terror, how would they know their common objectives and the strategies for achieving them? When a sermon that included both the name of McVeigh and the admonition "Love thy enemy" so offended a parishioner that he switched churches, is there a functioning model of American identity in which there can be respect for both pastor and parishioner, instead of just highlighting their dissension?

A hyperindividualized America cannot come to grips with its differences and its collectivity at the same time, only its differences. Dead or alive, Tim McVeigh can only hold America hostage to the heart of the current cultural dilemma of how to relate the individual to the society if it allows him to. After 9/11, people started talking about not letting terrorists win, which was progress in the way that America thought about terrorism. That sensibility should be dialed back onto Tim McVeigh and applied to other homegrown terrorists, in order not to let them win either.

The sensibility should also be dialed forward into the American future to combat an atmosphere of endemic interpersonal anger in America, even among those who do not chose terrorist action. American terrorists display that anger spectacularly, but Americans who are not terrorists display it in milder forms everyday. Road rage is minor league jackal behavior.

Hypercompetition is enshrined in American business. Internet chat rooms drip with vituperation. It is hard to tell what citizen might go "postal" next, from an intolerable build-up of emotional and social pressure. A comfort zone of complacency will not move Americans out of their growing tendency to victimize one another in minor ways on an everyday basis.

Post-McVeigh and post-9/11, Americans would do well to sign up for "Remedial Social Thinking 101," a course with no tuition, no classroom, and no professor. The course can be self-taught in every interaction in American social life, with Americans learning that not all of their problems can be blamed on outsiders, and that they have the power themselves to reorient the balance of individual interests with stable community in America's homes, schoolyards, and workplaces. America's potential domestic terrorists are, after all, American coworkers, American children, and the next person in line at the convenience store. More socially constructive American interaction would improve both American cultural character and its odds of peace in the face of domestic terrorism. There is a post-9/11 cultural window of opportunity for culture change that Americans should use, keeping in mind both the victims of Tim McVeigh and the victims of 9/11.

SURVIVING THE UNABOMBER

Early speculation was that the perpetrator of the anthrax attacks following 9/11 could not have been an American. Whoever it was must have known what they were doing, with weaponized anthrax, not delivered by any one person, or anybody in America. The breadth of the early assumption was striking, and teaches a lesson about American culture and terrorism. The speculation that anthrax terror could not be homegrown was not just a hangover of 9/11 anxiety, a state-sponsored terrorism hypothesis, or negative commentary on the intelligence or resourcefulness of Americans. It was also based in a cultural stereotype of Americans as people who do not do that sort of thing. America had still not wrapped its mind around the fact that Americans could be terrorists. America is still stunned and surprised whenever one is. The matter rested there, with all bets on an outsider, during the national therapy of the 2001 World Series. Only after October slipped into November was there an up tick in intimations that the anthrax perpetrator might be local. Then, the FBI profile of the anthrax letter writer released in November read much like a profile of the Unabomber.

In the fall of 1995, I had submitted a profile of the author of the Unabomber Manifesto to the same FBI agent who released the anthrax profile. The Manifesto itself was a lengthy intellectual fingerprint, and my analysis focused on what its author had read and referred to, his psychology, and how his social attitudes dovetailed with the subculture of Berkeley in 1970. In addition to sources identified in the Manifesto, the unidentified sources on which it was built were an interdisciplinary hodgepodge of dated and current resources, at least one of which is identifiable to a specific page reference. Later, with the search warrant producing all of the evidence from Ted Kaczynski's Montana cabin challenged in court, the Unabomber case turned on a linguistic comparison of the Manifesto to Ted Kaczynski's earlier writing. The warrant was upheld when the comparison was upheld.[6] A cross-check of my analysis and Ted Kaczynski's revolving purchases from the used bookstore in Helena, the written sources in his cabin, and his local library records, might well have produced a parallel result.

I narrowly missed Ted Kaczynski a couple of times. He left Berkeley in the spring of 1969, before my arrival in the fall of 1970 as a graduate student in cultural anthropology. I narrowly missed him too, when I analyzed his Manifesto. The author of the Manifesto was not the man I had known at Berkeley at the outset of the 1970s. That man, though, was also one of a number of radical alienated academics from the same time and place.

The house north of the Berkeley campus I lived in had an eclectic mix of nine people, including a couple from New York, a woman from Georgia, a strange guy who lived in the garage, a nurse and her husband, and two guys who lived in the basement. One of them was a musician. The other was hard to categorize. He had an odd little shop, and few social contacts with anyone in or out of the house. He had no visible means of support, the polite assumption at the time being that he was dealing drugs. He read books about bombs, and understanding him was a challenge. He, the nurse's husband, and I, had long conversations on sunny afternoons on the roof. We talked about politics. We talked about society. We talked about gender. We read counterculture comic books. When he came back to visit, a few months after having moved out of the house for no particular reason, it was apparent that he was not living far away. It was strange. He was an odd combination of fire and reclusiveness, and always a bit of a mystery.

Over two decades later, I discovered that he was Leo Burt, another American terrorist. Burt, though rumored to be dead, is still wanted by the FBI for a fatal August 1970 bombing at the University of Wisconsin at Madison. After his disappearance from Berkeley at the end of 1971, people heard that he had blown himself up while building a bomb. Nobody believed it. It was just the sort of story he would have made up to cover his movements. There are now more recent rumors of his death. Despite his tongue-in-cheek pseudonym "Jeff True," there was more to him than met the eye, and it was not easy to figure out what was true and what was false. He had much in common with Ted Kaczynski, similar social philosophy, social isolation, an interest in bombs, and depression.

We argued about the impact of technology on culture. He did not think it could ever be good. We argued about gender roles, and when I read the Unabomber Manifesto, I thought I recognized those conversations in the author's complaints about feminist anthropologists. While some of the anthropological references in the Manifesto appear to be to classic works by female anthropologists, Margaret Mead included, the author was sufficiently meticulous that he probably would not have described women who predated feminism by several decades as "feminist." One of the references in the Manifesto might have come from a book I had given Leo about technology and social change. It did not, after all.

In hindsight, Leo would not have been quite the writer Ted was. That thought did not occur, though, during the Unabomber investigation. The match between them was much too close for comfort, and I was too busy sweating to think that clearly. Even the composite sketch of the Unabomber was chillingly similar to my housemate's features. The sketch could easily have represented either of them. I could see a gregarious young graduate student, practicing her budding professional style of creating conversational rapport with all types of people, as one of the few people to come into significant contact with this secretive and isolated man.

The writing in the Manifesto, like the personality of the man I had known, is filled with incongruities. Its author is preoccupied with technology and depression. The references to technology are prominent, front loaded, and central to the author's thesis. Then, references to psychology and depression increase in the second half of the document, until depression becomes the literal centerpiece of the final diagram. Besides manifesting symptoms of depression in the Manifesto, the author is very taken with it as a topic. His commentaries on technology and on expert and experiential perspectives on depression remain significant in American culture, even though his terrorist bombing run is now over.

For me, a fast forward from 1971 came in July of 1995. Over twenty years later, and after almost twenty years as a college professor in Minnesota, I suddenly found that I was still in the same story. A student put the July tenth *Newsweek*, with the composite sketch of the Unabomber on the cover, in front of me. The issue also had an article titled "What Is An American?" that asked about a national identity crisis in a country where everyone had their own niche but no sense of what they had in common anymore. The appearance of the sketch and the article in the same issue was not exactly a cultural coincidence. The questions about who the Unabomber was and what drove him, and what was going on in a conceptually disjointed America were related. That day, though, it was the cover that got a rise out of me. The resemblance of the face in the sketch to the man I had known at Berkeley flitted across my consciousness. If I had known that the latest cocktail party game in California was "I think I knew the Unabomber," I might have joined in right then and there.

As it was, I made an interesting mistake by saying to myself that it could not possibly be the same man. The odds against it were too great. I dismissed the thought on numerical grounds. It turned out later that I was objectively correct and it was not the same man, but my working assumption had still been flawed. It almost kept me from pursuing a pattern that could help lead to the right man, even if I had not known him as an individual. An FBI agent on the case later made the same mistake of presuming that the odds apply to each individual lead or phone call. They do not. Ask any dyed-in-the-wool lottery ticket buyer, or anyone with a post-9/11 fear of flying. Your specific case is the one that matters, not the odds.[7] Numbers, important as they are, cannot get at patterns, and they do not inform emotions. During the terror generated by the beltway sniper, psychiatrists told Americans that although their chances of becoming a direct victim were extremely small, their anxiety was going to escalate anyway. The psychiatrists were right. Given its quality of virtually randomized attack, terrorism always seems to have the odds in its favor. Getting out ahead of it is going to take more than just numerical thinking. It is also going to take pattern consciousness. Overapplied quantitative thinking can actually get in the way. Finding a perpetrator is not about finding an average. It is about finding a person. Statistical odds can serve in the hunt, but they can also mislead.

In protecting against terrorism, outstrategizing the single most resourceful terrorist is as important as keeping most terrorists out. A high percentage of success is good, but the goal is also to thwart the toughest terrorist. In doing that, the great trust in American culture for numerically based thinking can also be a bane. It sometimes is for American intelligence collection bureaucracies, overwhelmed by the sheer amount of information they deal with and failing to envision unlikely possibilities. Intelligence can end up with both the quantity of information and their tendency to always think about the problem in quantitative ways out against them. The Oklahoma City bombing did begin to move some security thinking in America away from an exclusive orientation to the statistical likelihood or probability of a terrorist occurrence, which is always small, and toward models of possibility instead. That movement in consciousness was reinforced by the experience of 9/11.[8]

The FBI, however, commonly responds to criticism about its shortcomings by reference to the number of phone calls or documents or leads that it is dealing with, instead of in terms of the need to adjust the quality of their system for handling quantity. Quantity cannot get to pattern. It is a different phenomenon, and the smartest prevention and enforcement systems will deal effectively with both. The FBI agent trainee who refused to believe that John Muhammad was who he said he was when he called repeatedly did not fail because of the volume of phone calls she was handling. She failed because the quality of interaction she was using in those phone calls was wrong. When looking for a "crackpot," not every one who sounds like one is going to be a hoaxer. One of them may well be your man.

My own state of numerically based mental bliss was not to last. In August of 1995, a colleague sent me excerpts from the Unabomber Manifesto, which had been partially published on the Internet. The Manifesto was originally sent to the *Washington Post* and *The New York Times* in June, and was fully published in print in September. But reading those excerpts one mid-September morning before the full document came out, my jaw almost literally dropped onto the desk. The language in the text reverberated with memories of the sketch and a sunlit roof. Statements about technology and social change read just like conversations with Jeff True.

The Manifesto seemed to have been written as an intellectual puzzle meant specifically for me to solve. He was the professor, I was the student, and the Manifesto was a big trick question written for me. Otherwise, maybe its author was just looking for anyone to beat him at his own game. Walking into class that morning with the color drained from my face, I told my students that I thought I had just identified the Unabomber. Many of them also turned several shades paler. Meanwhile, the FBI had issued a special request to hear from people who might have had some contact with the Unabomber based on his ties to the University of California at Berkeley.

A hot line had been set up for tip calls. The full text of the Manifesto was due out within days. I thought about the fact that I agreed with some of the author's arguments about American culture. I thought about the risk to my students, family, and my own well-being if I got involved. I thought about the relative safety of not making the phone call. I thought about the victims. I thought about my inability to enjoy the freedoms of a culture that I did not help to defend. I thought about errors in the Unabomber's analysis, and how they needed intellectual as well as moral debunking. I called. My call on September 13, 1995 was one of tens of thousands that the FBI received in the case. The woman on the phone that day said she thought the lead sounded "hot," and that she would forward the information to the special task force investigating the case.

I had begun an American odyssey of my own. Maybe I could help catch him. I could at least field test his hypothesis that individuals could not have an impact on bureaucracy. I could make myself into a test case demonstrating that he was wrong. The Unabomber had forgotten something important about American culture. While he was right that bureaucracies everywhere are run by rules, he had missed the human element in how those rules are applied. He had also missed the fact that one of the greatest cultural games Americans play is how to bend, twist, or otherwise turn any rule system to their own personal advantage, based on the fundamental American cultural rule of serving self-interest.

If I could not help get to him physically with fingerprint evidence, I could at least provide a counterexample to his thinking, by making headway with the most notoriously secretive and intransigent of American bureaucracies, the FBI. Working with the same bureaucracy he had worked successfully against for so long, I could prove him wrong. Maybe I could get to him two ways, both disproving him and helping to catch him. The weekend came. I plied my memory and my old journals for information about the man I had known. Some memories resurfaced. Some things were written down. I called the FBI again, this time bypassing the hot line number and going directly to the task force.

It would be a couple of weeks yet before the information from my original phone call would reach the task force. People tend to forget what you can accomplish, though, by using the U.S. mail or a phone book, if you put your mind to it. I got through to the task force. If I had the key to the case locked up in my memory somewhere, the people at the center of the investigation and my mental process needed to be linked. As an investigator of cultures rather than criminals, I knew that a skilled interviewer asking the right question might be just what was needed to bring the key information out of an archived consciousness. Difficult cases demand creative tactics, like putting up with assertive informants. What the case needed, from my perspective, was an FBI agent with adaptive creativity and intelligence. I found one. He was not a bureaucracy. He was a human being. Right off the bat, I had the Unabomber's ideas about individuals being ineffective in the face of faceless bureaucracies on the run.

I did have to vault some bureaucratic hurdles to get to the creative and extremely hungry agent. It was not hard to hear over the phone how badly the bureau wanted the Unabomber, but being swamped with thousands of phone calls was a new experience. Talking to the public at the public's initiative was a reversal of traditional roles that some agents were not ready for. One task force phone-answering agent, mired in a traditional FBI culture of agency-centered and quantitative thinking, was not going to put my call through to the task force. He was not prepared to accept the incursion of an assertive informant into his sense of professional control and identity. I just sidestepped, and went where I needed to go in the bureaucracy by a different route instead. When you cannot go straight to California, go via Virginia. The phone-answering agent angered me enough, though, that the FBI almost lost an assertively cooperative informant who might have had the key to the case, and who did produce a highly touted profile. He had not adjusted his sense of how to interact with people calling in, the people who composed the haystack in which he was trying to find a needle.

The phone-answering agent said, using the same numerically based thinking I had when I first saw the composite sketch, that he could assure me that the people staffing the Unabomber hot line knew more about the psychological profile of the Unabomber than I did. What he said would be true for most of the people calling in. His problem was that the few callers who did know more than his staff were the ones he needed to be the most interested in. Trying to solve the case by assuming that the average applies to every phone call was poor strategy. Just like telling people who call an FBI hot line saying that they are the beltway sniper that they are hoaxers, you will be professionally correct and in command every time, except for the one phone call that you really care about.

The concept of the average, applied to a high volume of calls, gets in the way of solving the case. It is not the average that you are looking for. It is a particular human being. The agent who took my call had not thought about the importance of the exceptions to his rule, that being right 9,999 out of 10,000 times was not good enough. It was that 10,000th caller that counted, with an agency with $48 million and eighteen years into solving the case, unless you wanted to risk dropping the needle right when you had it in your hand. While the economies of limited resources and the need to pursue numerous leads in investigations are givens, giving up the power of being open to the unexpected is not. It pays to remember, and incorporate into your social role, that you investigate because there is something that you do not yet know.

The FBI had another problem in the Unabomber case. The million dollar reward may have encouraged more people to call in, but the money also discredited them with the assumption that the calls were made in self-interest. The default cultural assumption of financial self-interest left no motive to sort out callers' motivations. As it turned out, the call that did solve the case, originating from Ted Kaczynski's brother David, had nothing to do with personal gain, and everything to do with personal integrity and self-sacrifice.

The lesson of never ignoring the small numbers, the "minority data," even when you are overwhelmed by "majority data," also applies to American culture as a whole. While American terrorists are few in number, for the rest of the culture to ignore them on that basis hides the solution to larger cultural problems. American terrorists are trying to communicate with the rest of the culture, and their "phone calls" really should not be missed. Those calls are needles in a much larger cultural haystack of confusion. Ignoring "minority data" can render important patterns invisible, and is especially risky when dealing with something as elusive as terrorism. It was the human factor that kept me sufficiently motivated to keep fighting the Unabomber's social hypothesis after I hung up with the task force phone-answering agent. The agent who had sent me to him in the first place had finer-tuned human sensibilities. Him, I trusted. Him, I called back. He made the necessary connection.

Like the phone-answering agent, another agent on the Unabomber task force bemoaned the number of calls he had to deal with during the investigation. He was tired of talking to women who thought their ex-husbands were the Unabomber (the beltway sniper investigation, too, produced a surfeit of women with information about their ex-husbands). Unaccustomed to dealing with a flood of volunteered information, his desire to catch the Unabomber made him dependent on talking to anxious women.

I pointed out that the calls were not necessarily throw-aways, and could be productive instead of frustrating. Listening carefully to each one to discover social patterning in what the callers had to say might generate understanding that could refine the existing profile, and help solve the actual case. The women's composite experience, recorded anonymously into a database for sociological analysis, might point to precisely the right question to ask of someone interviewed later, someone whose best friend actually had dated your perpetrator. Wrong leads could still provide information about cultural patterns. "False" leads weren't necessarily worthless or useless. They could not be if my profile, which was based on a false lead, had the kind of value I was told that it did.

Several things in the Unabomber investigation happened around the same time. At the end of September, I faxed to the FBI a fourteen-page single-spaced analysis of the short and long forms of the Manifesto. The next-day response was that it was the best profile the bureau had seen, even compared with those from over a hundred other academics and the agency's own panel of psychiatrists. It was being distributed throughout the agency immediately. Still, it turned out that I was wrong. The Unabomber was not the man I was writing about. While I missed the specific identity of the author, my analysis did document a pattern of time, place, mental health status, and political orientation that encompassed both the man I had known and the Unabomber. I had profiled a pattern, rather than a person.

The power of my "false" lead but good profile was in its combination of perspectives, (1) cultural and sociological knowledge of American culture and the radical subculture of Berkeley at the time, (2) an interdisciplinary academic approach to documenting the references in the Manifesto, which themselves included sources from history, anthropology, psychology, biology, etc., and (3) personal knowledge as a depression sufferer. While my profile addressed who Kaczynski was socially and academically, I had a particular resonance for who he was psychologically. In Americans who suffer from depression, American cultural emphasis on the self and the focus on the self produced by depression compound into an extreme. That extreme was written all over the Manifesto.

Depression is, coincidentally, also addictive in its nature. It grows by feeding on itself, in an individual, or in a cultural psyche, as it does now in fertile ground in America. Recovery, as for an alcoholic or a gambler, requires constant effort not to slip back. Whether it is an individual person or a culture fighting depression, the only way to keep winning is to keep blocking it and holding it back. My experiential knowledge of depression, which differs in quality from the expert knowledge of psychiatrists, was one of my tools in approaching the Unabomber's text.

That there is a difference between those two types of knowledge is, in fact, one of the points he makes in his text, along with the observation that American culture puts too much value on the expert perspective, and not enough on that of the experiencer. As an experiencer, I could disconfirm the Unabomber's depressive railings about the lack of power of individuals in American culture with an authority that no expert could muster. At the same time, I could debunk the false elements of his argument about America's overemphasis on professional expertise, as well as underscore the true ones. Professional expertise is overrated in America, in part because the people consulting the experts allow it to be.

Critiquing the Manifesto is not hard. It is a poor piece of writing, internally contradictory and morally indefensible, even though it does include cogent cultural commentary. Kaczynski was wrong about having to be violent to get published. Violence-based notoriety may have made it easier for him to get published, but even after bombing his way to fame, he did not manage to publish a book. Fame in hand, his social dysfunction still prevented him from getting his memoir out. He could not come to terms with his publisher. I set out to prove wrong the man who thought you had to kill to get your message across, the book with the counterargument that was a precursor to this volume was titled, in a variation on the pen and sword theme, *The Book is Mightier than the Bomb*. Now, the Manifesto's test of me has been set to rest, but the test it presents America is only partly over. Its author is incarcerated, but if one measures the culture in relation to themes in the Manifesto, a sense of individual disempowerment, how humans relate to their technology, and how social fragmentation and mental health problems relate to cultural dysfunction, the test also clearly continues.

Kaczynski's idea that technology is always harmful was easy to refute. Technology is a double-edged sword with potential for good or ill, depending on how human beings use it. The unquestioning devotion to technology that supersedes trust in people and has come to characterize contemporary America is a cultural problem, not a technological one. Technology is tools. People run tools, not the other way around, at least until they build a cultural belief system that allows them to forget that they are in charge. Technology only runs people when they allow it to, passively submitting to the environment that they have created with their tools, instead of commanding it. Do not concede authority to the computer, and it does not have it. The computer is not the issue. The issue is how the computer is defined in the minds of human beings. Hating, blaming, or depending exclusively on the machine only feeds the erroneous sense in American culture that it is technology that counts, rather than people.

Like other Americans, Ted Kaczynski aggrandizes technology out of proportion to its importance. He just does so negatively instead of positively, in the belief that technology has robbed Americans of their ability for social change. The American ability to adapt culturally has not gone anywhere, and technology is not in the driver's seat, even though there is a cultural myth that it is. Bureaucracy is not unequivocally in charge, either. Bureaucracy will run you if you let it, but it is not necessary to concede the point. Nor do you have to bomb your way out. There are other ways to have an impact. Any bureaucracy is made up of human beings, although Americans ensconced in culturally generated assumptions about the powerlessness of the individual have forgotten that fact.

America's tendency to glorify technology is as much about devaluing people as it is about worshipping tools. Technology and bureaucracy, even in combination, do not dehumanize. What does dehumanize is the thinking that accords them supremacy over people. That thinking is reinforced every time a human concedes authority to a machine without considering the human being behind the machine, or refuses to try to have an impact on "city hall" because doing so is impossible by definition. Everyday Americans did not seem to buy the Unabomber's technology arguments. Internet responders to the Unabomber's Manifesto said that the problem in America was not computers, but how people thought about them. They should be tools for work instead of sources for value judgments. What was wrong with the idea that the computer could not be wrong was not wrong with the computer. It was wrong with the people using it.

Ted Kaczynski did not really fight the misguided idea that technology takes primacy over people. He used it instead, and victimized people with it. Arguably, both Kaczynski and anti-gun activists succumb to an extent to an American tendency to identify a problem with the technology that represents it, rather than the humans behind it. Kaczynski's poor formula first gave in to the idea that technology defines American culture, and then tried to fight it. People have choices. If they want to organize their lives without a particular technology, they can. It is not easy, but it is possible. He did it, but at the same time he made the strategic mistake of giving in to the assumption of the supremacy of technology. He did that, not the technology.

People are not wrong because a computer says so, even if it does have a voice. The computer may or may not know what it is talking about. Person-free and human solutions to problems do not live in two separate vacuums. They intertwine. Contrary to contemporary science fiction themes, the relation between humans and machines need not be conceived as adversarial. Thinking in other terms requires social imagination, but technology is not always the answer, and it is not always the villain. Technology has become a surrogate in America, taking the blame for problems that are, at their foundation, social in nature.

Problems of social organization surrounding the use of technology, such as how the introduction of a new technology will reorient human social relations, require social imagination that is seldom applied. It is easy to understand that the people Ted Kaczynski calls "technophiles" are attracted to the social status they receive from being closely associated with computers. Info-tech priesthoods are no different from any other. Those priests, like any others, work to keep the power that comes from being close to objects of ritual worship to themselves. Bombing the priesthood will not get the focus back on the fact that the problem is fundamentally a human one, and not a technical one.

Ted Kaczynski exemplifies the problem he identifies, mentally vesting excessive power in sophisticated tools and the people closest to them, and misattributing a growing sense of lack of control in American life to technology rather than to people. We have met the enemy, and it is not our PCs. He could have bombed for a century, and never scratched the surface of a pathology he was part of himself. The human-technology relationship in American culture bears rethinking, but not via Kaczynski's methods of destroying life or terrorizing a nation. The CIA's recent object lesson in how technology can empower and disempower simultaneously, in its post-9/11 realizations about the irreplaceability of human intelligence, reconfirms that the human element is central and indispensable in fighting terrorism. Kaczynski's extremist perspective still serves as a cultural mirror, as the tendency to relinquish the importance of human identity to the power of technology is a powerful force in contemporary America. America would do well to extract wisdom from Kaczynski's argument, once the twists and the moral bankruptcy are taken out. It does not have to like the messenger.

Kaczynski's Manifesto asserts that "the human race with technology is just like an alcoholic with a barrel of wine,"[9] in other words, addicted to it. Recent cultural commentators echo that thinking, asking whether increasingly plugged-in Americans are addicted to their data and their devices.[10] One way to view terrorist violence in America is not as an extension of techno-fantasies, such as violent video games, but as an attempt to regain a sense of the physical human self. "Game-inspired" violence may also be a protest against a growing tendency to remote and disembodied communication in contemporary American culture.

With face-to-face or even direct phone contact becoming less normative, Columbine bombers Eric Harris and Dylan Klebold may have not just been acting out video games, but also trying to get away from them, reclaiming an embodied sense of self from a cerebralized one by bombing. Maybe Britney Spears is not "hot" because she resolves virgin-whore dualism, as some cultural commentators have maintained. Maybe she is "hot" because she has a body and knows how to use it, capitalizing perfectly, with old-fashioned primate display behavior, on an impulse to bring American cyberselves back to earth. Maybe what she resolves is mind-body dualism. That would be plenty of fodder for a latter-day sex goddess to work with. American bombers may be trying to do the same thing in a different way, in a culture plagued by a deep strain of division between ideational selves and physical selves. Addiction to technology in America bears further thought, despite Ted Kaczynski's counterproductive methods for getting attention on the subject.

On the subject of "experts" in American culture, Kaczynski mistargets again. His criticism is based on the fact that scientists, academics, and other professionals are not the perfect expressions of principles of objectivity and empiricism that they are often taken for, but fallible human beings. He forgets the same fact himself, though, and falls right into his own trap. His cultural training as an academician is written all over his questioning of everyone's fallibility but his own, and his disingenuousness is in his belief in the powerlessness of humanity, including that of the experts he derides. His belief in human powerlessness supports his willingness to destroy humans. Forgetting that scientists do not embody or personify science but practice it, as a good scientist will admit, he conveniently forgets their vulnerabilities, except when he chooses to use scientists as targets. While the culture confers social status on scientists, just as it does on "technocrats," bombing professors does not touch the problem of the excessive valuing of expertise.

Kaczynski confuses the map with the human territory. He does not strike at his target, a "system" that disempowers people, but only at the human beings who symbolize it for him, in a ritualized sacrifice to his ideas. Kaczynski could not damage the American cult of expertise, because he never attacked its foundations. He only attacked people who happened to be scientists or engineers, and other people nearby, like their secretaries. There was only service to his own tortured consciousness in what he did, certainly none to humanity or American culture. The cultural overvaluing of expertise is a problem that requires a different solution. Kaczynski's defense of American humanity by destroying parts of it just created a lose-lose scenario for him and the culture. So far, Kaczynski is 0 for 2. He missed on the technology, and he missed on the experts. Besides, he had his own addiction. It was to bombing.

In anthropology, Kaczynski scores another ill-informed zero. As usual, though, it is an instructive zero, with something to teach contemporary America. Kaczynski's social philosophy is a simple twist on the old, and equally oversimplified Social Darwinist theory of cultural change. All that nineteenth-century anthropologist Lewis Henry Morgan needed to know in order to rank the evolutionary status of a culture was how advanced its technology was. Nothing else mattered. Separated by a century, Morgan and Kaczynski are Americans with not entirely dissimilar views of their own culture. Morgan's now academically outdated evaluation of the superiority of his own culture based on its technological sophistication still lives on in American popular culture.

Kaczynski simply turned the Morganian perspective on its head, making technology, by definition, bad instead of good. The more you have, the worse off you are. Kaczynski's perspective could also be viewed as a kind of techno-Marxism, based on the idea that technological supremacy will lead to the eventual breakdown of society. On either Morgan's or Kaczynski's trajectory, though, the idea that technology is the be-all and end-all of culture is faulty. Both perspectives neglect to take human beings, and not just their tool kits, into account when evaluating culture.

Kaczynski is 0 for 3, with technology, experts, and culture. With the subject of depression, he appears to be headed for 0 for 4. His arguments about it are faulty, too. It is tempting to disregard them, but this time another interesting near miss turns into a serendipitous save. Depression in America is a growth diagnosis, a growth pharmaceutical industry, and a growth conceptualization of American consciousness. Its close relative, anxiety, actually regarded by some in the field of psychology as the same disorder, also belongs in a discussion of terrorism in America. After 9/11, anxiety became even more au courant in American cultural consciousness than depression. Zoloft commercials for depression before 9/11 became for a time afterward commercials for post-traumatic stress disorder, an anxiety diagnosis, before they went back to being commercials for depression.

My practical training in anxiety came in the fall of 1995. After turning in my profile to the FBI, I had to manage mentally all of the possible outcomes I had created by involving myself in the investigation. One was that I had identified the right man, and that he would find me before the FBI found him. Depression changed to anxiety, and comedic scenes ensued. A box would arrive. Was it safe to open? No box appeared innocuous. My family members and I were some of the earliest terrorist mail-screening citizenry in the country. When mail actually did arrive later from the Unabomber, with his name and address at the Supermax federal prison in Colorado written on it in meticulous block letters, opening it was still a little exciting. In the interim, there was a scene in which an FBI agent and I discussed the case on the phone. A woman, whose depression was one of her calling cards in her ability to profile the Unabomber, had to surmount her own anxieties about bureaucracy to assert her perspectives to the FBI. The FBI were the professional experts in this case, but it was my family and students who might be on the line.

Having provoked my own anxiety by getting involved with the FBI, I had to reach past the stigma of being identified as mentally ill in order to manage my dealings with them. Facing up socially to my mental health status was my job. The FBI had their own problems. To solve my personal problem with American terrorism, I had to reach inside, take the pathologies there, and put them fearlessly on the table. Facing fear was not optional. It was required, while dancing with both the Unabomber and a bureaucracy with its own complicated configuration of emotion and rationality about the case.

The moral of the story is not to leave anxiety in charge of the situation. The bureaucracy was not left in charge. The terrorist was not left in charge. A human being, determined to take control of her own fate, was in charge. There is a lesson for the nation in that, a lesson about anxiety being a poor master when combating terrorism. Then things got quiet on the phone until spring break of 1996, when a Unabomber suspect was arrested. My lead had not been the right one, and my relief was profound. There would be no testifying in court, and no media attention. I could settle down to writing about a Unabomber saga that had separated itself from my own.

Ted Kaczynski's postarrest experiences confirmed that he does not do well around people. His social problem, based on a combination of his personal history, his extreme intelligence, and his mental health status, may be his most fundamental problem, and his example of social maladaptation is one for the culture to heed. From his official psychiatric evaluation, to his relationship with the judge and his attorneys, his ill-advised use of the media, his dysfunctionality as a book author, and his failed bid for a new trial, he did not manage well. While his is a failed story of management of depression and anxiety, his deepest failings can be viewed as not having made the social connections he needed to get his message across, despite the violence he used to promote it.

Experts do not always agree, as Ted Kaczynski would be the first to point out. They certainly did not agree about his psychiatric diagnosis. Of the small army of personnel who offered diagnoses, some thought he was delusional. Others did not. If the question was whether he was schizophrenic, the answer came back both yes and no. Furthermore, the social distribution of expert opinion did nothing to support the concept of total psychiatric objectivity. The experts linked to a defense team determined to use a mental health defense viewed him as acutely ill—meeting the standard for legal insanity. Those tied to the prosecution saw him as clinically ill perhaps, but not legally insane. Kaczynski himself agreed with the prosecution. Every time he received the diagnosis of paranoid schizophrenia, his anxiety level must have gone up, as aversive as he was to accepting the idea that he might have a mental health problem. He appeared to fear nothing so much as the social stigma of mental illness.

The psychiatrists who tied Kaczynski's aversion to psychiatrists to their evaluation of his schizophrenia were citing social as well as psychological phenomena as a basis for diagnosis. The fact that Kaczynski did not accept the members of the profession was one criterion used to determine how ill he was. That is expert power. One of them became a social leader among those evaluating Kaczynski on behalf of the defense, with Kaczynski's attorneys echoing his diagnosis of paranoid schizophrenia to the press.

As the process of defining Kaczynski's frame of mind continued to unfold afterward, it was easy to miss the fact that the psychiatrist's idealized expert objectivity, combined with his socially-situated power over Kaczynski, was a perfect expression of Kaczynski's own arguments about experts. In theater of the absolutely absurd, Kaczynski was caught in the plot of his own text. Psychiatric diagnosis does occur in a social context. Psychiatrists are social actors, as well as detached professionals. Ted Kaczynski's eventual official diagnosis of delusional paranoid schizophrenia was rendered in a framework of social dynamics richly illustrating that mental health evaluations are the products of social as well as scientific processes.

Psychiatrist Sally Johnson, sought by the same attorneys who had already labeled Kaczynski delusional in the press, produced diagnostic reasoning for defining Kaczynski's state of mind as "delusional" that rested in society as well as what was inside Kaczynski's head. She thought that his "nonbizarre delusional beliefs" might be the result of social isolation, noting that such beliefs are measured in relationship to what almost "everyone believes."[11] Her diagnosis was made in relationship to his own social history, and how far his thought was from social norms for consciousness. She attributed to him a personality disorder that was "an enduring pattern of inner experience and behavior that deviates markedly from the expectations of the individual's culture."[12] In other words, nonconformity to cultural norms was a benchmark for determining psychological pathology.

Since one of the arguments in the Manifesto is that mental illness is defined in relationship to the rules of the culture, at least they agreed on that point. A person "disordered" in one culture might not be in another. Alternatively, if a culture changed, an individual's diagnostic status might change along with it. He objected to her diagnosis. He would rather have died than be defined as crazy.

Since critiquing your own culture strongly can contribute to being diagnosed as delusional, one of the factors in play in diagnosis is the expert's opinion of what "everyone believes." Different experts, with different views about society, might well come to different conclusions about the same person. What looks delusional to one psychiatrist may just look radical to the next. Deviant action can also support a diagnosis of delusions, and Johnson's evaluation was made in a social setting where Kaczynski's conduct, including fighting with his own attorneys, made him the odd man out. Both the social processes surrounding a diagnosis, and the socially based nature of the diagnostic categories can affect it.

Such unremarked aspects of "objective" expert opinions about an individual's state of mind are what Kaczynski abhorred. Dr. Johnson's social, as well as professional, power in the situation is exactly what drives Ted Kaczynski, to put it in the vernacular, "crazy." Interestingly, her evaluation also attributed Kaczynski's depression solely to situational adjustment to his life in prison, ignoring his self-reports and professional diagnoses of depression from a period spanning several decades, the centrality of the concept in his Manifesto, and his family history.

Kaczynski helped make his own ideas about the system disempowering the individual work on him like a charm, through the way he handled his relationships with his attorneys and the judge, and others. Given Kaczynski's palpable mental and social problems and his fixation on American attitudes toward mental illness, the diagnosis of delusional paranoid schizophrenia must have been sheer torture, a psychological punishment worse than death. Following his failed underwear suicide attempt during the trial, he continued to seek death through the mechanism of a retrial. He must have found the entire process depressing. The power of mental health stigma in Kaczynski's mind was such that the prospect of dying while regarded as sane was preferable to living while regarded as insane.

FBI profiler John Douglas, another sort of expert, rendered another opinion of the Unabomber's psychiatric status based in society, as well as what was going on in Kaczynski's head. Douglas said of Kaczynski that: "anyone who would walk away from (a tenure track job at a top department in his field at the University of California), after working so hard for so long, to live as a recluse without amenities or conveniences must surely be psychotic."[13] The decision to leave Berkeley was not a lifestyle choice, a social failure to conform to norms of professional achievement, or an adaptive response to levels of stimulus and stress that a depressed Kaczynski could not cope with. It was psychosis. Giving up the brass ring was not a strategic personal choice. It was nuts. Seeking an environment with peaceful solitude instead of high status was not tactical. It was crazy. Douglas's view reflects a tendency, even among profilers, to stereotype terrorists as mentally ill. It happened that Kaczynski actually was ill, although arguably not as intensively ill as Douglas thought.

Kaczynski did not leave society out of his psychiatric commentary either. In a 1999 *Time* interview, he presented himself as sane and not delusional, while acknowledging that he had problems with "social adjustment" that some people would call a sickness.[14] His state of mind would not have been "organic" like "schizophrenia or something like that." He should check his own Manifesto, where he identifies depression as having genetic (the same as "organic") origins, as well as environmental causes. Given his self-identification as depressed at several points in his life, in the 60s, 70s, 80s and 90s, there are gaps in his thinking on the subject of his own mental health status. He is not coming to grips with it. In being confused and ambiguous about mental health, including his own, he is closer to being typically than atypically American. His aversion to the idea that anything could be wrong with him is rooted not just in his own psyche, but also in the American cultural aversion to acknowledging or dealing with mental illness. In beating around the bush, instead of realistically evaluating himself mentally, he engages in an activity that is all too common in the culture as a whole.

In the flurry of newspaper reporting that took place after the tragedy at Columbine High School, there was a call for a new attitude toward mental health issues in America. The call for more support and less stigmatization of depression sufferers was issued, in order to help prevent a future Columbine at the hands of other depressed American teenagers. Kaczynski suffered from an acute case of resisting the stigma associated with mental health in America, and the specter of the same problem stalked America at Columbine. At Columbine, it was not just Klebold and Harris themselves, or just their parents, their peers, their counselors, or their social environment that was to blame for them crossing the threshold into suicidal violent social protest undetected. Stigmatization of mental health issues in America was also a contributing factor.

At Columbine and elsewhere, forthrightly acknowledging American weakness could have helped promote American strength. There was tragedy instead. One of the potentially problematic things about depressed people in America is that they are creative. Their creativity is not always applied constructively. Little happened to change American attitudes about mental illness after Columbine, despite the warning signs posted on the national psyche.

Kaczynski's opinion was that society helps induce mental problems, and that: "when one does not have adequate opportunity to go through the power process the consequences are . . . depression, anxiety."[15] While he may have a point, one does not "have" opportunities to have an impact on society. One makes them, seizes them, or creates them, as he did. A depressed person is short on a sense of initiative or perceived ability to do anything. It is not necessarily the ability itself that is lacking. It is the sense of having the ability that is lacking. Thinking that you do not have it can help steal it from you.

Besides stigma, another problem for depressed individuals in contemporary America is that they live in an environment that encourages depression. Not only is the environment socially fragmented, it is also characterized culturally by the presumption that individuals are powerless to do anything. That cultural presumption itself is an indicator that the national psyche, too, is at risk for depression.

There is other evidence that the national psyche has become passive and depressive in character. Even healthy people are socially passive, and positive models of social action are hard to find. If depression gets a grip on a particular individual, stigma feeds that grip. Stigma, like the disorder itself, helps to create more social isolation for the individual, which in turn supports their depression. If social isolation is a norm in a group, the psychological tenor of the group (in this case, the national psyche) itself will circulate in the same emotional arena. Group and individual depression will support each other. Kaczynski, far from being a "nut" to be dismissed, is both an ironically astute analyst, and a perfect example of problems in American culture with mental health. He presents a puzzle for American consciousness to solve, not to shun.

The 1999 U.S. government report on profiling terrorists, *Who Becomes a Terrorist and Why* gives an interesting counterpoint to the drama of psychiatric consciousness that evolved during Kaczynski's trial, noting that terrorists come from a population that "describes most of us." In other words, terrorists are less freakish than most people like to think. The personality of the terrorist often has "a depressive aspect to it," characterized by an inability to maintain relationships, and a focus on death.[16] The report concludes that the personality profile of terrorists varies, and that contrary to the stereotype that terrorists are always psychopathological, "the terrorist is actually quite sane, although deluded."[17] Stereotyped as crazy, terrorists can be nonetheless quite sane.

Whether any one terrorist's "deluded" state would rank as a psychiatric diagnostic category would be a matter for a psychiatric expert to determine, but that expert would still be a member of a culture in which terrorists are stereotyped as psychopathological. In practice, and certainly in the Unabomber case, social stereotyping of terrorists, clinical definitions of insanity, the state of the society itself, and depression are combined in an almost inextricably muddled mix.

Kaczynski's ideas about personal disempowerment are commonplace in America in less extreme forms. People who are not clinically depressed are often what might be called culturally depressed. Perfectly mentally healthy Americans still think that there is nothing they can do to have impact on their own society. They do not vote, think only celebrities count, and that only money talks. Watching the daily news is a daily challenge to mental balance, and some Americans show a classic symptom of anxiety, avoidance, in not accepting the challenge of digesting news. They prefer instead to immerse themselves in the pleasures of sports and entertainment. Ted Kaczynksi put his finger on a truth about the self-centered, consuming, "pleasure-seeking," civically passive American, when he talked about a depressive "leisured aristocracy" that needs goals toward which to exercise its power.[18] He was absolutely right. A clearer sense of and pursuit of ethical and moral goals in contemporary America would leave the collective psyche both less depressed, and less at risk of serious victimization by terrorism. He was right that the benefits of antidepressive drugs for individuals do nothing to affect the social environment that helps encourage depression in the first place. This Prozac and Celexa and Paxil nation arguably does overmedicate its individuals, as it undermedicates its collective social consciousness. Focusing on the individual, as psychiatry must, leads to the treatment of single cases, but leaves questions about treatment of the social psyche and social environment unasked and unanswered. Clinically depressed or not, socially passive Americans live in a culture with a rising rate of clinical depression, and a collective psyche in the danger zone. So do their socially active counterparts, some of whom are American terrorists. Despite his blind spot with respect to himself, Kaczynski came close enough on depression that his final score has to be 1 and 3.

Add an anxiety-provoking experience with terrorism to a depressive psyche, and you have a genuine challenge on your hands. It happened to me with the Unabomber. It happened to the nation on 9/11. America's already compromised collective emotional state became more so, but Ted Kaczynski, like Tim McVeigh, only holds America thrall to the psychological passion play of always thinking in terms of the individual and ignoring society if we allow him to. Kacyznski, while both psychologically disordered and socially maladapted, is correct when he points out the existence of problems in the cultural psyche. In another place and time, he might have been regarded as a mad prophet, but people would have listened. In America, his story dead-ended in an unsuccessful legal appeal after his original conviction on a plea bargain, and his publisher's cancellation of plans to publish a book-length memoir *Truth Versus Lies*.

CHAPTER 2

CAN'T KEEP TRACK

THE BOYS ON THE BLOCK

Y ou can't keep track of terror in America without a scorecard, but let's start with the boys on the block. Tim McVeigh and Ted Kaczynski became friends at the Supermax prison in Florence, Colorado, where they lived on the same cellblock with 1993 World Trade Center bomber, Ramzi Yousef. The two American bombers were clearly a pair. While the close quarters apparently smoothed out any differences, friendship did not keep them from criticizing each other. Ted thought that Tim was intelligent, but Tim got into Ted's moral no-fly zone with what Ted termed the indiscriminate slaughter of Tim's bombing. Ted thought that the amount of collateral damage was unnecessarily inhumane,[1] which made the bombing less than effective as an antigovernment protest. Actually, Tim's bombing had served to move public opinion regarding Waco quite effectively in the direction of his own views.[2] Ted was the minibomber, and Tim was the maxibomber. They may even have talked about whether the Oklahoma City bombing fueled Ted's decision to send off his Manifesto for publication just two months later, a decision that led to his arrest.

Tim got Ted back by criticizing him for poor legal strategy. Both stated a preference for execution to life in prison, but Kaczynski lost the opportunity for a retrial that would have brought a renewed possibility of the death penalty. Tim got what he wanted. Tim said of Ted's October 1999 *Time* interview "I Don't Want to Live Long. I Would Rather Get the Death Penalty Than Spend the Rest of My Life in Prison": "Ted messed up . . . If one is serious about it, you never show your hand."[3] Stating his intentions had been a poor strategic move. There was also no shortage of arrogance in Kaczynski's telling everyone else in his Manifesto that they could have no effect on bureaucracy, and then publicly announcing his own intentions for personal use of the justice system. Besides that, Ted was playing with mental health fire. The judge in his case had other ideas about the system being used by someone self-announced as suicidal, had already ruled on the point, and had his ruling upheld on appeal.

Whether or not Ted's October publicity did anything to turn sentiment on the three-member panel of federal appeals judges who reviewed his motion for a new trial the following January, the panel did deny his motion. Being portrayed as a "gross and repellent lunatic" in a mental health defense may have looked like coercion to him, but it did not to them.[4] They upheld the original ruling denying him the right to represent himself. The dissenting justice asserted that Kaczynski should have the right to represent himself, even if he was "seriously disturbed," and could face execution. The fact that Kaczynski wanted death and a public platform for his ideas was beside the narrow legal point of competency.

The original trial judge had opened himself to criticism of having ruled off the narrow legal point by explaining that allowing Kaczynski to represent himself could impugn the integrity of the criminal justice system, "since it would simply serve as a suicide forum."[5] Still, his ruling, together with his sense that the integrity of the system was more important than the integrity of the individual, held.

Ted had been put on a suicide watch during his trial. The trial judge's rationale of keeping society uninvolved in Kaczynski's suicidal plans effectively extended that watch from his cell into the courtroom. Kaczynski could be sane and technically legally competent, but none of that mattered. He was scarcely going to be granted a position of social responsibility in a courtroom if he acted suicidally. Being suicidal made him socially, if not clinically, insane. At the same time that the ruling went against Kaczynski, it offered support for his theory that the system takes precedence over the individual. The judge was a human being and not a bureaucracy, but he was a human who arguably erred in favor of protecting society as a whole from a "disturbed" individual.

Kaczynski had a problem with his social perceptions, and sabotaged his social status again with the release of the *Time* interview shortly before filing his motion for a new trial. Producing suicidal ideation or action before trying to gain responsible status in a courtroom began to look like a pattern in Kaczynski's life. After a final failed appeal to the Supreme Court, Ted Kaczynski's bid for a retrial and his practical options for having an impact on society were both dead, and he was alive for the foreseeable future. In pre-appeal correspondence with Kaczynski, I advised him to reconsider his resistance to being thought of as a "sickie," and not to let the social stigma of depression get in the way of his best strategy to get a new trial. It was an argument I suspected he would reject, (and did, along with further correspondence with me), but felt it was necessary to offer. I asserted that cultural forces might cause judges to respond more to his depressive actions than to his legal competency.

In a culture where Kaczynski thought himself "widely assumed to be insane," the sanest move he could have made would have been to admit a level of mental health difficulty that did not meet the standard of taking away his right to represent himself.[6] Claiming that he was psychologically well made him look crazy. He ignored my advice, honing to denial of his personal mental issues and succumbing to anxiety about his mental health status. Whatever the problem, it was fundamentally society's rather than his. He lost the appeal. The moral of his story is the same as the moral of mine. If you have any level of mental health challenge operating in relationship to terrorism, you are better off owning up to it and dealing with it than denying it. It does not matter whether you are a victim or a perpetrator. The principle holds. It also applies to American culture as a whole, which has much that it could learn from the Unabomber's mistakes.

The appeals history was another sequence of stunning social failure for the Unabomber. He could not win in the court of public opinion. He could not win in the court of psychiatric opinion. He could not win in the court of judicial opinion. He could not win in open court. So why even think about this "loser"? What does he have left? What he has left is the fact that the arguments in his Manifesto are not all wrong. His critiques of

American culture are cogent. His processing through the legal system supports some of them nicely: "The system reorganizes itself so as to put pressure on those who do not fit in. Those who do not fit into the system are 'sick,' to make them fit is to 'cure.'"[7]

His personal scorecard on his own hypothesis was quite good. Refuse psychiatric evaluation. Be labeled as paranoid. Deny that you are mentally ill. Have your own attorneys label you publicly as delusional. Attempt suicide. Lose your right to defend yourself. Become a threat to the integrity of the system. Find that the integrity of the system is more important than your integrity as a person. Have your evaluating psychiatrist, who agrees with the attorneys she regards as your "main support system" about how your fears rank diagnostically, be the final arbiter of how your consciousness is defined. It would be enough to make a guy paranoid, if he weren't already.

Ted is always meticulously busy. When Tim McVeigh appeared on national television in a bid for a retrial of his own, Tim looked and sounded like he had been coached by his block mate. There was no retrial for Tim either, but the system also handed him a level of bureaucratic vindication before his execution. The FBI had failed to transfer all of the relevant documents to his attorney during the discovery phase of the trial. Many of the documents had remained in local field offices, unconveyed to headquarters. Nor would the McVeigh document fiasco be the last the American public would hear about failed relationships between FBI field offices and headquarters, with the Phoenix memo, Coleen Rowley, and more on the horizon. When McVeigh went to his slightly delayed execution in 2001, after a failed appeal process based on the document snafu, it was undoubtedly with another degree of assurance in his mind about the righteousness of his opposition to the government.

Their personal failures aside, both McVeigh and Kaczynski saw their ideas about the government confirmed in their own cases. If their arguments about the culture are right, they are not pure losers. They still "win" to a degree. The system does tend to recreate itself in outcomes, causing a sense of powerlessness familiar in American culture to build up in those individuals who allow it to. While these two American jackals did not beat the system, together they illuminated it, sacrificing themselves to society along with their other victims. These jackals are defanged, but not refuted. They have not been extricated from the heart of America. The game is not over, and America is still in a squeeze play between them and other American jackals who still have their fangs. As long as their perspectives and arguments are outstanding, Kaczynski and McVeigh remain a threat to American character and consciousness, even if no longer to American property or persons. Learning from their histories can still help America do what it needs to do to fight back terrorism from within.

Ted Kaczynski thought that if he were optimistic about life in general then you might have a case for concluding that he was mentally ill.[8] He was not the one who was nuts. The rest of the culture was. The oversimplified argument nevertheless had some wisdom in it. The American national psyche is increasingly emotionally challenged, its pathologies showing in everything from road rage, domestic terrorism, spectacularly pathological interpersonal crime, conspicuous corporate malfeasance, to rising rates of clinical mental illness. Dead or alive, Ted, Tim, and their acts and perspectives remain in the hearts and minds of Americans, helping to coach the dark side of American culture.

In a 2002 publication of material that Kaczynski managed to convey outside of his cellblock at Supermax, "Hit Them Where It Hurts," he guides radicals on how to target "the system" effectively by promoting attacks on communications, computers, the biotech industry, and the "propaganda" industry that renders people docile and conforming.[9] The problem with the last part of his argument is that attacking media will not make people less docile or conforming. They have to do that themselves. In the meantime, the docile would just continue to be horrified and enthralled while watching sensational terror. American culture is not nuts, but it does have a need to recognize where its challenges are, and do something about them.

TERRORIST DU JOUR

Turn from Ted and Tim's sagas of destruction to other news of domestic terror, and things only get worse. The news is about a stressed culture with stressed, angry, and depressed individuals in it, who are beginning to provide a perverted leadership of emotional despair. Abortion clinic terrorism continues. American secondary schools remain the scene for youth who feel disenfranchised enough to plan violent social statements. Radical animal rights groups, environmental, and militia groups can be cast as a backdrop to America's "lone" anti-heroes, or vice versa, depending on one's literary tastes as a story writer. Spring was the most brutal season in American schools in the late 1990s, not just on school grounds, but also for a public required to absorb report after report of violence. The nation has recovered less from Columbine and a series of similarly disturbing, if less destructive, incidents than left them as unprocessed emotional baggage. America did get itself an international reputation, though. A 2001 Columbine-style school shooting in Germany brought the comment that Germany had been "Americanized." It also brought the observation that the environment of American schools had to be changed, not just to screen weapons out, but also so that the social environment was such that students did not feel that they needed to bring them in. That was the much tougher challenge. Searches could never get to the heart of a social problem that needed to be mastered, not just beaten.

In the spring of 1999, when Columbine became a new icon of terror in the heart of the nation, the generational range of the jackal clan in America effectively expanded. While Columbine-era high school students grew up on a news diet of Ted Kaczynski and Tim McVeigh, today's high school students have Eric Harris and Dylan Klebold as part of their cultural legacy. Each perpetrator of American terror becomes, via terror's public nature, a self-martyring mascot for future American jackals. While some Americans are horrified by the course of this developing history, others are impressed or inspired, taking note as they conceptualize and craft violent responses to their own American social situations.

The turn to the year 2000 remained punctuated by violence in American schools. A sixteen-year-old from Kansas showed her understanding of how culture works when she observed that with Columbine and other shootings, it was inevitable that something similar would happen near her. She was paying attention. She was ahead of some people's teachers. American terrorism was not going away. It did not go away, even with 9/11 compromising its memory. September 11 just created one more risk factor for domestic terrorism from its victims within America, and enhanced the likelihood that internal problems would go ignored.

In November 2001, the jackal clan showed its teeth in American schools again, in a culture too traumatized to take much notice. High school students were arrested in New Bedford, Massachusetts for conceiving an event "bigger than Columbine," reportedly having planned explosives, mass shooting deaths, and a public suicide ritual on the roof of the school. The report was not the big news it would have been if the plan had been carried out, but observers still said that even the mention of Columbine sent shudders through post-9/11 America. The building was short and the plan was truncated, but the young woman from Kansas would not have been surprised. She may even have been less likely than others to gauge the importance of this terrifying moment by the fact that no physical damage was done. No destruction was caused, but that does not mean that nothing happened.

New Bedford is the home of Herman Melville and his novel *Moby Dick*. A newspaper reporter covering the arrests was inspired to connect American patterns over time, observing that Melville had turned his depression to creativity rather than destruction. She wondered if Melville could have stood up to the stresses of dealing with the "geeks," "preppies," and "jocks," at the current New Bedford high school. She wondered how the dark "genius" of the plan's coconspirators could still be sculpted to constructive purposes.[10] She wanted to know how to take their pain, and their determination to spread that pain outward, and turn it from the path of the jackal to the path of the phoenix. It was a question that could be asked about many people in many places in contemporary America, before they get as far as planning to shoot or blow things up.

The mother of one of the arrested teenagers said that they would not have caused any harm, despite their violent speech and ideas. They were good kids. Whether Susan St. Hilaire was objectively right about her son, Steven Jones, or not, she is on the wrong track. Even if the argument serves to protect him as an individual, the social cat is out of the bag. Even without acting, her son had been transformed into a minor league American antihero, when the threat of violence became public. Even if he is a "good boy" in private, he is a "good boy" mixed up with terror, in an increasingly bad cultural context. Even though he may not be very much unlike many of his peers, she is still in a form of denial. Some would call her crazy or troubled like her son, but there is more to the situation than blaming or labeling either mother or son. That does not get the whole picture. It does not do anything to create a consciousness that a society with good boys at that kind of risk and parents in denial about their level of risk both live in a society with some problems of its own.

After the plan was made public, the social "box" she had lived in was peppered as full of holes as the New Bedford high school would have been if the plan had been carried out, but she could not see it. She tried to adapt by retreating further within. Acute unaddressed problems of psyche and culture brewed in her offspring, even before a trigger was pulled or a bomb detonated. Defending him as an individual, and being dismissed by others for doing so, simply ratcheted up the culture's penchant for denying its collective problems one more notch.

She and her son are both creatures of a culture of fragmented consciousness, resistant to seeing the problems in the pattern right in front of them. How can "good boys" in America act so badly? Susan St. Hilaire did have the craft to invoke changes in American culture in defense of her son. Expectations for teenage consciousness have changed in recent years, as terrorist threats of violence have become more common in the daily life of American high schools. That change helped her to mount a defense of him as a "good" boy. He is only a good boy, though, in a compromised culture. Ideas about what ranks as deviant, or even delusional, in the culture are shifting in the wrong direction.

If "good kids" in America have persistent violent ideas and speech, America has an increasingly troubled culture as well as increasingly troubled youth. Are such young people less disturbed now simply because there are more of them? Move the "expectations" of the culture, and the boundary where individual psychological pathology begins moves with it. The fact that both the psychology of individual Americans and the psychology of the culture as a whole are pointing down the path of the jackal is largely obscured to American consciousness. Individuals and the culture are both showing signs of emotional distress. No matter Steven Jones's psychiatric or legal status, there is a civil war going on, both in his head and in his culture. Maybe Ted Kaczynski is less delusional now than he was at the time of his own trial. Either way, blame teachers, blame counselors, blame Susan St. Hilaire, blame her son, and, like her, you will miss the bigger picture.

John Walker Lindh, known at the American Taliban, Clayton Lee
Waagner, alleged abortion clinic anthrax letter hoaxer, and Eric Harris of
Columbine, were all in the news on the same day, December 6, 2001. Later,
it would be Charles Bishop, Luke Helder, John Muhammad, Lee Malvo, and
others. Sorting out America's post-9/11 "new normal" from surreal was a real
challenge. You couldn't keep track of the jackal clan without a scorecard.
Walker's guest spot as America's newest antihero, if not domestic terrorist
per se, was short. His father, Frank Lindh, echoed Susan St. Hilaire's statement
of the previous week, saying that his son was a "good boy."

There would be more such good boys on the horizon. The simple fact
of these parental assertions left the rest of America struggling to understand
where good left off and bad began within America, or just dismissing the
parents. The reality of the behavior pattern in these good American boys
seemed not to sink in to cultural consciousness. On the other hand, maybe
the "good boy" phenomenon was intensifying in America to the point
where the pattern would finally become noticeable. Both Ted Kaczynski
and Tim McVeigh had also been described as having been "good" boys
in their youth.

Government officials told Americans that anthrax hoaxers were
terrorists too. It was just that their damage was psychological instead of
physical. The jackal clan in America diversified, with sociological twists
of age and gender. Anthrax hoaxers included a 58-year-old woman from
Pennsylvania and a 69-year-old woman from Washington State. Clayton
Lee Waagner's arrest for allegedly sending over five hundred anthrax
letter hoaxes to abortion clinics in October and November of 2001
provided a completely updated version of American terrorism. A little
abortion clinic bombing atmosphere, a little Unabomber mail
methodology, and a little post-9/11 anthrax fear were all whipped up into
a new American recipe for psychological terrorism. September 11 had not
just taken America beyond the movies as metaphors for life—the movies
could not possibly keep up with this pace. It was more like the coffee
flavor of the day, or the terrorist flavor of the day, or week, or month.
Terrorist du jour. Shortly thereafter, media focus was on militant animal
rights groups, and the jackal clan marched on.

Even as time went forward, American terrorists came back from the
past. Eric Harris's diary found its way to the surface of the media the same

day as Walker and Waagner. Maybe America was back in a movie and it was a Stephen King movie. Had Harris and Klebold survived Columbine, Harris wanted his follow-up act to be to "hijack a hell of a lot of bombs and crash a plane into New York City." Jackals think alike. January 2002 brought fifteen-year-old Floridian Charles Bishop, who stated his sympathy for Osama bin Laden, and then piloted a suicide Cessna into a Miami high-rise in the hopes of injuring or killing others, as well as himself. Although Bishop's suburban Florida community was a perfect place for social isolation to thrive, and his tearful teacher said there was no way she could have known, she still seemed tortured by a sense of individual responsibility, with no way to think past it. In May, there was a twenty-one-year-old Minnesotan, stuffing bombs into mailboxes. Just trying to keep track of the hits was a chore, but there were more, and they belonged to us.

THE ENEMY WITHIN STRIKES AGAIN—HAVE A NICE DAY

Spring, time to brace again for American school violence, so grin and bear it. In 2002, the syndrome went on the road in the form of college student Luke Helder's self-confessed spree of rigging American mailboxes with pipe bombs (later to be replaced with announcement of an intended not-guilty, insanity plea). He inscribed a huge smiley-face design right across the middle of the country, and kept moving America in the direction of the jackal. America responded by doing its best to ignore him. Contrary to profiling punditry, Helder's target was clear. It was just too big for most people to see. It was the culture as a whole. Profilers professed themselves perplexed by the case. Helder was an enigma if one tried to understand him based on his choice of specific targets. He did not fit into recognizable previous patterns upon which profiles had been built. People could not figure out from the smile on his face, or the one he carved across the heart of the nation, that what he was after was the big picture. That was his point in the first place. Nobody was seeing the big picture.

Helder did little damage physically, but his psychological targeting was brilliant. He hit America squarely both in its rural roots and in its inability to think about itself as a cohesive entity. Most Americans could not see him either coming or going. It was easy to forget him, in part because the physical damage was minimal. He had nothing of the impact of a Harris, Kaczynski, or McVeigh. Still, some argued in Helder's wake that America needed to return to traditional values, which was another way of saying that it needed to return to a time when people could see how things fit together into a meaningful pattern. That analysis was right, but Helder's unsolved taunt of contemporary America's remedial pattern consciousness remained masterful.

The focus went predictably instead, to what was in his head, which presented a puzzle just as defiant as Helder himself. For a few days, divining his thought was a new cultural game. What was he trying to say? The picture was hazy, confused, and had missing pieces. His written work did little to clear matters up. America's attention, after registering shock, bafflement, and fear, fuzzed and faded within a week. Even when your message is clear, which Helder's was not, bombing has a way of turning people off. His own jumbled thinking aside for a moment, the irony of his attack is that Americans could not figure it out, because their vision of themselves does not fit together much better than Helder's disjointed prose. Americans who terrorize each other in small ways every day are shocked when Luke goes on the road to make a real impact.

People wanted to know what set him off, what caused his thought to turn to action. Identifying a single event that was the spark to his tinder would have fed the American appetite for simple and sensational explanations, but it would not have told anyone how his terrorist fire was laid, only how it was lit. Whatever "dot" of specific information answers the question of what set Luke off still needs to be connected to other "dots." He is not an isolated "dot," as an individual either. He is connected in a pattern to other American terrorists and to other American youth. Take a clue from his design. He was connecting dots. National press said his attacks had dredged up painful memories of the Unabomber and the anthrax terrorist, but let's connect some dots. The anthrax perpetrator was still at large, with the call for public assistance still out. Anthrax was not exactly history, but the reporter's ability for mental fragmentation seemed as prodigious as anyone else's in America.

Was Helder a "good" boy? He had a loving family and friends. He came from a good American social environment. Since his personal world and private context seemed to be perfectly in order, this time the jackal shocked as much with who he was as with what he accomplished. Thinking beyond Helder as a private individual was what made his actions make sense. The larger cultural context in which he had that loving family and those friends was intolerable to him. Helder is largely forgotten, but he is not history, and he is not a mystery. Instead, the lesson in his story is as prominent as the face he inscribed. Terror lies within the heart of good American social environments. The message could scarcely be any plainer.

With other American jackals as guides, Luke Helder put his need to convey his message over other people's pain. He threw it right in America's face. How could he grin like that while being arrested? That the smile offended seemed to be precisely his point. The smile offends. Why does the nation smile when there is so much wrong? Helder etched the false smile in pain in order to point out the problem.

People who took personal offense at his personal smile missed its larger commentary. Didn't he realize that this was serious business? He had hurt some people and terrorized others. He must be crazy. The cure-all to social consciousness of labeling him as a "nut cake" was predictably applied. In whatever way Helder is clinically psychologically disordered, the cultural dynamics of labeling him as nuts go beyond his individual mental state to also scapegoating him as an individual for the problems of the culture. Some thought that meting out harsh punishment to him would solve the cultural problem by deterring others. It will not solve the cultural problem, any more than tightening up discipline in the chain of command at the FBI will. The problem is not rooted in chain of command, or even in how "good" American families raise their children. It is rooted in the extreme individualism that pervades the culture, and that is the place to counterattack. Helder's dramatic assertion of extreme individualism is, after all, what most terrifies Americans about him. It is what causes them to hate him. The answer to Helder's riddle is in the mirror.

To revile the grin is to miss his mockery. That the smile is not real, either his or America's, is his point. The smile masks disconnected turmoil beneath. The jest is about both facades being false, a twisted statement of ironic social solidarity with a public that Helder deems to be less "with it" mentally than he is himself. If Kaczynski is America's mad prophet, and McVeigh its corrupted soldier, Helder is its ironic jester. He seemingly shares the Unabomber's opinion that it is the culture and not him who is crazy, along with a perverted perspective of how to fix it. Befuddling as his message and targeting are, viewed at the individual level, viewed through a cultural lens both are strikingly clear: "Pay attention to me and the problems in this culture." The FBI practiced some very active listening, but only until the moment that Helder was caught. Then everyone breathed easier, and proceeded to forget both him and his message. The continued "attention-getters" that Helder promised would not come from him once he was in custody. But there was a nagging problem. He was right about more attention-getters being on the way. It was just that someone other than him would produce the next attention-getter.

America's slow learning curve on its own terrorism came to a halt after Helder's arrest, when his power to baffle only increased. The combination of Helder's acts with his dead-ringer normalcy should have raised an extremely red flag in American consciousness, not just about him, but also about America. If Luke Helder can choose terror, just about anyone can. The flag should, in fact, be red, white, and blue, with Americans working to understand it as well as wave it.

Seeing Helder as dangerous was also a stretch for his family and friends. Some of them flat out denied that he was dangerous, even after his arrest. There was no putting together in their minds their personal experience of him with what he had done on the road. His age-mates could not muster a social imagination that included him as armed and dangerous.

Helder's fantastical view of the world was not entirely unshared either by his pained and upstanding father, who also assisted in his apprehension. As solidly pro-American as Cameron Helder's role in the drama was, and as tragically similar to David Kaczynski's, he too was culturally duped in his thinking. Cameron Helder was right about the fact that Luke wanted people to pay attention to his ideas, but he was wrong about his son not being dangerous. Cameron Helder is another American parent with a son who, viewed up close, was a "good boy," but his son's actions as an American were entirely different and definitely dangerous. Cameron Helder may have seen his son clearly at a personal level, but he had blinders on about Luke's place in American culture. The mental "disconnect" that does not allow some American parents to understand that their good boys can promote terror works against them, and against America.

Delores Werling of Iowa took a bomb hit from Helder. Her husband said that she was a wonderful person, someone without an enemy in the world. What he did not see, even after her injury, was that she did have one. It was Luke. The riddle came with the fact that his enmity had nothing to do with her as an individual. It was depersonalized. He was her enemy only because she was an American at the wrong place on the map, and because she was easier to attack than someone famous. Luke Helder was an "every man's" terrorist. The terror in this case is partly precisely because his attack was not about her as a person. Luke did not attack celebrity. Her mailbox could have been anyone's. Delores Werling just lost an American cultural lottery as Helder designed his smiley-faced pattern. She became a dehumanized symbol, and not a human being, just as McVeigh's and Kaczynski's victims had been for them. Helder's depersonalization of her is a logical violent extension of the trend to dehumanization in American culture.

Another of Helder's victims claimed a year after the attack that her life would never be back to "normal." That concept was gone. While it was precisely that sort of personal powerlessness that both Helder and Kaczynski protested, the details of that powerlessness were clearer in the Unabomber Manifesto than in anything Luke Helder wrote. What Helder contributed intentionally to the American tradition of terror was his refinement of the fear factor in random victimization, a fear factor soon to be perfected by the beltway sniper. Helder struck in the nation's rural heart and the sniper at the heart of the beltway, but both targeted the heart of the culture.

While Luke Helder's cultural profile is clear, his psychological profile remains mysterious. Publication of the details of his public defender's intended insanity defense, as of this writing, awaits the beginning of his trial. There are keys, though, to the mystery of that profile in culture. A former FBI profiler leaped to conjecture that Helder was a paranoid schizophrenic. It was hard to tell if that assertion was more about Helder himself, or more about associating him with Ted Kaczynski, who had been attributed with the same diagnosis. Perhaps the projected diagnosis was a cultural response in the profiler to just how "crazy" Helder's actions seemed. Psychological experts projected possible schizophrenia because of communicative problems apparent in Helder's writing, but the FBI profiler also worked in a cultural environment under the influence of Helder already having been compared to Kaczynski in a number of ways. Helder's writings had been dubbed as his "manifesto" in the media and by profilers.

While Helder's and Kaczynski's writings do have clear philosophical similarities, more than those parallels may have contributed to the instant tendency that emerged to compare the two terrorists. Kaczynski's status as an extremely powerful icon of American terrorism, a ranking antihero, may also have been a reason for the FBI profile of the anthrax perpetrator to be so strongly reminiscent of him. As profilers compared Helder to Kaczynski, they may not have noticed the possibility that they were using cultural as well as psychological consciousness to build psychological profiles.

Whether Helder is paranoid schizophrenic or not, depression also appears to be in his mental mix. With a gun to his head during his arrest, and writings full of assertions about the irrelevance of death and entry into paradise, Helder was placed on a suicide watch. The self-centeredness associated with depression was no stranger to Helder, with his all "about me" concept of how to connect with others. His vision of connection to fellow citizens had been reduced to becoming famous by killing them. He even had trouble maintaining that level of mental connection, declaring that he "didn't mean to hurt" the people he could have killed. Helder's hero was a depressed and suicidal Kurt Cobain, and one of his central issues was feeling pressured toward conformity. Helder's generation lives with intense multiple pressures, to succeed, look good, be accepted, and manage personal trauma, and many of his age-mates are customers in the burgeoning American market for antidepressants. If the culture kept itself together better on their behalf, fewer of them might need drug therapy, or turn up on the evening news after turning hatred of American culture into a ritual of sacrifice.

Cultural consciousness could have refined the profiles of Helder. Profilers were shocked after his arrest, and not just because the profiles were wrong about specific characteristics like age. Profiling is not perfect when it comes to pinpointing specific social attributes. It is a technique for generating a reasonably likely pattern of characteristics, and cultural variables are often neglected in generating those patterns. A former FBI profiling consultant rendered the opinion that the disjointed thought apparent in Helder's writings could not have been part of the profile of a person who was socially connected to others. He would not have been accepted. She was painting a picture of a generalized American. Generalized Americans do not exist any more than numerical abstractions like statistical averages. Helder was not a generalized American. He was an American from a specific regional subculture. Her presumption would have held some places in America, but not in Helder's home state of Minnesota.

Minnesota's regional subculture has many socially well-integrated people with the characteristically disconnected thought associated with depression, because the social environment is one in which social cohesion is high and depression is common. There was a blind spot in her profile, and Helder was right in it. Fueled by generalized American cultural assumptions, she projected a prototypical, stereotypical American "loner," which Helder was not. A profile is two edged; it can lead you toward or away from the perpetrator. If Helder had not been apprehended so quickly, that profile would have led away. The national television commentator who interviewed the profiler made things simple for popular consumption by just referring to Helder as a "sicko."

In a perspective that was not helpful, the fact that Luke Helder was a profiling challenge was cited as evidence of the limits of profiles. If Helder did not fit the profile generated by existing techniques, the solution is to refine the techniques, not to fault profiling. Cursing a dull tool does not improve its performance. Sharpening it works better. If, as Helder's math professor asserted, there was nothing in his behavior that would have predicted his actions, profiles need to be rewritten in ways that incorporate emergent, evolving, and unexpected cultural patterns, as well as the characteristics of past perpetrators.

Just what is it that is not being seen by American teachers, and by profilers who have challenges in perceiving culture? The nation had not seen the precise configuration of Helder's contradictory and unexpected combination of characteristics before, but his dark and light makeup is a part of the nation's dark and light makeup that is often being missed. American consciousness, both in profilers and the public, has some stretching to do around what America is now. After Helder's apprehension, FBI agents said that they still did not know what had caused him to do what he did. The total picture he presented was that opaque.

While Helder's target was clear, and his psyche remains a mystery, his arguments are undeniably muddled. In the letter he stuffed into mailboxes along with his bombs, and a longer letter he sent to a student newspaper before starting his wild weekend, apathy and conformity are central concerns. Death, for him, was preferable to a life of conformity. Underneath the garbled convolutions in his texts, and beyond the psychic rant, there is a kind of contemporary American sense in what he writes.

His problems with apathy are about individual powerlessness and passivity. Sounding a little like a combination of McVeigh and Kaczynski, Helder wants Americans to know that technology and complexity will never satisfy them, and that both allow the government to control American actions and minds. He views practical personal freedom as limited in a nation where "1% of the nation controls 99%" of the wealth. Anyone who is angry about recent corporate financial scandals in America might agree with him on that point. America does not like his methods, but that does not negate the cogent elements of his muddled message, their similarity to the messages of other American terrorists, or their ties to the discontents of many Americans.

The longer letter, "Life on Earth," has technological dependence, government and bureaucratic control, environmental immorality, and greed and materialism as its primary themes. Helder thinks that Americans conform out of fear and use money to relieve their pain, thereby allowing the government to control them. The text reads like American freedom turned inward into a nightmare of anything but independence. Helder thinks that Americans lose track of themselves and their ability to dream or project their consciousness to make things happen. That argument sounds somewhat like Kaczynski's ideas about an interrupted power process and lack of goals, except that Helder has a spiritual twist on the same theme, and a particularly finely tuned rendering of a sense of groundlessness. The arguments, though garbled, will not be totally unfamiliar to Americans of any age who feel disempowered in the face of big bureaucracy, money, or celebrity. Even if Helder's arguments seem off the wall, they are not entirely off the analytical mark.

Helder wants Americans to learn from their mistakes and change society accordingly. If American terrorists are cultural "mistakes," can America learn something from paying attention to their messages as well as their deeds? Leaving American perpetrators of terror as mysteries compounds their damage. Vilifying or dismissing them as nuts or deviants leaves America complicit in its own terror. Complacently accepting their existence provides support to the next one. To be like phoenixes, Americans need to start traveling dark American passages of thought, in order to get back to the light. Those passages are darkest and in clearest relief in America's terrorists. Without Americans going to ground in that way, trauma and complacency (Helder would say apathy) will evolve into more darkness. Thinking about Luke Helder as personally misguided, confused, troubled, or mentally ill does not solve the mystery that can help take the terror away. Analyzing his childhood or citing his psychiatric status in an insanity defense cannot relieve the anxiety caused for everyone else by his existence within the cabal of American terrorists.

He made himself into a pained short-term icon of the turmoil bubbling below the positive exterior of this culture. America should listen to his cultural voice, instead of just smiling back. Letting go of Luke's enigma leaves the jackal smiling. It is America's enigma to decode. If his mental chaos becomes just one more unexamined stroke for turmoil in the cultural subconscious, America may incarcerate him, but it will never get the smile off his face. The easy road for Luke was to bomb his way into American consciousness. The easy road for the rest of America was to drop him right back out of it. The harder road is to come to grips with American terror, by coming to grips with who and what he is, as he has so pointedly asked America to do.

TERRORISM, OR JUST TERRORIZED?

The beltway sniper case was a crazy case in a mixed-up culture. John Muhammad, Lee Malvo, and Luke Helder all appeared as ushers into a new age of terror in America, one in which the distinction between terror and terrorism blurred in a post-9/11 cultural haze. It was the age of the intentionally random victim. People also started defining cases of terrorism in more victim-oriented than perpetrator-oriented ways. The anthrax perpetrator was a partial participant in the new age, with targets chosen ideologically, but actual victims randomized. Unintentionally random victims rapidly became old school. The new strain of perpetrators either had no clear ideological agenda, or did not communicate it clearly if they did. Helder's writing was largely incomprehensible. Muhammad's vague anti-American, pro-Al Qaeda political agenda was equally vague in terms of how it applied to his actions. Both cases fit well with a general cultural state of confusion about terror.

Most importantly, though, targets became non-specific. Anyone who happened to be in the right place could be a victim. Loosely anti-American agendas and scattershot victimology were a new cultural order in American domestic terror, in what began to look like a jackal's retort to the culture's symbolic countering of 9/11 with increased respect for humanity. Whether the smiley-face marked target locations on Muhammad's planning map were a cross reference to Helder's jaunt is impossible to know.

Snipers Muhammad and Malvo (self-confessed in Malvo's case, and not technically speaking snipers in either case) upended classic categories of criminal killers, as well as the boundaries between terrorism and crime. Their rampage was too slow to be spree killing and too fast to be serial killing, a weird blend of characteristics distinguished mostly by the fact that it fit no previous mold. The demand for money was out of place, the communication routines unprecedented, and the sidekick unexpected. The sniper's motive was described as absent, a mystery, or as simply to create terror. He did not just challenge profiling as Helder had; there was absolutely no box to fit him in. One profiler devolved into interpreting the motivation as "sport," essentially human hunting. Another described him as a new specimen of terrorist.

There was plenty of terror, whether Muhammad's anti-American sympathies reached the threshold of a terrorist political statement or not. The post-9/11 shift among some experts and in the media in the use of the word "terrorism" to describe only foreign and group activities did nothing to slow down the effects of that terror. The defense argument at Muhammad's trial that the terrorism law under which he was being tried was intended to apply only to foreign conspirators like Al Qaeda did not hold sway. The jury, convinced of his intent to intimidate the public, convicted him of terrorism anyway. One investigator, asked if the shootings were the work of terrorists, was not concerned with fine distinctions such as whether the terrorists were local or global, "The terror is here, and that is terrorism."[11] The America that the snipers hit had terror on its mind, as well as in its heart.

Muhammad was not just angry about authority, but also about disorganization. Like the Unabomber, he aided in his own apprehension with angry communication. It took Muhammad many phone calls to get through. As in the Unabomber investigation, authorities were also inundated with calls from women who suspected their ex-husbands, calls that could be anonymously data-mined to help sharpen the profile.[12] This case went too fast, though. While huge volumes of calls were heroically condensed into leads by round-the-clock efforts of investigators, there was also evidence that quantity was being dealt with, but quality was being ignored. The fate of Muhammad's series of calls to the maniacally busy office of Police Chief Charles Moose of Montgomery County, Maryland was one thing, but the bureaucratic "not my department" response of the Rockville, Maryland dispatcher who had Malvo on the line was something else entirely.

The dispatcher did not try to keep him on the line, or offer to connect him to the office that was investigating the crimes in Montgomery County. Instead, the dispatcher offered to give the correct number so that he could make another call.[13] Malvo hung up, the quality of the telephone reception apparently totally out of accord with a sniper's sense of importance. The unmitigated threat to the safety of children came on the heels of more fury—at a phone bank FBI agent trainee who refused to believe the caller was who he said he was. The supervisor of the phone bank was later called to task for not distributing information about an "indicator" Muhammad had said he would use in communications. A post-9/11 culture of bureaucratic connection and collaboration was clearly not yet fully in place.

Given Muhammad's communication patterns, authorities should have taken any self-declared perpetrator seriously, with or without a pre-established indicator. Any caller claiming to confess could have been the right one. The FBI publicly represented the missteps as inevitable due to the volume of calls, but the problem was not one of scale. It was one of the quality of interaction used in the phone calls. The scale argument reflects not just investigative realities of scope. It is also an American cultural problem, often used in bureaucratic self-defense. As a blanket excuse, it leads away from perceiving and correcting investigative problems. In this case, by repeatedly angering the one caller they did not want to hang up on them, the FBI earned a death threat for five more people. Luckily, Muhammad was so persistent about identifying himself that he conspired in his own apprehension before he could carry out the threat. He just kept calling different numbers until he got what he wanted.

Terrorism became surreal with the beltway sniper case. While what went on in Muhammad's mind might not have constituted domestic terrorism, his acts further blurred the distinction between terrorism and terrorist crime in a nation with an anxiety-ridden psyche. Those who called the sniper a domestic terrorist made the categorization more with an emphasis on the eye of the beholders than on the perpetrator's mind's eye. Even at trial, evidence presented to support the charge of his "intent" to intimidate the public came in the form of statements from people who felt intimidated. His "terrorism" has no clear specific political, religious, ethnic, or "single-issue" motivations. The psyche of the culture, via intimidation, did seem to be the target, though. While Helder was a puzzle, the clear conjunction of his critical statements on American culture with his actions place him firmly, if not spectacularly, in the category of cultural terrorism.

The sniper and his effects, together, were just one big cultural puzzle. The anti-American statement made came partly in the very fact of creating the terror. There were no written statements of doctrine. Terror was the form of articulation, as terrorism seemed to evolve from being a means to an end, a self-referential act that fit the self-referential culture that it terrified. While experts could not agree on whether the sniper was a terrorist, anything lacked in specific intent was more than made up for in impact. The sniper was dubbed, if not a terrorist, at least the most terrifying American killer to date. The accomplishment of fusing crime and terror in American consciousness was substantial progress in the direction of the jackal for a couple of week's work.

In an already depersonalized culture, Muhammad dehumanized his direct victims further into a new height of human expendability. Indirect victims were anyone within eyeshot or earshot of a newspaper or television. This new version of randomized American terror confused. The October 10,

2002 headline of *USA Today* asserted that this time the terror was personal. Actually, one of the most terrifying things about it was that it was not. It was not about any of the direct victims personally. Therein was the depth of the chilling message, the more terrifying for its negation of the post-9/11 renaissance of a sense of the importance of humanity in America.

Some said that there was no pattern in what he did, only fear. The lack of apparent pattern, despite the possibility that in his economic destitution, he was targeting primarily people who were spending money, at malls, at gas stations, or at restaurants, demoralized as surely as a clearly stated agenda would have, perhaps more so. Jackal thinking was in full flower, even if the formal writing on the terrorist calling card was smudged. Lee Malvo, by his own report, was simply amused by the killing he had done. That mind frame does not reflect the intentionality of a classic bona fide terrorist. What it does is to boil terrorism down to its antihuman essence.

Profilers, challenged both by the Helder and the sniper cases, started speaking openly about the limitations of their craft. One of the fundamental assumptions of profiling, a tool used to narrow a pool of suspects, is that past patterns help to identify current perpetrators. What profiling does not do, in following the past and numerical odds, is to invoke the sociological imagination, look for the unexpected pattern, or project changing patterns of perpetrators. It is a tool for combing a haystack that does not incorporate awareness of changes in the haystack. In the heat of anxiety generated by a terror case, though, the profile becomes not just an investigative tool, but also a symbol clung to by a hungry public and investigators.

In the sniper case, the vehicle "profile" of a white truck pointed in the wrong direction. In the Unabomber case, a profile projected him to be working class, based on the fact that most woodworkers are. As a minority middle-class woodworker, Kaczynski fit into a profiling trick corner. Profiles also reflect the consciousness of those who construct them. The answer to a postarrest profiler's question about who would have imagined that the Unabomber would be a college professor is that I would have. The presence of a college professor on Helder's profiling team was what directed profiling consciousness toward a college student.

Like psychiatric diagnoses, profiles have their social influences. Since profiles do not target people who are breaking past behavioral modes, they leave original perpetrators, like the sniper, with an innovative sociological edge. The sniper case, despite the added use of geographic profiling, challenged profiling by breaking modes in every possible direction. Even so, the public was in no position to criticize the problems of professional profilers in the sniper case. The public's problems of "profiling" consciousness were worse. Only a minority of serial killers in America are African-American. Envisioning an African-American perpetrator was still hard for many Americans who were thinking by numbers and social stereotypes, even after Muhammad and Malvo had been arrested.

One commentator observed that the sniper has an assured place in an American culture of notoriety, unlike his soon-to-be forgotten victims. In treating his victims as non-persons, he won a perverted cultural game of social notoriety, in which their deaths bought his celebrity. The more of them that died, the greater his celebrity. The dynamic redelivered the message that everyday American individuals are powerless in the face of terrorism. That message was practical, and it was also symbolic. The dynamic also reaffirmed an American addiction to celebrity. All American terrorists want press. So do other Americans, an artifact of the general attitude that you are not anybody unless you are famous.

Serving a terrorist's fame with your randomized death is the ultimate new American put-down, as well as a terrorist-produced form of reality TV. The fact that the next American terrorist might climb to notoriety over your dead body is an attack on both individual and cultural self-esteem. Muhammad's notoriety looms larger than that of his victims, his own personal social existence, and his own condemned life, following a death sentence. Like other American terrorists, he uses the culture, including its media and law enforcement to victimize himself, his direct victims, and the culture as a whole. If the American public misses everything but the impact on direct victims, it also misses that his eventual execution will do no more to solve the cultural dynamics of terrorism than the execution of Tim McVeigh. John Muhammad and other American terrorists, in their personal and cultural self-hatred, all use the same formula. Until the formula is replaced, American purveyors of terror will just keep plugging it in and using it.

Muhammad's gruesome reaffirmation of the darker side of American culture earned him credit for redefining reality TV, which itself was rapidly evolving after 9/11. The sniper was hailed for creating the ultimately interactive reality show. During the investigation, the media was dragged, mostly kicking and screaming at Police Chief Charles Moose, more closely than ever before into a loop where the perpetration and reporting of terror were tightly interwoven. The case made Kaczynski's time frames for feedback between the media and his actions absolutely archaic. A case where rapid feedback from what authorities or others said on the air could influence the actions of the killer created a rapid-fire, new plot twist in the story of terror in America. The sniper became instantaneous popular culture, a very low budget horror saga for the post-9/11 American millennium. Chief Moose shifted his own realm of action eventually by resigning his position together with its code of communicative ethics, in favor of writing a book about the case.

The entire sequence became an exercise in a newly readjusted post-9/11 relationship between reality and the media. In the aftermath, beltway residents readjusted their sense of "normal" to include a new sense of vulnerability, shifting America's national character again slightly in the direction of anxiety.[14] Muhammad would declare later, in August of 2003, that "America got what it deserved" on 9/11. Some money-minded Americans took that statement as the first indication of a possible non-financial motive on his part. They had not been watching him very carefully.

The apprehension of Muhammad and Malvo on Thursday, October 24, 2002 brought profound relief from the emotional chaos imposed by terror. But after a quiet weekend with Muhammad and Malvo in jail, America encountered terror again in the actions of one of its own. On Monday, October 28, Robert Flores's mass murder-suicide, which claimed the lives of three nursing professors at the University of Arizona in addition to his own, was no act of political terrorism. As with Columbine, the motivation for the act was substantially personal. But also like Columbine, Flores's act had elements of social protest about social exclusion. This time, the particulars were race and gender, but the anger in both cases was about feeling excluded in American society. Flores's act was a curtain call to the beltway performance immediately preceding it. His communication was a lengthy angry letter, delivered posthumously. While more autobiographical and less doctrinaire than the writings of Helder or Kaczynski, the common thread was that it came from an American who was terminally disconnected from the social threads of his own society.

Robert Flores, like Ted Kaczynski, did not want to be seen as irrational or as a "lunatic," despite his self-admitted depression. He wanted the world to know that he was not misanthropic, and had not been inspired by the sniper or by psychological issues from his childhood. The sniper did, however, make it into Flores's correspondence in an extremely short turn around time. Perhaps Flores had set his timing when he could get to the center of the American cultural stage, right after Malvo and Muhammad were apprehended. Flores did not need to have been inspired by any particular perpetrator of American terror in order to be making similar choices in solving the cultural puzzle in front of him. It was just that, unlike the sniper, Flores stuck to victims he knew.

Strictly speaking, even the weekend was not quiet, and Flores was not the next purveyor of terror in America following the arrest of John Muhammad and Lee Malvo. He was edged over the weekend of October 26 by an eighteen-year-old Oklahoman named Daniel Fears. Fears's anger rampage began with neighbors he knew, and proceeded to victims he did not. He killed one of each. Like Helder, Fears was described as "polite." By the time American consciousness turned itself back from Fears and Flores to trying to make sense of Muhammad and Malvo, thoughts about patterns of instability in the culture had begun to emerge. The observations were not just about Gulf War veterans, a group that includes Flores, McVeigh, and Muhammad. "Evil" began to replace "crazy" as the pat explanation for an increasingly vexingly elusive pattern. But it was Walter Kirn of *The New York Times* who touched the real cultural nerve, with his observations about combat stress (or post-traumatic stress disorder) in "real" vets being coupled by a virtually induced form of the same problem in America's media witnesses to war, trauma, and falling towers.[15] Reality and media danced closely in post-9/11 America.

A GIFT A MONTH

Leading up to the second anniversary of 9/11 in 2003, American news vaguely resembled a monthly gift of flowers or fruit, except that the packages for the American public contained terror. March of 2003 brought a doubled-up geographic twist on the concept of domestic terror. One incident took place abroad, in the Iraqi desert. Sgt. Asan Akbar of the 101st Airborne

Division of the Army was arrested for a grenade attack in camp that killed one and wounded fifteen. He reportedly had an attitude problem, and an unidentified retributive motive against his compatriots, rather than any treasonous association with Saddam Hussein. Akbar's geographic location for terrorizing America was novel. Another March innovation was geographically stunning. A disgruntled tobacco farmer occupied the National Mall in Washington, DC, with his tractor. Dwight Watson professed himself to be willing to use explosives to get his message out about the impact of the reduction of federal tobacco subsidies. The incident was an object lesson in the power of one American individual to make a difference by disrupting America from within. His impact on Washington traffic was substantial, drawing the observation that one of the purposes of terrorism is to divert resources. The incident reawakened again the sense of the impact that a single American with terror in mind could have.

April took terror in America back to school, when a "normal," "nice," "average," fourteen-year-old boy, who was "no problem" and "friendly with everyone" chose to kill his generally well-loved junior high school principal and then himself. Danny Dulin pricked American consciousness again, but commanded less than half a column on the bottom half of the twentieth page of the next day's *New York Times*. One might call that national habituation. May did not bring shooting or bombing on the school front, but did offer another indicator of a heightened atmosphere of hostility and dehumanization among America's youth.

The nation received another object lesson in the role of ridicule and humiliation in American schools, when a group of high school senior females initiated their junior counterparts with feces and intestines. The incident, a gender-shocker to some, was more shocking still in the attitude of one of the perpetrators that the cracked head she had perpetrated was not "that big of a deal." She sounded like a milder version of Lee Malvo, in her disregard for the suffering she had inflicted. The legalized aftermath of the incident was as roundly adversarial as the hazing itself. For a culture already in a post-9/11 haze, and warned about possibly delayed violent outbursts from its victims, especially in children and youth, hazing itself became a hazy concept. The hazing ritual was not just brutal. It was senseless. Into what were the juniors being initiated? Even if the incident itself did not seem terrifying, the question certainly was.

June brought a rare score for the home team with the arrest of Eric Rudolph, suspected in the 1996 Atlanta Olympic Park bombing, an abortion clinic bombing, and a gay nightclub bombing. Rudolph was another American with a spectrum of complaints about American culture who was remembered as a "polite" young man. With overtones of white supremacism, anti-government sentiment, extreme Christian fundamentalism, and American isolationism in his philosophy, Rudolph's motives did not fit readily into any single category. Hate groups and militias were not his style. He appeared to be another essentially "lone" American terrorist. If he did have a support network during his years in isolation, it was informal and loosely structured, rather than a systematic organization. That his self-sufficiency as a survivalist surprised so many authorities is itself a comment on current American individualism. They had difficulty imagining an American individual with that much skill.

In July, the young American jackal clan accented the Fourth of July weekend with the most recent "bashful," straight-A American student to assemble an arsenal and plan a rampage of terror. Eighteen-year-old Matthew Lovett of Oaklyn, New Jersey, and two younger companions, a group styling themselves as the "Warriors of Freedom," were reported to have planned to kill three local teenagers and then kill randomly, in what authorities described as a "Columbine-style plot." The selected victims had ridiculed Matthew and his younger brother. The inclusion of random victims gave an insight into how Matthew's model of local community extended out to a larger community.

Take your anger, and spread it outward. Whoever happens to be in front of you at the moment is there to kill. Matthew's father described him as a withdrawn homebody who did not get along well with peers because of having to defend himself and his brother from social derision. Immersion in video games and modeling on movie characters also folded themselves into the organization of Matthew's consciousness. High video contact, low social contact, and anger brewed up into the newest exercise in intended terror in a corner of America that God seemingly had not blessed, despite the date and Matthew's use of freedom metaphors.

America needs to understand what freedom is in Matthew's mind. It is freedom from this society, according to the letter that he left explaining himself. What is the cultural connection between Kaczynski's concept of freedom and "Freedom Club," and Lovett's "Warriors of Freedom?" Lovett, like his (and Lee Malvo's) *Matrix* movie hero "Neo," and like Ted Kaczynski, saw himself as saving humans from a dehumanized system. Lovett's and Kaczynski's concepts of freedom reveal the dark side of the contemporary American concept of freedom, which involves rejecting and terrorizing American society.

Lovett's uncle sounded familiar, when he described Matthew's actions as a "call for help." He sounded like Helder's father, who had said that Luke wanted people to pay attention to his ideas. Perhaps America needs to improve its listening skills, with the price of communication consistently becoming human life. Local residents were reportedly shocked, not expecting anything like that would happen near them. The question, in an America with an impaired learning curve on domestic terror, is why they did not. Perhaps in a cultural psyche suffering from post-traumatic stress, the standard symptoms of emotional numbing and avoiding issues that provoke fear are part of the cause. The American psyche is not facing the fact of terror within.

August brought two "gifts." The first came in headlines for the Earth Liberation Front (ELF), with arson that caused $50 million in damage to an apartment complex under construction in San Diego, California, the destruction decorated by their banner statement: "If you build it, we will burn it." The ELF followed up shortly thereafter with vandalism of $2.5 million worth of SUVs. This time, the social statement accompanying the crime was: "Fat, Lazy Americans." A person representing the views of the group displayed a typical American capacity for conceptual fragmentation. ELF had never harmed one person. People and their property were radically separate in his mind. The only way to harm a person was to harm their body, but torching development property or a high-consumption vehicle was an act of angry "liberation."

August also brought a series of sniper killings in West Virginia that were said to echo the beltway sniper case. Locals favored a drug-based theory of the crimes, but as August gave way to September, the investigative task force formally forwarded the notion that the shootings were random, putting them in the realm of intended public intimidation. The next death from a randomized shooting spree would occur in Ohio.

The cultural mix of crime and apparently terrorist-related thinking got stranger in September. A Pennsylvania pizza deliveryman with a bomb strapped to his body blew up after robbing a bank. The case presented a hopelessly muddled set of criminal and terrorist metaphors for incorporation into American culture. The image of an American suicide bomber had finally presented itself in the convoluted configuration of American crime. Before September was out, it also gave America an intensely shy, quiet fifteen-year-old John Jason McLaughlin, known for being teased, angry, not associating with people, and being paid no attention by his fellow students. The cost of raising that level of attention was a fellow student's life. Motive was unclear in the Cold Spring, Minnesota shooting, but some students at his school thought that people might start being nicer to each other afterward. At least there was a plan to turn the awful lesson to an advantage. Americans should expect more such "gifts" to come, even though they are disinclined to see them coming, or to put them into use.

CHAPTER 3

PSYCHOLOGICAL GROUND ZERO

WE'RE ALL A LITTLE CRAZY

We are not all a little crazy as individuals. We are all a little crazy as members of American culture, and denial is never any help when it comes to dealing with mental health issues. It plays into the hands of the problem. Americans are in denial about a national psyche that is increasingly characterized by anger, passivity, and fear. Denial helps make the culture a little crazy. September 11 was no help. "New normal" became just plain normal, along with habituation to a ratcheted-up level of unease. The social psyche of America is not clinically ill, but "normal" is more fearful now, and American national character continues to shade toward anger and passivity. In some ways, popular awareness of individual mental health issues in America has improved since 9/11. News magazines have abounded with articles about mental health, stress, anxiety, and depression in everyone, and the prevalence of those and other disorders in teenagers. Popular authors have forecast a national nervous breakdown, and scholarly authors have compared the American lifestyle to the symptoms of attention deficit disorder. Still, coming to grips with the emotional challenges in the national psyche is relatively uncommon.

The post-9/11 rush to reclaim a sense of normalcy, even one that incorporated feelings of vulnerability and uncertainty, included a strong impulse to recalibrate "normal" without confronting America's new level of emotional challenge. The new emotional homeostasis was in a different place, but Americans enamored of the concept of normalcy created for themselves a post-9/11 trap of not attending to the new level of challenge. The national psyche, which remains the benchmark for defining individual pathology, moved. Enhanced post-9/11 anxiety either elevated the bar on defining a formal state of pathology for individuals, or made Americans as a group a little more nascently ill. Maybe it did a bit of both. Ignoring social psychology because Americans do not think collectively, or because they are tired of "psychobabble," supports denial of collective emotional challenges and the relationship between the national psychological profile and domestic terrorism.

Americans cannot build psychological security for themselves with just airport security procedures or a Department of Homeland Security. They have an angry and depressive American social psyche to fight as well as terrorism. In a depressed brain, failed connections between synapses make it impossible to keep thoughts together or emotions on an even keel. In depressive American social psychology, failed connections between individuals make it impossible to keep a sense of a unified society together, or the behavior of its members on an even keel. The nation's emotional health is at risk. An environment characterized by social passivity and disconnection is also one in which it is harder for individual Americans suffering from depression to be cured, or for any American to have a sense that they can make a positive social impact. Such an environment also encourages the emergence of more individually depressed Americans. Americans are not connecting social dots, and they are also not seeing the relationship between America's problems with social connection and its psychological challenges.

One way to deny the serious reality of depression is to give it cachet. In some places in America today, depression has become a fashionable aspect of identity. Better than stigma, cachet still does not get at the roots of social insecurity in America. Depression has a creative side, in addition to its darker side, but mostly it continues to hide in dark American corners.

Even when individuals are treated, as the Unabomber observed, the roots of the problem of depression in the society are not being addressed.

Fear and anxiety are growth concerns in the national psyche, a pattern that Americans will not discern if they think only in terms of individual mental health. Barry Glassner's *The Culture of Fear* documents how Americans systematically translate small risks into large fears.[1] Glassner argues that Americans vastly overate risks of everything from pedophilia to plane wrecks to road rage. He identifies the media as playing a role in creating hyped-up fear in America. Another key to understanding national fear is that emotions do not respond to numbers or odds. They respond to cases. Statistically, the number of child abductions can go down, but a few high-profile, horror-tinged cases will cause anxiety to go up. Emotions are not rational. While sensationalistic violence like Columbine is unusual, its very occurrence within the range of American behavior alarms. The images of even a single horrific event emblazon themselves on the brain.

There is also the matter of degree to consider. Road rage is overrated as a cause of death, as Glassner demonstrates. But road rage does not have to be lethal to be real. Road rage is indicative of an emotional tenor shifting toward anger and fear on America's roads, even if it is unlikely to kill you. Another current analysis of American fear is that people exaggerate rare and spectacular risks over more common ones, and that the "disconnect" between actual and perceived risks has come about because of the influence of both technology and media on the society.[2] Simply meditating on the worst that America has to offer, without thinking through the root causes of fear in America and doing something about them, also helps Americans to give in to fear. America's propensity for frightening itself is just one symptom of a cultural problem with anxiety.

The impact of 9/11 on the mental health of Americans was underrated in some places by individuals who did not recognize their own needs, and overrated in others by predictions that did not take American resilience into account. The rates of the clinically diagnosable mentally ill fell off rapidly from a peak that followed 9/11, but even with resilience as a general rule, not everyone bounced back. Those who did not created a new class of emotionally vulnerable Americans who also lived in an emotionally changed atmosphere, with the feeling tone of the culture's personality shifting further toward vulnerability and anxiety. While it was important after 9/11 not to confound "normal" emotional reactions in individuals with clinical illness, it was also important not to bias against understanding how mass emotional experience subtly shifted the mental health profile of the culture as a whole.

An America already disposed not to see its collective problems of social psychology found post-9/11 denial of the mental nature of mental health in odd places. Speaking about the anthrax scare, Dr. Nadine Johnson, President of the American Psychological Association, told America on October 13, 2001 that what it faced was a health problem, not a mental health problem. A call-in questioner to CNN asked if government services could be improved in response to so many people feeling overwhelmed. The CNN commentator slipped in a question about how much need there was for post-9/11 counseling. Johnson responded, "Yes, I do think it is a role of government, because this is a health problem. This is not a mental health issue. This is a health problem. People are reacting in very normal ways to a tragedy and a terror and a trauma that is ongoing. And if somebody had a cold or strep throat, they would be allowed to go for treatment. People are reacting normally, and they ought to be able to go and get appropriate help for it."

In other words, people were not going for mental care, but for "health" care, because their reactions were "normal," even though emotional care was exactly what they were seeking, and some would have reactions that ranked as clinical. While those experiencing combat stress may be having a "normal" stress reaction to an abnormal situation, they still have an emotional challenge to surmount. Their challenge needs to be faced, whether it ranks as clinical or not. The language of normalcy may allow the challenge to be faced without also facing the stigma of mental illness in America, but it also directs attention away from the challenge.

In Johnson's parlance, the code of reacting normally to abnormal circumstances left the concept of "mental" entirely out of the needed care. Her statement had a paradoxical cast, appearing to mean that people should feel free to go for help without feeling "crazy." On the other hand, seeking mental care while denying that it is what you need can have a poor outcome. Not seeking mental health care when you need it can also have a poor outcome. Commentator Daryn Kagan caught what was unusual in Johnson's perspective given its source, and noted that a whole show could be done on the subject of America's acceptance of mental health issues. She was right.

Nadine Johnson tried to skirt the stigma of receiving mental health care by conveying permission for people to receive such care, while denying that it was what they needed. Maybe the help they needed was only short-term. Maybe they were not clinically diagnosable, but the help they needed was emotional. It was mental. The danger zone they were in, though, was social, as well as in their own psyches. Circumstances had moved them into a volatile area of stigmatized social identity. Facing your own fears at the same time that you face the culture's fear of mental health problems is a big job. It was the second part of that burden that Nadine Johnson tried to relieve, en masse, for people traumatized by 9/11, so that the first would be more likely to receive medical attention. Her expert advice could not simply bypass culture, however. Experts cannot take on social stigma for their patients. The patients have to do that for themselves.

Johnson's verbal equivocation put the needed care in the realm of the body rather than the mind. Maintaining the concept of normalcy was more important than distinguishing between the two. It was an odd strategy in a culture so firmly philosophically rooted in Cartesian mind-body dualism, but in post-9/11 impulses to holism, other Americans joined her in identifying the mental as physical. Western cultural traditions of separating mind and body notwithstanding, there is a connection between the two. Anxiety and depression are related to the physiology of pain in the brain. After 9/11, busy emergency rooms in New York City filled with patients complaining of physical ailments, rather than the mental ones from which they actually suffered. They misidentified their experience, and went for treatment of physical symptoms.

America's denial that it had suffered a collective cultural trauma solidified as daily routines returned to "normal." With many finding comfort in choosing to ignore their emotional responses, denial helped create a mental haze in collective American consciousness. *Newsweek* in December 2001 published a claim that the "age of denial" was over, having gone out with the travails of Congressman Gary Condit, but the cultural situation remained unclear. Denial was not entirely dead. As the culture took a largely unconsidered shift in the direction of anxiety being more normative, it became harder to tell where normal fear left off and disorder began. Medical study indicated that general psychological distress was within normal limits, despite increases in individual cases of post-traumatic stress disorder (PTSD),[3] but the reassurance of normalcy was also misleading.[4]

The 25 percent projected rate of PTSD for direct survivors of the World Trade Center bombing was conservative in relation to the 34 percent that had developed in Oklahoma City survivors, but after the Oklahoma bombing, it was not just rates of individual mental pathology that went up. It was also social problems, such as rates of divorce and drug addiction that went up in the surrounding citizenry. After 9/11, the entire country was the surrounding citizenry. By June of 2002, New York City schoolchildren had a reported 10 percent rate of PTSD. The accompanying 8 percent with depression and 10 percent with generalized anxiety disorder surprised psychologists, who had not expected those figures to elevate as well. The nation was at a different point within the "normal" range after 9/11. When "normal" moved, so did "abnormal." American culture became a psychological moving target.

Dr. Johnson's framing of post-9/11 emotions guarded against overpsychologizing the issue, or swamping the mental health care system. She slipped mental health care in under the cultural radar, which sounded, in an America where anxiety had become a cultural problem as well as an individual one, like a form of denial in an especially unlikely location.[5] Not recognizing anxiety as a collective phenomenon robs Americans of the ability to heal themselves as a group. While the concept of a national psyche saw a post-9/11 resurgence among psychologists, it was still a tough sell at the popular level. One news commentator asserted that the national psyche was no more than a statistical average, just a metaphor for averaging out millions of individual psyches.[6] What he missed was the fact that a collective phenomenon is more than the sum of its individual parts. Culture has integrity as a system, whether people in an individualistic culture discern that fact or not.

When the concept of combat trauma was developed after World War I, it incorporated ideas about mass civilian trauma. Anthropologists and psychologists cooperated to produce concepts of trauma as both a group and an individual phenomenon.⁷ After World War II, that dual interdisciplinary perspective was largely missing, and the concept of trauma continued to develop with a focus on the individual. Recent work in psychology now directs attention again to how mass trauma damages the social body of a community by rupturing bonds and undermining communality, and represents a return to the earlier perspective. That work has been applied to the effects of the Oklahoma City bombing, and is relevant again after 9/11.⁸ To the degree that America was collectively traumatized by 9/11, there will be worsening rifts in the American social fabric, unless the national psyche finds a way to heal.

America experienced communal grief and group loss, and it responded collectively. People attended funerals of people they had never known, and cried over the deaths of total strangers. Commonalties in American grief could become a psychological asset used to sustain a sense of community, instead of allowing social rifts to deepen, but American consciousness will have to change to reach that state. Ignoring the collective mental health component of the nation's battle with terrorism is counterproductive. This Prozac Nation needs to wake up and smell the collective psychological coffee.

Another challenge that contributes to the American need for psychological self-examination is that mental health issues often hide themselves. Even trained people on the lookout cannot always spot them. Six months after 9/11, an American child psychiatrist was surprised to discover his daughter's ongoing concern about the event. He had not thought that it would be there. He communicated his experience publicly to parents of other children who might be struggling with unidentified grief or fear. Other mental health care professionals cautioned after 9/11 that teenagers might self-medicate for fear about the future with risky behaviors like drinking or violence, a new American red flag.

Charles Bishop was not just another disturbed, depressed American teenager, to be forgotten after the media coverage of his suicide Cessna flight into a Miami high-rise at the beginning of 2002 was over. He embodied a new twist in post-9/11 American cultural character worth pondering. Bishop was described as a quiet loner from a suburban Florida community, itself described as a place where it was easy to disappear and keep to yourself. Social atomism creates a good environment for the development of both individual mental health problems and jackals. If Bishop did not know anyone in his community, that was partly because of his conduct as an individual, and it was also partly because of theirs. Part of the social context of his death was that he had not reached out to other people. Another part of it was that they had not reached out to him. Being on the evening news was how he chose to make social connections. Having his death broadcast was how he achieved social ties.

Psychologists attributed his actions to depression rather than political motivation, despite his note of praise for Osama bin Laden. Bishop's lack of Taliban training notwithstanding, Osama bin Laden too was part of the social context of his death. While he was more alienated and despondent than politically sophisticated, Bishop still chose the jackal clan to signify his personal suicide attack on American culture. A straight-A, flag-carrying, U.S. Air Force-aspiring student, with a loving family, low self-esteem, and a poor choice of hero, Bishop also showed a great deal of underlying pain and references to depression in his earlier writings. The pattern was not unfamiliar, and Americans would see variations on it again soon. Descriptions of him as ordinary or little different from an average, middle-class, suburban teen, and statements that there are a million out there like him should be more bone chilling than forgettable. The statements have much too familiar a ring. There are a million like him, who need to have the culture start offering them dreams about life, instead of the one that he chose to live out in death.

Cultural denial of mental health problems is one factor that makes it difficult to provide care for psychologically at-risk solitary teens. The culture's social fragmentation also denies them social support. While both mental health care and a more supportive social environment are worthy of pursuit, the latter is easier to provide. Teens can be provided with a better social environment for free, and there is no stigma attached. Working to create a better social environment would mitigate the relentless American conceptual focus on the individual. People are at liberty to make social connections.

Social connections do not cost anything. They were what Eric Harris and Dylan Klebold craved deeply. Bishop was described as delusional, but tracking the social baseline against which his delusional state was measured is not as easy as labeling him. He had no connections to terrorist organizations, but they clearly had a connection to him. People said that Charles Bishop would be forgotten within weeks. The problem with forgetting him is that it does not make Americans less vulnerable. It makes them more so. Bishop, like other American terrorists, had his "tendencies to depression," as Kaczynski called them, left free to simmer to an undesirable conclusion. It was the wrong type of American freedom, and the culture is complicit in the situation. Bishop's tearful teacher, who protested that there was no way she could have known, actually was less individually responsible than her guilt told her she was.

Mental dysfunction in America relates to social structure as well as trauma. It was within American culture that the diagnostic concept of "Acquired Situational Narcissism" (ASN) was produced.[9] A disorder of celebrities and sports heroes, its associations with depression, anxiety, anger, and social isolation make it similar to classical narcissism. In the case of ASN, though, everyone around the celebrity feeds a sense of social isolation by setting the celebrity apart, responding to them as though they were anything but normal. American teenagers like Bishop and Harris have perhaps a social inversion of ASN, something that could be called "Acquired Situational Low Self-Esteem" (ASL). Their sense of social isolation from normal life makes them angry, anxious, and depressed. People set them apart, the message being that in their complete lack of social noteworthiness, they are anything but normal. It does not matter that the people around them are not interconnecting socially. To them, it looks like individual rejection. They are just at the opposite end of the social scale.

Did Americans like Harris and Bishop and Helder try to move from ASL to ASN, so that they could have celebrity status along with their mental suffering? Domestic terrorists aspire to fame, but on the top or bottom of the social scale, the mental health issues look very much the same. Greater social cohesion would make ASL more difficult to achieve.

Like other shock waves, the effects of mental stress emanated outward from Ground Zero. This time, the surrounding citizenry was in not just the Oklahoma City area, but also the entire nation. Americans did get healthier again afterward, but the part of the picture that was largely missed was that there also was a subclinical residue of anxiety and fear in the psyche of the culture. People geographically distant from the 9/11 crash sites quickly put away the idea that 9/11 might continue to affect them, along with the idea that there was anything that they could do to respond, but they were wrong on both counts.

Six months later, a woman from North Carolina struggled to manage her anger and her fear for traveling family members, but did not succeed. The only solution to terrorism she could think of was simple and violent, to "nuke" anybody who might create a problem. Dealing with the complexities of other solutions to terrorism was not of interest to her. She had no nonviolent strategy for facing her fears in a post-9/11 world. If there are many like her, the culture that post-9/11 Americans generate as they interact with one another is likely to be neither very peaceful nor very much based on trust.

Professionals said that healing would take time, and that Americans would be feeling and showing emotional effects, long after such effects might appear to be gone. The illusion of "closure," on the other hand, had the potential to keep Americans from finishing their emotional healing. Psychologists told Americans that long-term emotional recovery would depend on tying recovery to values and ongoing behavior. The sense of that connection, however, was quickly lost. Long-term connection of emotional and behavioral dots was easier to project than achieve.

In the same interview, Nadine Johnson cautioned that 9/11 could retraumatize people with previous psychological trauma. They might need additional care. The perspective the nation largely missed was that such people might also become a cultural resource, the healthier among them being survivors with experience, people who could show the way to inexperienced trauma victims.

Vietnam veterans who successfully manage Post-traumatic Stress Disorder (PTSD) could be post-9/11 emotional leaders. Their experiential credentials make them resources, even in a nation unlikely to identify them as such. America would have little difficulty finding students for them to teach. They would have a great deal to say to American teenagers who feel like they live in a cultural war zone all the time. Then add the Gulf War veterans who have handled stresses of both combat and reintegrating into American society successfully. America has been victimized by the ones who were not successful, so it would be advantageous to pay attention to the ones who were. Then add resilient survivors of the Oklahoma City bombing, of racism, domestic abuse, or anything else, and America's grittiest citizens could, in the wake of national crisis, be reinterpreted as a national resource. America would be smart to learn from the phoenixes in its ranks, instead of just paying attention to the jackals in the news. In order to create a less anxiety-promoting environment for the people around them, patriotic citizens can rally around their fellow citizens, as well as the flag. They can reduce their own anxiety, and seize a greater sense of control over their social surroundings by being active within them. Americans can choose to create the closer-knit America that would serve to help curb the numbers of clinically diagnosable mentally ill among them, or they can become more hostile and fearful themselves, as they watch those numbers go up. Salving fear with material wealth or power was not a good social equation before 9/11. It is a worse one after.

A better approach would be to root out American fear and anger, and start addressing America's negative collective emotional backlog from extreme individualism, including that expressed in domestic terrorism. Conceptually leaving the responsibility for individual psychology entirely in the hands of the individual is part of the American problem. Individual psychology is affected by the social environment, and can affect it in turn. Those dots need connecting. President Bush's post-9/11 call for the cumulative effect of a million acts of kindness, followed through upon, could do as much or more for America as new federal bureaucracy. If Americans began believing that they could have an impact on their own culture and paying more positive attention to those around them, they would create an America less likely to produce Tim McVeighs and Ted Kaczynskis.

The location of the dividing line between "crazy" terrorists and the rest of "sane" America is becoming less clear. While American society is not crazy, as Ted Kaczynski asserted, "normal" in America is moving in the direction of increased emotional challenge. Like Kaczynski, America has not learned that it is at least a little "crazy" to live in a borderland of emotional unwellness without admitting it. A culture in which football fans perpetrate head injuries by throwing heavy projectiles onto the field, and the incident is reported, as it was on the December 17, 2001 CBS Evening News, as a post-9/11 return to "normal," cannot stake a perfectly clear claim to sanity.

If national recovery from an immediate post-9/11 state of "niceness" incorporates into "normal" acceptance of violence that would not have been normal by pre-9/11 standards, that is just a little crazy. A culture that accepts in itself a more violent nature in the aftermath of trauma is a culture whose lease on sanity has been undermined. Domestic terrorists emerge from the borderlands of America's psychological unwellness. The bigger the borderlands, the greater the risk of domestic terrorism. To combat terrorism internally, the national psyche needs to be vibrantly healthy, instead of marginally so.

Individuals may take a long to time to recognize or resolve psychological problems stemming from trauma. The same is true for the culture. Collective healing from the psychological effects of terror can only take place if Americans keep envisioning that healing and counteracting the effects of terror, instead of ignoring them. America needs to find the guts to admit that it has become a little crazy. If American culture were completely sane, it would not be producing American terrorists on a regular basis. There is power in acknowledging who you are.

NATIONAL PSYCHE CHALLENGED

The concept of normalcy continues to get in the way of America's consciousness about itself. "New normal" has an ethos of uncertainty, and a sense of powerlessness and fear. While reassuring, a focus on normalcy also invites Americans to do nothing. The psychiatric research community acknowledged that the nation was in uncharted psychological waters after 9/11, with little known about victims of trauma who live with an ongoing threat, but many Americans did not.[10]

A year after 9/11, a proliferation of polls told variations on the same story about fear and social inaction.[11] There was more fear in America, especially of flying. The percentage of respondents reporting that they were worried about how terrorism affected their own life had risen slightly from just after 9/11. Elevated levels of trust and faith had been retained, but not the translation of those feelings into social action. Except for continued flag display, the translation into behavior was getting lost. Fewer people reported avoiding others, but fewer also reported altruistic behavior.[12] The national psyche was still compromised. The response to the situation was a hazy combination of social avoidance and social outreach. Unfortunately, one form of social outreach in America is not altruism, but terrorism.

The recovery of psychological well-being in Americans was distributed in sociologically identifiable patterns. It was lower for Americans with lower levels of income and education, and for African-Americans.[13] Behavior like avoiding crowds persisted for minority groups, women, and people in poor health.[14] People with pre-existing social vulnerabilities seemed to predominate in the group of Americans who were now also newly psychologically vulnerable. Are there also phoenixes among them? Popular American consciousness paralleled the scientific polls, acknowledging that the society was fearful, uncertain, cautious, and struggling with anxiety and a sense of vulnerability that was around to stay. The "new normal" of a cultural environment haunted by low-level anxiety was the first normal a generation of American children and youth would experience.

Seeing where a culture that had vague anxiety coupled with extreme individualism might be headed was not easy. Fear, together with a sense of personal powerlessness, could predispose more Americans over the long term to try to create a sense of control through tragic violent gestures, managing their own terror by perpetrating it on others. The rhetoric of recovery, according to a September 11, 2002 editorial in *The New York Times*, could be a trap.[15] The title of that editorial was about America enduring. Actually, it needed to do more than endure. It needed to improve.

"Terror management theory" is a psychological theory based on the idea that terrorism undermines the psychological balance coming from a cultural world view that the world is a stable and orderly place.[16] That world view is basic to daily functioning. Even in America, where the cultural world view is based in individualism, people get their psychological security from being valued by others who share the cultural self-esteem encoded in the world view.[17] When terror strikes, a culture's world view and its self-esteem require protection, as well as its citizens and its physical assets. Stressed, members of the culture communicate the world view among themselves for psychological protection. In post-9/11 America, both the world view and the social connections through which it could be communicated needed bolstering, partly because Americans who choose terror do so not only from a lack of individual self-esteem, but also from a lack of cultural self-esteem.

The authors of "terror management theory" observe that since high anxiety and low self-esteem go together, self-esteem is a buffer against anxiety.[18] The low cultural self-esteem of a society that produces its own terror will help to promote anxiety, as well as the threat of terror itself. The pattern fits together like a puzzle, and it is not a healthy one. The National Opinion Research Center's October 2001 report "America Rebounds," on the response of the public to 9/11, indicated that despite the profound impact of 9/11 on Americans, it "did not destroy confidence in America, or elicit shame and national self-denigration," but the report also noted that anger was the most profound response.[19] The interpretation of the survey results was silent on the question of whether America had turned the strike into an opportunity to improve national self-esteem.

A related question, given the paucity of research on how people respond to ongoing threats, is just where all that anger is going to go. A long-term cure for fear and anger is not simply to project both onto Osama bin Laden, but to create a cultural environment supporting a high level of national self-esteem. Denial of hidden problems of cultural self-confidence, problems stemming from the ravages of excessive individualism, will not make that happen.

The evidence of such problems is all around, in American scandals, in American terrorism, and in the erosion of American ethics. The cultural rule of looking out for the self has done much to create a hostile social environment in which maintaining a positive cultural world view is a distinct challenge. In their heightened sensitivity to the need to maintain a positive cultural world view, some Americans adapt by violently rejecting any criticisms of their perspectives on America at all. In post-9/11 America, it was difficult to tell to what extent American flags flying from vehicles expressed self-esteem, and to what extent they covered up avoiding it.

Mental health care professionals said soon after 9/11 that it had been a massive mental health catastrophe. A panel of experts reported to Congress that average Americans who had not been in direct contact with the tragedy were full of fear and anxiety. Mental health services across the country were going to be stressed, in a nation no better prepared to deal with catastrophic mental health problems than other health problems in case of national emergency. One of the opportunities of 9/11, and a need created by it, was to become proactive about the nation's long-term mental health. The alternative was for the nation to face future emotions about terrorism essentially unprepared, leaving the cultural world view that protects individual psychology weakened. A national psyche is hard to treat. The only people who can do the treatment are the people who jointly comprise it.

Fear produces chemicals that kill neurons, and psychological warfare literally makes the brain into a battleground. Fighting back fear is part of holding back the terrorist opponent. After 9/11, Americans battled the sense of helplessness brought on by the emblazoned recurring images of falling towers. First, the images recurred on the television screen. Then, they recurred in people's minds. The images triggered reactions in other areas of the brain. People were touchy after 9/11 because of the image of the Twin Towers in flames in their brains. They were not just kinder; they were both kinder and more irritable. They experienced emotional numbing, interspersed with "hyperaroused" hair-trigger anger. Family members of victims, with their own deeply engraved mental images, criticized the rebroadcast of collapsing towers in the docudrama *9/11*. Trauma, stress, fear, anxiety, insomnia, feelings of helplessness, and a new sense of vulnerability and uncertainty all edged the nation closer to depressive territory. Americans did recover, but as they battled to regain a sense of control, they were hit again and again, with anthrax and financial scandal and sniping.

Part of the tactical beauty of psychological warfare is that it does not just debilitate individuals. It turns the opposition in on itself. Already weakened American psychological territory before 9/11 was vulnerable to infiltration by terrorism. Fighting back means not just retaliating, but also fighting back against problems in American culture. Complacency serves the jackal. The target on 9/11 was a national psyche already at risk, with escalating use of antidepressants, and a populace largely absorbed by self, screens, and consumption. Then terrorism threw that emotional profile further into anxiety territory, and the national emotional danger zone intensified. Whether terror gets you on the street or not, terror in the mind will not go away on its own. You take it, or it takes you. The mind has to be reclaimed from a hostile colonizing force. The counterattack can be in opening the mail, getting on an airplane, staying informed, daring to behave with economic confidence, or caring enough about American culture to keep making it something you want to defend.

Fighting terror involves giving others social support. People with mental challenges who have social support while they fight them instead of being discriminated against, are more likely to stay out of the violent range. When having the guts to grapple with mental challenge engenders respect, community is built two ways, in those respected and in those doing the respecting. Americans should not wait for community to come to them, but go and make it. People can get their own emotional support by giving support elsewhere.

Helping or being helped, community is under construction either way. Social connections can heal America's collective psyche and individual psyches along the way. Close-knit communities have lower health risks for their members.[20] Social cohesion is a free and universally available health insurance policy for any type of health risk. The invitation that the American cultural sense of the importance of everything "big"—business, government, technology, and media—gives to a sense of individual helplessness, and the accompanying cultural low self-esteem and despair is a pattern that can be broken, but it is a pattern that can only be broken from within.

Americans can beat back cultural depressiveness with positive social connections, or continue to terrorize each other in small ways from their individual bivouacs. Kaczynski's bombs never made him feel better. They were just one more step down a path of addictive American self-indulgence, with his isolated cabin in Montana a perfect symbol of how not to live. The rest of America can choose a substantially different path. Instead of feeding fear and anger, Americans can heal the collective psyche by getting out from behind their individual doors watching TV, and going instead to new social destinations.

Unless Americans bond socially to give themselves back a sense of social control, fear and low cultural self-esteem will grow. Fear levels will remain dependent on the news instead of on freely taken social initiative. Individuals may not be in a position to help law enforcement directly, but they can always take the principles involved in fear, such as the bankrupt social ethics of hoax attacks, and turn them to education instead. If you cannot help to catch a hoaxer, you can help prevent one by teaching about personal integrity. You can take indirect action against terrorism, even if you cannot take direct action. The target area in America is endless. Americans have an underlying impulse to do something; they just lack a road map for doing it.

Since terrorism is fundamentally an attack on humanity, anything that supports humanity counteracts the spirit of terrorism, and its psychology. Read stories to children about courage and cowardice. Deny the sense that there is nothing to be done. Lose the sense of hopelessness that induces social paralysis. Think about problems in America. Take them apart and put them back together in your mind. Then go and do something about one of them. If you cannot be part of a direct short-term solution to the problem of terrorism, be part of an indirect long-term solution instead. It is good psychology.

Terrorism threatens everything, and the effective social psychological response is to strengthen everything. September 11 victims can be honored indefinitely by endlessly reinforcing the worthiness of the culture they lived in. Serve soup. Mentor a kid. Visit a shut-in. Bring the concept of initiative back to the center of American character by doing what you can to take America out of the inactive depressive danger zone. Knit your own well-being and that of your culture back together at the same time. Substitute healthy social connections for self-focused addictions. Fear is hard to sustain when you are too busy to think about it.

Some of the anxiety in America is distinctly orange. While a campaign of shock and awe in Iraq moved some American fear and anger outward, there was still plenty to go around internally. In February of 2003, unreliable informants translated, via a government alert, into duct tape mania and commentary on the deleterious effects of chronic alertness. An alert intended to galvanize the population was more chaotic in its effect. The most sobering thought in that connection is from anthropologist and psychiatrist Arthur Kleinman, who observed that non-specific alerts can make things worse by deepening social anxiety, especially if they come as reinforcement for ideas that there are technological solutions or quick fixes for terrorism.[21] Those ideas only increase the sense of a lack of control that terrorism instills. Failed communication in alerts and faulty modeling about solutions to terror plays right into the hands of the jackal.

SKIP THE PSYCHOLOGY?

Some say that the last thing to do to respond to terrorism is to think in terms of psychology. They are fed up with psychology, pop, traditional, or any other kind. Rejecting psychology is a way for a culture that already has too much focus on the individual to react, but it is not the psychology that needs curtailing. The focus on the individual does. One of the costs of America's addiction to the individual is the conviction that working on the self can solve any problem.[22] Individually focused psychology cannot solve the problem of too much focus on the individual, and psychological warfare cannot be overcome through strengthening individual psychology alone. Bolstering social psychology is a far better strategy, but coming to that realization without falling into the overemphasis on psychology that pervades the Unabomber Manifesto and the culture in general is a subtle task. Falling into the trap of ignoring psychology, though, puts America at a disadvantage in fighting the psychological warfare intrinsic to terrorism. Denying a mental challenge because of conceptual saturation with psychological concepts still leads in the wrong direction.

The American psyche was affected by 9/11. In a national Rand study published in November of 2001, nine of ten Americans reported some degree of stress after 9/11.[23] Generalized, the findings would project that something on the order of 270 million people in America had disturbed thoughts and dreams, had difficulty concentrating or sleeping well, or experienced angry outbursts. In the first days, some oscillated between a euphoria of patriotism and lows of pessimism and dejection. There was wild variation in behavior, from acute kindness to astounding aggression. Philanthropy and violent crime both went up. Those who thought that everyone in America became nice after 9/11 were not paying attention to the other end of the continuum. A volatile, agitated, filed-tooth, overreactive American cropped up soon after 9/11. Aggressive responses came across the fax and on the highway. Messed with, people were definitely going to mess back. Fellow American survivors of 9/11 took their stress out on one another.

While aggression went up, tolerance for it went down. Aggression took on an uncharacteristic aura of taboo. It had a different tone, and was less predictable. Pushy tailgating fell off, replaced instead with more fly-off-the-handle, sudden, frustrated driving moves. People ignored each other less and paid attention more. Civil disregard came back into full force later, but right after 9/11, conflict rankled. A postal worker's union official announcing his intention to file a lawsuit with the goal of providing postal workers the same level of anthrax protection as members of Congress, had perfect social semantics for post-9/11 America. The common worker in the war on terrorism should have the same protections as the powerful. But the voice quality was as wrong as the action seemed right. The tone did not fit the anticonflict tenor of American culture at the time.

A caller to a public radio show had a point. There was a lesson to be learned in his connection of mistreatment of minority women in America to hypocrisy about concern for women in Afghanistan, but the lesson was lost in the anger and agitation in his voice. Commentators replied in non sequiturs, instead of engaging his point. His argument ignored, he was doubtless angrier yet after getting off the phone. There was also a banner example of low post-9/11 tolerance for anger in the stunned reaction to belligerent responses of New York fire fighters, after policy changes degraded their ability to recover human remains from the World Trade Center site.

The subjects in the Rand survey painted a picture of American coping mechanisms. The picture presented a folk version of a professional recommendation for dealing with individual anxiety. The rehabilitative actions that Americans took were not recommended by experts. They came naturally. Anxiety in an individual can be treated with changes in imagery (which at the cultural level would be a change in symbolism about cultural identity), a restructuring of assumptions (or for a culture, a rewriting of cultural values and rules), and resulting changes in behavior (or overall patterns of social interaction), in order to combat a sense of vulnerability.[24] The national psyche set about combating anxiety right after 9/11. Americans talked. Talking about thoughts and feelings topped the list in the Rand survey at 90 percent. As they talked, their cultural symbols for themselves changed. Two-thirds used social activity to combat stress, while one-third gave blood or money.

The behavioral folk therapy was good, but brief. The wisdom of what Americans did in early days paralleled a psychological course of treatment for anxiety, but Americans did not stay on course. Cultural self-assessment, changes in imagery and values, and more social connectedness all needed to be kept together in one picture and retained over the American long term, but that was a stretch for American consciousness. If Americans continued to talk, expanded the set of people they talked to, and kept creating new strands of social connection, they could give the national psyche ongoing therapy. General philanthropy was up over the 2001 holiday season. Ongoing philanthropy of both money and conduct would sustain healing to the national psyche. Keeping track of initial responses to 9/11 and keeping them up would provide upkeep for American society and character, if Americans could remember and sustain those responses, and realize that the responses were in part about national psychological care.

Continuing to exert the same force of will to fight fear in daily American life that it took for Americans to get back onto airplanes and into large public gatherings after 9/11, could move America into an uncertain future with anticipation instead of dread. Americans could stay out of social reactive mode, using instead social assertiveness and unexpected kindness as an element of surprise. Americans have the power to make culture change by treating fewer people like adversaries and more like partners. They can drum anxiety out of the American landscape by giving people around them less reason for anxiety. The geography to be conquered is within the self and within the society, and Americans can work their social environment, instead of succumbing to it. They can break a culture of anxiety by giving fear its due, and then beating it back.

Do not skip the psychology. Psychology is a valuable piece of the complex cultural puzzle to be solved. By six months after 9/11, the language of vulnerability and fear were everywhere, and a general inability to get a conceptual handle on the aftermath of 9/11 had begun to wear. Some thought shock therapy was in order, possibly in the form of another tragedy that would again galvanize the nation. Others thought the visuals in the docudrama *9/11* should have been more graphic for shock value, and that people were incapable of remembering the event without ongoing stimulus from the media. Casting the media as psychotherapist to the nation was new, and the media's psychotherapeutic methods for combating depression were definitely outdated. Americans, meanwhile, faced the idea that shock therapy was the only prospect for producing clarity and unity. Even a new attack might be just a temporary fix. The challenge was to dig deeper and find ways of improving odds instead.[25] One of the ways to dig deeper into the roots of contemporary American culture is to deal with the psychology of terrorism. Americans need better care than shock therapy, and they need to muster that care for themselves.

POST-TRAUMATIC GROWTH

Fear moves. It does not stay still. Left alone, it grows. Confronted, it gets the adrenaline flowing. Then the response is both to the fear and to what caused it. Americans will move with their fear, but in what direction? They can surmount it, or let unresolved emotions of fear and anger remain extensions of their terrorist opponents within themselves. Being subdued by an enemy that is not even fighting at the moment is not a good position to be in, and transforming victimization is always up to the victims. President Bush pointed out that terrorists "hope that America grows fearful . . . forsaking our friends." He may have had international friends in mind, but the admonition works just as well when applied to people down the block. He was onto an important principle in dealing with fear. It can be fought effectively with social connections.

The work of psychiatrist Sandra Bloom identifies the phoenix's answer to post-traumatic stress disorder (PTSD), post-traumatic growth.[26] People who come through the fires of trauma can emerge into a stronger state of being, wiser, more resilient, more optimistic, and more socially connected than they were before. The catch for America is that the social connectedness that is a key element in post-traumatic growth is hard to achieve in a fragmented and depersonalized society.

Sandra Bloom told the nation after 9/11 that it did not need formal professional therapy, that being only for the most troubled individuals, but the concept of post-traumatic growth can still be profitably applied to a national psyche already challenged by violence. In a 1997 volume, *Creating Sanctuary: Toward an Evolution of Sane Societies*, Sandra Bloom described the pre-9/11 national character as suffering from "cultural post-traumatic stress disorder." She characterized pre-9/11 American culture as fragmented, dissociated, emotionally numb, alienated, and self-destructive.[27] The nation may not need professional therapy, but the key to achieving post-traumatic growth for the national psyche through folk therapy is in creating social connectedness.

Post-traumatic growth enables the resilient to strengthen after trauma by developing a greater appreciation for life, growing closer to others, pursuing unexpected paths, deepening spirituality, and developing feelings of being stronger and more effective. That formula bears use in American culture, even among people who do not themselves need psychological care, on behalf of the national psyche that all members of the culture take part in generating. One of America's challenges in achieving post-traumatic growth is facing the permanent stress of another possible trauma, but social psychologist Ronnie Janoff-Bulman instructs that shattered assumptions have to be rebuilt after trauma.[28] The shattered assumptions that needed rebuilding after 9/11 were about America's cultural identity, as well as its safety and security. If Americans continue to redefine their culture so that it reflects the power of individual humanity in strengthened social ties, prospects for national post-traumatic growth will be good.

New York fire fighters, who said in December of 2001 that giving to children in Afghan orphanages helped them deal with their own grief, had a solution. Americans can heal the collective psyche by also applying the same principle internally within America, but such healing will require restructuring assumptions about the American individual so that they are removed from the realm of social powerlessness. What is confusing about post-9/11 national process is that there are no specific recommendations for behavior to follow. Narrow instructions, such as the World War II charge to give up nylon stockings or grow victory gardens, are missing.

This time, the challenge is broader, and the social charge is correspondingly broad. Any socially constructive behavior will help to get the job done. Conceptually compartmentalizing the responsibility for dealing with the threat of terrorism entirely into the hands of law enforcement and government will not. The solution to the mental puzzle of what to do to strengthen America is that Americans should not depend on the media, the government, or experts to generate the culture. They should also do it themselves. The American people fought right after 9/11, on the mental battlefields of the mail, the economy, and flying.

The mail gets to everyone. So did anthrax mail anxiety, and facing it was a universal challenge. Post-9/11 holiday postal workers were overloaded in more than the usual ways. First, the anthrax terrorist jabbed, and then the mailbox pipe bomber reverse punched America in its mailbox. Having to dare to receive mail was part of new American "normal." Abortion clinics had anthrax mail hoaxes, and Kaczynski watched the saga from prison. The solution was not to leave the fear in the mailbox, but to take it out and fight it.

To open or not to open the box was the question. To spend or not to spend was another question. Like receiving mail, spending money is something almost every American does. At the same time that post-9/11 Americans were inclined to modify their often-addictive overuse of credit cards, based on economic uncertainty, they were being asked to keep spending to bolster an endangered economy. The equation was a tough one to figure out. You could use restraint to serve your own psychology of caution and fail to support the collective economy. Alternatively, you could spend, and feed the stereotype of the morally vacuous, consuming American, even in the face of 9/11. It was not a pretty position to be in, but America adapted. Like travel destinations, shopping destinations changed. The collective cultural solution to the thorny problem was to spend money—at Wal-Mart. Cash register bells rang incessantly in the 2001 holiday season, and although the average purchase price may have gone down, the bells chimed in synchrony with a shift in cultural symbolism that highlighted the everyday American.

America seemed less consumed by its own consumption, its appetites directed toward craving the simple human connections at the core of giving relationships, with simple material accessories to match. Upscale shopping, along with other forms of extremism, was not where the cultural viscera were, the high end and the high risk less appetizing than the well known and the close to home. The local and the ordinary went into growth mode everywhere. There was less Aruba and more roller rink, more cocoon and less Cancun. Sales of basic durable goods rebounded quickly, but lavish luxury was a tougher sell. Still, the local mall was wall to wall in December. Everyone and their cousin were out, wanting beauty, magic, and shoulder rubbing. On the Fourth of July

2002, a sense of connected community still held, as did celebratory healing in public gatherings where people made a defiant point of feeling safe.

There was the fear of flying to navigate. Being on any ship shrinks the world. There is only the ship, the element you are moving in, and your company. People rethought the risks inherent to air travel, faced new fear, and adapted to delay and inconvenience. The sense of individual entitlement to perfect mobility was replaced, grudgingly but successfully, with a sense of personal limitation and social control. Humility, patience, and tolerance became sudden social requirements in a significant area of American cultural life. Anxiety in security screeners and pilots, as well as passengers, became part of a new cultural obstacle course. Adjusting American individualism was not easy, but adjust it did.

Culturally speaking, the air became a very interesting place. While the new "national community" headquartered in New York City had little practical outreach on the ground, there was one face-to-face place the new American sense of community functioned daily—in the air. People flying together after 9/11 constituted community, and they knew it. They had become newly interdependent in enforced exercises in social cohesion. They shared risk and responsibility for the social control of their membership.

These new communities functioned with uncommon solidarity, showing Americans that tight-knit mutual social support was a quality they could achieve. Controlling miscreants in the communities was not much of an issue, from stewardess-abusers to shoe-bomber Richard Reid. President Bush described the Reid incident with the phrase "culture of . . . ," after a pause filling in the blank with "alertness." A few days later, he described it as a culture of vigilance. The concept of a culture of vigilance ran into civil liberties problems on the ground, though, and another important cultural question remained. That question was whether Americans could take any cooperative sense of community with them back off the plane and onto the ground.

Complacency keeps Americans from fighting for the post-traumatic growth that will forearm them psychologically against the next terrorist attack. America's weapons against fear are not just new technologies, bureaucracies, or psychotherapy for individuals. They also include reconceptualizing the American individual into a constructive rather than a hostile relationship with the next American on the block, in order to fight a cultural atmosphere characterized by a compartmentalized America and a passive and depressive social ethos.

Psychological growth for America will involve making the social connections that will give America a better social-psychological baseline to work from as it faces terrorism. The process is not entirely unlike an individual recovering from depression because of increased neurological connections in the brain. In this case, a society needs to recover by making more connections between its individuals. Terrorism challenges American consciousness beyond trauma to growth, and the nation does not need a fully certified case of cultural PTSD to set about transforming shock and horror into collective post-traumatic growth. It does need to do work it already had to do before 9/11, in order to get back a sense of social control in America.

America does not yet have a clear plan for how to wage a psychological battle with terrorism. A lot was up in the air in the aftermath of 9/11. Uncertainty was up. Hope was up. Kindness and flash point aggression were up. For the pattern that settles to be one of growth, the nation needs to keep giving itself therapy for cultural anxiety. There needs to be continued talk about experience, a changed model of itself, and altered cultural rules and behavior to fit new cultural imagery.[29] There is a coherent vision for transforming America in the shifts in its symbols for itself after 9/11, a vision that can help draw a map for taking America to where its cultural self-esteem will be more resistant to the impact of terrorist attacks. America was resilient after 9/11, but the game is not over. If America can find the honesty and courage to capitalize on the chinks in its own psychological armor, it can forge a stronger national psyche. Serenity can no longer be bought individually in America at an expensive spa. It is on the other side of collectively facing and battling fear.

There is yet another reason to collectively combat PTSD in America. Individual cases often do not surface until long after a traumatic event. They did not after Oklahoma City, and will not after 9/11. Far from having psychological closure on 9/11, the nation has a shift in emotional tone and a new pool of individuals with unresolved trauma to confront. The pool contains potential jackals, and the phoenix clan would be well served to do something proactive about them. There should perhaps be special concern about America's youth, since the prevalence of PTSD in children traumatized by community violence or war is well established.[30] Post-9/11 research in America also indicated a prevalence of probable PTSD associated with a high number of hours of watching television coverage of the attacks.[31] Put it all together, and one of the internal populations America should especially be reaching out to is screen-oriented, emotionally troubled, and socially challenged youth, people, for example, like Matthew Lovett.

CHAPTER 4

SYMBOL SHIFTS

RITUAL SACRIFICE AND . . .

Ritual has political implications. Ritual is about getting, keeping, and exercising power.[1] It is also about making emotional connections between people. Terrorism is a theatrical form of ritual, and the World Trade Center, the Pentagon, and the airliners were all elements of a mass sacrifice on 9/11. The icon of American economic prowess was down, the citadel of American military power was assailed, and Air Force One was scrambling. The only significant symbol the attackers neglected was the lady who represented liberty. She stood firm, but the concept of freedom that she embodies did go into a level of cultural arrest. The deaths on 9/11 had riveting symbolic significance. Ancient Aztecs who extracted human hearts atop pyramids, and Jim Jones with his Kool-Aid death cult, also knew something of the emotional power of rituals of mass human sacrifice. They, the Taliban, and American terrorists are all aware of the power of public execution.[2]

Viewed as ritual, 9/11 was a bid at symbolic ethnic cleansing of American culture. It was attempted genocide on an identity. The staggering visual power of the attacks, focused on the sheer spectacle of collapsing towers, caused America to reel, not just its government and economy, but also its very understanding of itself. American psychological self-defense included fighting back with symbols and with counteracting rituals. President Bush's first weapons in his war on terror were symbols, deployed against a much greater impact on cultural consciousness than Tim McVeigh or the Ted Kaczynski had ever had. Bush termed "sacrificing human life" as an expression of the terrorists' will to power as they tried to "remake the world in their own brutal images."[3] Image was the issue, and fighting back required opposing images. As a nation, America set about creating funerary sacrament that negated the meaning of the sacrificial ritual. As it did, it reached beyond the funerary into redefining the living.

The Taliban reiterated its symbolic challenge verbally late in September, saying that Americans were people who believed in weapons and wanted material things, rather than people who believed in what was in their hearts. Al Qaeda and the Taliban did not get capitulation, or an extinction of the American sense of self, in response. They got American symbolic adaptability instead. Post-9/11 America did not cleave to an individually self-centered, high-tech, money-driven image. Even before the Taliban issued the second challenge, America's metaphors for itself had begun to shift from technology, money, and media, to humanity, community, and reality. The shifts were clear, sharp, and intense, if not enduring. American thought migrated in the direction of the power of the individual human being, not just the ones with political power or celebrity, but anyone. The obvious musical selection to accompany the bounce-back symbolic sense of America's collective self was Copland's *Fanfare for the Common Man*, and it was selected.

The post-9/11 cultural buzz in America was that power and size were no longer overpowering metaphors, and that the demise of the towers had taken America past the time when height signified superiority. The symbolic shift brought America's sense of itself closer to the human heart. America should not have been surprised at its impulse to symbolic transformation, since the same thing had happened on a more limited scale after Oklahoma City. Edward T. Linenthal documents the symbolic transformation of mass murder there into a form of "patriotic sacrifice," and represents Tim McVeigh's execution as a form of symbolic reversal in which America cleansed itself of his taint in a blood ritual "of civic purification."[4]

In a similar reversal, Ground Zero, which had been desecrated, became symbolically consecrated as a cultural holy site. The standards for symbolic propriety at Ground Zero remained high. Memorials that could be construed as signifying lost buildings instead of lost people were not acceptable. New symbolism was required to be about life rather than death. Daniel Libeskind's winning architectural design to replace the Twin Towers was criticized by detractors as "ghoulish," or a "death pit," for its preservation of ground where so many had died. His close competition was criticized for latticework towers that looked too much like "skeletons."[5] Evoking death rather than life was clearly taboo, which sounded like good news for the phoenix.

A cheap, low blow leaves a lot of room to rise above in response to an attack. The lower the blow, the more likely it is to arouse high-end moral responses, like "towers of courage." But that also leaves a lot of room to get lost in. While America found its human self definitively right after 9/11, whether it will keep on effectively counteracting the low cultural self-esteem invited both by the attack and the dehumanization in contemporary American culture is another question. The importance of humanity, community, and reality had all declined before 9/11, and need renewal in America's consciousness of itself. While America's post-9/11 defensive symbolic shifts were worth retaining, what they faced was the American impulse to dispose of things quickly.

Media, technology, and money were still there after 9/11, along with humanity, community, and reality, as ways that America thought about itself, but they had new problems and challenges. They had been tempered. September 11 was the source of the symbolic shifts, and was itself treated with the greatest of symbolic reverence. That reverence extended well beyond Ground Zero. Trying to sell shoes by invoking 9/11 was not a good idea. In a country where almost nothing outstrips the importance of profit, profit was trumped by a reverence that created an outraged sense of economic exploitation. Using 9/11 for political publicity was similarly fraught with danger. Having been a first responder was no way to begin a political campaign, and criticizing a political opponent for 9/11 responses was worse yet. The specter of exploiting 9/11 for power loomed as large as the specter of exploiting it for money.

The symbolic identity structure of America modified, but tempered more than it transformed. At least for a while, Americans thought of themselves less as outgrowths of their technology, expressions of their money, or reflections of their media. They reexplored the foundation of their culture in human beings, the connections of humans to one another, and collective human power.

People in America became a conceptual focal point, from which technology, money, and media flowed, instead of the other way around. Technology served people more and shaped them less. When a technological solution to a problem was not immediately available, it was possible to image a labor-intensive human solution. People could screen checked luggage. Customers more often became multifaceted people, instead of just what they were ordering. They could be talked with. Media reflected reality more and created it less, bowing more often to the possible effects of its representations on real life. Americans had been given an object lesson both by terrorists and emergency responders in the power of people—even just a few people. If sustained, the focus on the ability of an individual to make a difference in society had the makings of the cultural revolution that many looked for after 9/11. For the most part, that revolution did not occur.

Anthropologist Clifford Geertz observes that people in a culture interpret themselves with the stories that they "tell themselves about themselves."[6] Stories both spring from a culture and serve to recreate it. Part of America's symbolic defense against 9/11 was a change in the nature of the stories that Americans told themselves about themselves. The stories changed not because of grief for the victims, but because there had been a successful assault on symbols of American economic and military power by a small cast of socially well-integrated characters, low on technology and high on determination. New stories had to be written to counter that story, or American culture no longer made any sense.

Not just America's airplanes, but also its sense of itself, was turned against it on 9/11, and Americans fought back with the idea that their culture was about the power of people, not things. On 9/11, the media as a source of American-storytelling consciousness was effectively stolen. America was not planning the programming in broadcast images that seared pain and confusion. The new programming brought down the primacy of America's image of itself in its own mind, and demanded immediate rebuilding with new stories, long before brick and mortar could be brought to bear. What was not destroyed was the power to keep reshaping American consciousness in the wake of the stolen imagery. Unlike American buildings, America's self-image did not collapse. It flexed.

RITUAL REVIVAL

Some of contemporary America's most important stories about itself come from the ritual combat known as sports, from movies and television, and from elsewhere in popular culture. The ritual counterattack to 9/11 began well before military action in Afghanistan, as America worked to demolish the degrading opposing myth of itself as a culture of self-absorbed individuals, powerfully high-tech, but indifferent to one another and humanity. Americans created a revised myth of themselves instead. The counterattack started right away and kept coming. Candles and pictures and flowers and vigils with massings of mourners were a foregone first response to the tragedy of human loss. Nobody in New York needed a consultant from Oklahoma City to know how to stage that part of the comeback. Later, the two cities would team up to fight their joint pain in a shared ritual that reaffirmed the hope and determination of survivors, but did not distinguish the nationality of the terrorist perpetrator. Part of the Oklahoma City commemorative survival tree came to New York, and New Yorkers went to Oklahoma City in the spring of 2002 to observe the seven-year anniversary of McVeigh's bombing.

Articulate but unbowed widows of 9/11, most notably Lisa Beamer, began to sound like embodied versions of Lady Liberty, their status as icons secured by their ties to their lost loved ones. At the same time, professional sports faltered and fumed, and the entertainment industry struggled temporarily in order to regain its symbolic footing in new American culture. The post-9/11 American sports hiatus was only partly about security and decorum. It was also about regrouping a sense of American identity, before that identity could be put into play again. While celebrities and professional sports figures were assured a comeback, the comeback for the culture would have been stronger yet if more of their salaries had gone to philanthropy over the long term, or Super Bowl ad images of community-involved professional athletes had been sustained for more than a year.

Songwriters and celebrities appeared in a string of benefit concerts. They also appeared as clearly vulnerable human beings. Grief showed on usually relentlessly prefabricated faces. Cameras trained instead on people who were clearly in pain and humbled to the task of supporting victims. Stars looked like regular people. Even the supremacy of celebrity came down in America for a while. The Concert for New York City looked like entertainment, but was also a ritual that battled the effects of 9/11. Incongruously smiling mourners held up pictures of departed loved ones, or gave them to celebrities to hold. The attack was attacked with celebratory memorial both for those present and for those watching. America was back in control of American storytelling. While celebrities were partly in a process of reclaiming their status in post-9/11 concerts, for the time being, the gloss was off. "Reality" TV faltered, and almost died, but would later see wildly successful development.

Over the short term, though, all types of celebrities were resoundingly trumped by unscripted reality. The reality show *Survivor* itself had to adapt to regain ratings. The "reward challenge" for the show itself meant bringing cameras back to New York and promoting humanitarian causes, such as anti-AIDS activism in Africa. The show survived. The contestants too showed signs of adaptation to a post-9/11 world, extolling cooperative contact with Marquesan natives that made them feel like "a human being," in contrast to the cutthroat social algebra of the survival game, and talking about how their experience on the show had taught them how many belongings they could do without. "Reality" TV looked more surreal than real for a while, before it hit a jackpot of cultural adaptation.

The power of fame was not assured. It struggled. During benefit concerts, fire fighter's orphans outmatched top celebrities on stage. The celebrities clearly knew it. For a time, celebrities went into the service of the American public, instead of being the symbolic drivers of the public's image of itself. Celebrities had to recalibrate and reestablish their place in American culture. By six months after 9/11, the "luminaries" at the New York City St. Patrick's Day parade were said to have become accustomed to being upstaged by fire fighters. That was part of the new American way. Nine months after 9/11, a rash of celebrities showed up to testify before Congress about a series of humanitarian concerns, creating a real post-9/11 American scene in which celebrity and everyday humanity had become more closely tied. A power balance had shifted. News reports became ritualized events after 9/11, sometimes themselves a blend of representation and reality. Network anchors Tom Brokaw and Dan Rather gave bravura performances with their own offices under anthrax attack. Senator Tom Daschle seemed less a distant icon of power, and more like a neighbor when he was under anthrax attack himself. Watching news, concerts, and documentary drama became a painful but intensely important personal ritual for many Americans. People had to dare to face what they might hear when they turned on the news, but everybody in America craved news intensely. Movies, like reality TV, got in on cultural revitalization mostly later on.

Stories changed. Over the short term, humor froze. Then comedy storytellers reemerged with symbolically secure material in a security-conscious culture. America's new cultural myths changed along three dimensions, with its new stories about humanity and its technology, money and its community, and reality and its media. America practiced its new sense of itself in its everyday news rituals and on special occasions, like the Academy Awards ceremony. Keeping and building on the content of the early new cultural myths, and enacting them into ongoing American stories in everyday life would be medicine for the spirit of the culture, a prescription for transforming cultural post-traumatic stress into post-traumatic growth.

MACHINES FIRST, A HUMAN ERROR

Within a week of 9/11, Attorney General John Ashcroft appeared before the American public with a plea for broadened law enforcement prerogatives to assist in the pursuit of terrorists. The plea involved a clear shift in cultural presumptions. The change desired in regulations for issuing wiretap warrants was to create a focus on people, and not on the various telephone technologies that they were using. Issuing the warrant for the person and not for the phone was going to be a more effective strategy. Organizing investigation of people in terms of people instead of the machines they were using was going to yield improvements in security.

Ashcroft's thinking marked a shift from the thinking behind an ATT ad that appeared in *Newsweek* in 2000: "It's a very exciting time to be a TV, phone, or computer. Not to mention a human being." People had taken back the conceptual lead. By 2003, computer companies would work to sell their products by touting the concept of "humanology," or the study of how people related to their machines. President Bush made the same symbolic shift from technology to humanity in his speech to the nation on the evening of 9/11. It was not the steel in the buildings that was important, but the steel of resolve in the American people. American wealth was not in glass and steel, but in people. He identified American people, not corporations or capital, as the source of American prosperity.

The *CBS Evening News* had already beaten him to the punch. Dan Rather's September 11, 2001 references to technology and money were delivered as virtual asides. He noted that the attack must have required some money, but the focus of reporting was on the human ingenuity behind the attack and its low-tech profile. Americans were reminded often in the days and months afterward that they were not their property or their technology. Schoolchildren wrote that the fire fighters had seen people in danger rather than burning buildings. The fallen Twin Towers transmuted into people who rose in their place. The "other Twin Towers" were a New York fire fighter and a New York police officer.

The message counteracting the attack was that although the heart of American material prosperity had taken a direct hit, its human heart still stood. Former president Clinton got into the symbolic reformulation act at the Concert for New York City, telling the audience that they were not about mountains of money and towers of steel, but mountains of courage and hearts of gold. Later, *Time* magazine's Person of the Year for 2001 was Rudi Guiliani, a "Tower of Strength," and the twin light beam tribute recreating the towers was renamed to reflect its honoring of humanity rather than lost buildings.[7]

As military action against Afghanistan unfolded, American overreliance on technically based intelligence rather than human intelligence was publicized. The concentration on high-tech surveillance that left America out in the cold in terms of human intelligence was one of the imbalances the post-9/11 American intelligence community moved to correct, adjusting to focus on both human and technical strategies for intelligence collection.[8] Human determination and the Afghan social environment challenged a model of American intelligence based heavily on technological clout. Reworking American intelligence into a more people-oriented activity, where that was even possible, would take time and a paradigm shift that maintained a focus on human resource and human relationship, but such shifts were also happening elsewhere on the home front.

Americans started to think more often outside the technological box, their social imaginations expanding to include the people behind the technology and the mobilization of humans in the face of human problems with technology. "Technical" problems with smart bombs whose batteries had been jerry-rigged after hours with glue by employees of the Eagle-Pilcher Company in Missouri, leading to the friendly fire deaths of three American military, were traced back to their human roots. The problem was not really technical, and the sensibility that greeted the Eagle-Pilcher debacle was different from the one that greeted the pre-9/11 Firestone tire issue. An addictively applied profit motive leading to human injury or death was now on the run, along with the anonymity of the human beings engineering the problems. Human accountability was in. As post-9/11 American culture carried on, the work of a security expert citing overreliance on "foolproof" technology as a major stumbling block to creating truly secure systems was cited popularly.[9]

Ted Kaczynski had already told Americans that technology runs them. While it only does if they allow it to, one of America's cultural problems is that they often do. People craft culture and the place of their machines in it. It is also people who accept or reject the idea that technology is at the core of a cultural system. Technology may invite Americans to forget about the power of human contact, but the forgetting is theirs. The technology does not do it. The person-free checkout, the computer, and the automated phone-answering system do not take away the humans beings on the other end of the interactions. They just make them harder to get to directly, or think in terms of. The Unabomber's views on the overvaluing of technology in American culture still carry weight in a post-9/11 America with a chance to think about itself as a culture that is as much about people as their machines. Humanity can be kept over the long term as a larger factor in America's cultural self-image, if people choose to do so.

Doing so will not be easy. In a survey of public response to 9/11, not only did respondents who were proud of America for its scientific and technological achievements outstrip those who were proud of it for its social ethos (i.e. "fair and equal treatment of all groups in society") by more than two to one, technological pride proved to be more resilient than social pride from 2001 to 2002.[10] Behavioral adaptations to 9/11 moved both in the direction of technology and in the direction of people. Some Americans used e-shopping as a way to avoid places of shared space with unknown human beings. Others found job clinics at churches. Ads in 2003 for U.S. Army recruiting marketed the power of people. The ads were not about technology or numbers, but the difference that a single human being could make, "The might of the U.S. Army doesn't lie in numbers. It lies in people like me. An Army of One." The metaphor was designed to sell the power of individual humanity, not scale or tools.

CAPITALIZING ON CONNECTION

Advertising people move fast. The American economy and company profits were both at risk. The concept of American culture needed a new synthesis after 9/11 to keep the company, the economy, the product, and the American Dream all rolling. If money and technology had become sudden American metaphorical afterthoughts, what construction of symbols could be used to sell product? The advertising challenge was rendered even more difficult with the normally sanctified American concept of making money taboo if it came in connection with 9/11.

Taboos on making money were essentially new American cultural territory. In a morally critical tone, economist Paul Krugman noted that some people had actually made money off of 9/11 in the stock market. Upscale shoe manufacturer Kenneth Cole came under attack for exploiting 9/11 after using it in an advertising campaign. Either Cole was morally wrong, or criticizing Cole was unpatriotic because doing so was anticapitalist. No matter which way you cut the argument, it was clearly important to have post-9/11 patriotism in a right relationship to

capitalism. On that point, there was agreement. Citing 9/11 for political
gain did not go over well either, whether, like Andrew Cuomo, you were
forwarding your campaign by downplaying New York governor George
Pataki's role in recovery efforts, or you were attempting to take your New
York City fire fighter status into a political campaign for Congress.
September 11 became a cultural holy-of-holies, and capitalizing on it for
personal gain, either economic or political, was forbidden territory.

What stunned about Krugman's statement was the attachment of
negative stigma to the making of money. If this was America, it was
clearly another America. Even if the new economic taboo related only
strictly to 9/11, the change to the symbolic structure of a generally
unfettered for-profit culture was still dramatic. Any modification of the
powerful American money metaphor constituted some level of cultural
revolution. The sensibility that there were places where making money
was forbidden filtered into network news reports about unscrupulous
small entrepreneurs in the following months. The pursuit of money, still
central in American symbolism about America, lost some of its addictive
edge. A rash of corporate debacles reinforced the loss. The social "stock"
of the disconnection that facilitated corporate malfeasance went down,
and that of whistle blowers went up. At least in theory, money became
something that should serve people, and not the other way around.

President Bush was on cue again. American economy was about
community, not money per se, and the "hard work and creativity and
enterprise" of American people.[11] People loomed larger in the American
economic equation. Cynics said that the bottom line would always be the
bottom line, and were right, as far as the analysis went. What the cynics
missed is that movies with different themes, or goods produced for shifting
tastes create different bottom lines in a culture with changing sensibilities.
They also missed the attitudinal shifts in a culture where a lot of people
were doing a lot of thinking about the damage done to the many by
excessive individualism in the powerful corporate few, in the wake of
Enron and other scandals.

Some of those people were the same people who waited for hours at
airports for repeat security checks, after one person had violated
regulations. The thousands who waited for hours on the sidewalk outside
the Atlanta airport in November of 2001, after one man ran through a

security checkpoint, had the ranking consciousness that day, not him. Their consciousness about the effects of his self-centeredness countered his extreme individualism. Understanding of the capacity of any one American to have an impact on the system will have followed their anger and frustration.

Corporate America began playing the power of people differently. Future American business people adjusted their views of their futures, and when Oldsmobile listed the names of individual car buyers in a November 2001 television commercial, it used a strategy to attract customers inclined to think about their ability to have an impact on a system. It listed the names of individual buyers.

A simplistic association between money and moral shortcoming was a danger that had to be parlayed quickly, in the interests of both America's major corporations and the culture. General Motors took the symbolic and economic lead and got the formula right, right out of the chute, to the benefit of their bottom line, the economy, and the symbolic comfort level of many watching their ads and buying their trucks. They did it by capitalizing on the symbolic shift toward social connection in post-9/11 America. General Motors advertising people got their new mixed symbolic metaphor together very quickly, and embarked on a marketing campaign to sell vehicles with zero percent financing. The ad symbolism in the campaign mustered a sense of community in order to support capitalism in order to support community. American capitalism was not presented as being at the service of the individual, despite the obvious good deal that individuals would get, or at the service of what GM was doing for itself as an individual corporation. Ad narrator Peter Coyote plied an America with a revised motivational structure, in the interest of selling cars and trucks.

The surface level value presented in the ads was building community. While individualism and corporate self-interest were still part of the cultural "bottom line," they did not play up front. In the symbolic shuffle, self-interested individualism had gone farther underground. The people listening to the ad knew it, Peter knew it, and the text writer knew it: "The American Dream. We refuse to let anyone take it away . . . Believe in the dream. Believe in each other. Keep America Rolling." Not only was America on the move, the American Dream was a metaphor on the move.

It was not just about having the truck yourself. It was about having the truck in the service of your country and your American identity. Remarkably, given much American driving behavior, it was also about having the truck in the service of the driver next to you on the road. She had also bought her vehicle in your service. Even if you did cut her off in traffic, your sense of a competitive relationship with her had moderated at some level.

Redefined, the dream was still about having it yourself, but it was also about being socially connected. When the ads annoyed, it was because the hawking of community seemed disingenuous. Read as part of the old American cultural game of working the rules to your individual advantage, the ads were cynically self-interested instead of honestly reconstructive. Either way, using community as a concept to sell with was a shift. Benevolently construed, the ads were a combination of public service and sales, first and foremost about creating a context of economic recovery, and within that serving society by promoting sales. At a minimum, the ads provided effective cultural cover for a 9/11-related marketing campaign.

The ad makers knew that the rhetoric, in addition to favorable financing terms, was going to work, if the American Dream recalibrated from individual consumption toward community responsibility. General Motors put their money on it and won. They pulled out all the symbolic stops. The ads did not tout taking care of yourself in troubled times, or promote an enhanced comfort level from "cocooning" in the cabin of your new truck. They invited buying into a revised metaphor as well as a new vehicle, the aim as much about community as consumption.

General Motors's world had changed too, and they knew how to sell in it. Sell they did. The October 31 promotion deadline passed, and with it came a new ad and a new deadline of January 2. Those who had not yet jumped on the new rolling American bandwagon still could, as the earlier admonition became stated fact. "Keep America Rolling" became "America Keeps Rolling," thanks in part to General Motors and its first ad. "This country keeps rolling. It's not about to slow down," intoned Coyote. Pontiac ads were a little more inclusive of projected buyers, who were supposed to "help keep America rolling."

Shopping looked the same. With the exception of how many people were shopping where, there was no apparent difference, but those who felt odd about spending to help the new "war" effort could feel one. It was why they felt odd. Serving the greater good was, at least in theory, supposed to be in the equation. Shopping to self-medicate was temporarily taboo, even if true. The undercurrent of understanding that the directive to shop went in the direction of social responsibility was there, even if cynics delighted in denying it. Separating out cynical consciousness from a pre-existing perception of American national character as an addictive shopper was no mean task. President Bush's rhetoric was right there, reminding Americans that they were not simply "shallow materialistic consumers" who cared only about "getting ahead or getting rich."[12] The goals of economic strength went beyond individual consumption, at least at the surface level of American consciousness, but the self-interested American individual loomed as present as ever in the unstated American cultural rule structure.

Still, the scene seemed temporarily borrowed from indigenous Dakota culture, a cultural tradition in which the human relationship is more important in economic exchange than the value of the goods. When the Dakota became materially poorer after the arrival of "mainstream" American culture, the richness of the cultural value prizing people and the connections between them over goods was only enhanced. Prior to 9/11, mainstream America lived at the opposite extreme of that dynamic, with profits superseding people, incorporating people, and making people expendable. Culture understood as a sense of connection with other human beings was a foreign concept, especially understood as positive social connections that were realized in economic exchanges. Economic exchange in America is the archetypal arena for self-service. After 9/11, economic addiction to the self moderated slightly in America, in a culture striving to find ways to think of itself as rich in human connections. Economics is, however, the toughest sell as an arena for Americans to think about and make positive social connections.

It was not just self-centered economic behavior that became temporarily forbidden. Any bureaucracy related to the event, whether the Red Cross or the FBI, was also supposed to operate according to new and less organizationally self-centered social sensibilities. Charitable organizations generally were at the center of a new social mathematics.

The closer to the tragedy without being a direct victim, the greater was the injunction against making money. The Red Cross became the most conspicuous offender of this modified post-911 American cultural rule, with a plan to set aside 9/11-donated funds for other purposes. Money was temporarily about connecting human beings. Benevolence giving was stunning. Bureaucracies of benevolence came under intense scrutiny, undergoing new expectations for coordination and integration. The concept of community supported a call for charities to take on the organizational burden of creating a common application form, instead of burdening victims with multiple forms to fill out.

The organizations themselves were expected to adapt and function like a community, in the service of their clients. Bureaucracies as monolithic givens bowing to individual human needs was new American cultural territory. The FBI would answer for its bureaucratic disorganization later. There was an interruption in American presumptions about supremacy and size. America was rolling, and even bureaucracy could move.

As notable American corporate bureaucracies unraveled, creating collateral damage to trust in American financial institutions, Enron's two towers were pictured shrouded in mist. The stature of those towers had been lost differently from the Twin Towers, and the mist surrounding the standing but discredited towers was a good metaphor for post-9/11 confusions in American culture. CEOs regrouped to face a culture in which small investors and employees could not be cheated with the same degree of impunity, and in which exorbitantly high compensation packages for top executives became a personal survival risk. People thought about not just the stunning size of the bankrupt bottom lines, but also the stunningly dysfunctional social relationships that created them. There were angry, newly disenfranchised everyday Americans, and an emerging phoenix subclan of whistle blowers.

The Red Cross story became a American mini-tragedy, with the direct link between people who gave money for 9/11 and its victims disconnected for a time by the plan to set aside some of the funds for future attacks. That plan swirled into controversy, threats of legal action, and the resignation of culture-lagged Red Cross President Bernadine Healy. She trod into a new American cultural mine field, and become a casualty on the home front by breaking the new rules about people connecting to people, when she put her organization between the people who gave the money and the people they meant it for. It was not a good place to be. Americans were not having social distance or bureaucratic disconnection based on organizational priorities for future needs. The amounts of money involved were not the issue. The direct human connections in those exchanges were what was primary. The incoming president of the Red Cross announced that all of that money would go to current victims.

Money also played in another painful post-9/11 conflict that related human connections to bureaucracy. Money was the symbolic forbidden territory. A New York conflict emerged between Mayor Rudy Guiliani, representing bureaucracy, and fire fighters, representing human connections. When Ground Zero recovery efforts were cut, and switched from the fire department to the port authority, fire fighters expressed their passionate commitment to connecting with fallen comrades by physically recovering their remains. They did so by claiming that the mayor had elevated money over community. In post-9/11 American culture, the claim that the cutbacks were about economy rather than humanity was a powerful one.

Guiliani trumped their claim with another aspect of human connection and community, the safety of the living. He held the life card as New York, the core of the post-9/11 American community, frayed over whose interpretation of human connections was authoritative. That was not the only symbolic tension in New York City that week. The city was billed as recovering from a battle between its own mayor and fire fighter superheroes the day after Game 5 of the World Series. At least on the ball field, the opposition came from outside New York.

The American workplace quickly reshaped itself from Ground Zero outward, with a more human face. Not surprisingly, companies with the heaviest human losses at the World Trade Center were in the lead. As Cantor-Fitzgerald struggled to survive the loss of two-thirds of its employees along with its headquarters, its tearful CEO turned sharply to social metaphors. The relatives of those lost were to "stay in the family," with 25 percent of future profits pledged to them. The statement was combined with a request for enough new business to keep the company alive. The plea to do business with Cantor-Fitzgerald was not because it was in your best economic interests, but because it helped that "family" to make the social connections it needed to care for its own. Generally, making money in connection with 9/11 was dangerous territory, but Cantor-Fitzgerald's Ground Zero credentials of human suffering gave complete insulation from accusations of exploitation. The firm would soon again face cutthroat competition, but the story it told America that day about American identity was different.

Sandler O'Neill, also headquartered in the World Trade Center, had a similar story. Their corporate survival, although self-serving, carried no stigma of moral reprehensibility. The moral purity of the framework in which the two companies worked to survive was assured. Financial security they lacked. Social security they had in spades. If one moved away from Ground Zero, the newly humanized dynamic in American economic relationships became less clear. Consumers at the mall, authors with American flags on book covers, and manufacturers of new red, white, and blue products were on weaker moral ground. Economic exploitation of 9/11 did occur, most clearly in benevolence fraud, but there was also a new antiterror territory of human connection in American economic consciousness.

Shifts in social consciousness in the American workplace rippled outward from Ground Zero. The language of job-layoff changed. In a less-frequented Las Vegas, managers spoke about making post-9/11 layoffs humanely. Laid-off employees were referred to with compassion, and not just in terms of cold economic facts. Workers were not just cogs in an economic wheel. The same ones would be brought back later. What was missing from the old American cultural formula was depersonalization. The business downturn produced human stories, not just economic realities.

On the opposite coast from Ground Zero, workers and employers in Silicon Valley reconsidered the importance of business in relationship to the rest of life, many concluding that their previous focus on business had been excessive. Work hours were adjusted downward in favor of more time with family. Employers stated the expectation that the adjustments would be long term. Some CEOs, functioning as grief counselors for employees, had their own sense of business adjusted. Others found ways to adjust the bottom line without laying people off. Community gained some ground on money.

Awareness of communal life bloomed, even in constrained material circumstances. Highly individuated American families bonded more closely, with one American family of four reflecting the shift. Displaced and living in a single hotel room in New York City, their close quarters enforced a striking new level of social intimacy. There was no retreat from a noisy child or a grumpy mom, only immersion in a new sense of social connection, both amongst themselves, and with other families in the same hotel. They modeled immediate post-9/11 American family life to those who watched from multiple-room dwellings. The commentator was not facile in saying that one room would be big enough because they all loved each other. He had his finger on a shift in cultural sensibility from elaborate material circumstances to human connections. Whether America takes the renewed communalism generally visible in post-9/11 family life and projects it long term onto the culture as a whole, it did at least have an immediate effect on business.

Wal-Mart did very well during the 2001 holiday season. The holiday buying focus was Dakota-like, less on the luxury of the gift and more on the social tie it would make between giver and receiver. The economy of American holiday shopping was not just one of material uncertainty, but also one of increasing growth in the sector of social connections. Less disparate American families grouped themselves around the comforts of home. The market still had the proverbial last word, but society was dictating what that word was. The word was that people were staying at home more and not defining themselves in terms of expensive purchases. Pottery Barn and Home Depot executives who saw their bottom lines improve without increasing their advertising budgets knew that the American cultural word had changed. Shopping may have facilitated patriotism, but it was definitely facilitating social bonding at home.

People even tried to use economic exchange to create the social connections that would help fight terrorism. In July of 2003, the Pentagon's DARPA (Defense Advance Research Projects Agency) announced an elaborate extension of the idea that economic exchange could create useful social connections. A proposal to establish a policy analysis market, a public stock market-style exchange dealing in terrorism futures, as an investigative tool to garner information about terrorist plots emerged. In other words, people would put their money where their prediction of the next terrorist event was. The market would provide humanly generated counterterrorist information. The idea was based in the notion that markets have predictive value, and was quickly abandoned after being announced. The exchange was not one in which the possibilities for insider trading even bore imagining. For all of the proposal's faults, including its culturally predictable American reliance on economic exchange as a way to solve any problem, it also echoed immediate post-9/11 sensibilities about using economic exchange to create constructive social connections.

The "little guy" in America made some waves in big corporate bureaucracy. In a culture where corporations sell identity along with their products: "You are what you eat," became a battle cry for consumers, rather than a mantra for their manipulation. The overweight "little guy" was decried for not controlling his individual eating habits, and blaming weight gain on McDonald's and Burger King, creators of the caloric and cultural ethos in which the weight was gained, instead.

The assertion of the vulnerability of that "little guy" in relation to the big corporation was still a perfect expression of the contemporary American tendency to perceive the individual as powerless. Lawyers who extended the model of tobacco damages and the vulnerable American individual to food were criticized. Statistics about overweight American children and adolescents with sedentary, screen-oriented lifestyles that contribute to obesity were bemoaned, but the cultural outcome still boiled down to one conclusion. Big business put its wares on a diet in response to consumers, in an interesting script for the reempowerment of the notoriously passive American consumer. That script was part of the drama of the new American cultural scene.

Another dramatic subplot in post-9/11 American culture, the rebuilding of Ground Zero, also echoed with themes of life and death and culture and community, all in relation to the importance of money. Discussing the place of culture at the rebuilt Ground Zero in this connection, tying culture to museums, performing arts venues, and the power of human expression, Daniel Libeskind said that culture remained

important because life was about other things, no matter how much money
you had. Others organized symbolism relating life, money, and humanity
differently, cleanly contrasting the sacred and the commercial as
competing interests in rebuilding Ground Zero, and associating
commercialism with ongoing life. Money is life.[13] Human expression is
life. There was a toss-up between the two in post-9/11 America.

MERELY ACTORS AND REAL HEROES

Actor Tom Cruise may be fearless on screen, but he was positively
timid in the face of the audience at the Academy Awards ceremony in
early 2002. His post-9/11 reflections about the purpose of the acting
profession were humbled, but clear. He mused about whether what actors
do is important, and whether the joy and magic of movies should be
celebrated. He concluded: "Dare I say it? More than ever!" Cruise believes
in magic. After an initially awkward post-9/11 period, the movies became
important again to Americans, and with a difference. At the ceremony, a
visual fanfare to the common movie fan, apropos of the times, followed
Cruise's statement. The montage included fans both with and without
celebrity status, good social scripting for an America where the rigidity
of social distinctions between the famous and the unknown collapsed
along with the towers, and celebrities were known to tag along with
everyday people.

The Oscar for best picture went to a movie about the heroism of
overcoming a mental health challenge in a hostile social environment. *A
Beautiful Mind* was a parable about social diversity and a good metaphor
for times challenging vertical social consciousness. It was a good night
for diversity on the Oscar stage too, with an African-American-led
ceremony. All in all, the social metaphors that night were anything but
hierarchical.

Tom Hanks, like other members of his profession, humbled himself
to pay tribute to real-life, first responder heroes of 9/11. He and his
colleagues were merely actors. Sports figures were similarly self-effacing.
The status of American fantasy came down several notches, as people
with name-recognition and big salaries extolled people with anonymity
and small ones. Hanks had refused in 1996 to consider portraying the

Unabomber, but there was radicalism in him. That radicalism rested in the concept of "merely." I had written to Hanks insisting that Ted Kaczynski was less a villain and more a misguided tortured genius. His antihero American character, distasteful though it was to think about, was important to portray, because Americans needed to ponder who he was. A Disney movie in production on the Unabomber, in the mode of a Greek tragedy that focused on the drama between Ted and his brother David, never came out. Hanks objected to playing Kaczynski because he understood something of the relationship between portrayal and reality, and there were places he did not want to go with portrayal. Hanks knew that what actors do is not merely to create entertainment.

The rub for Hanks was that as he deferred to everyday heroism right after 9/11 by trying to bow out of a misplaced overimportance of movies images in America, he could not discount the tie between the audience and the action on stage at a single stroke. What is on stage or screen affects the audience in real ways. But right after 9/11, people wanted to forget about having invested their consciousness into screens to the point of degrading it elsewhere. Hanks was one of those people. As a human being, he was stuck on screen trying to radically deconstruct that American cultural dynamic, but the power of screen enactment could not be taken away with one radical statement. Like the power of the dollar, it was still there. The significant cultural question, more precisely put, was about what forms that power would take in the movie images of post-9/11 culture.

In November of 2001, Hollywood conferred with Washington about how its productions would represent American culture abroad. Having Hollywood take the national interest into account in making production decisions was definitely a cultural plot twist. The movies had been upstaged on 9/11, when reality superseded anything seen on a screen, even when it was seen on a screen. Americans Dayna Curry and Heather Mercer, in Taliban captivity around 9/11, had hardly watched any movies. They had the shifting American media dynamic figured out, though, the minute they were released. Something in Heather Mercer's imagination, not anything she had seen on screen, made her comment that she did not think that Hollywood could have done better than her actual experience. Her story was ahead of Hollywood, not behind it.

Like money, media had a bit of its power edge taken off right after 9/11, and had its relationship to the rest of the culture changed. Its importance in relation to ordinary people shifted. Theater was still ritual, however, and new screen rituals would be part of America's ongoing symbolic recovery. People who were merely actors, paradoxically, were about to become more, rather than less, important.

If theater in all of its forms did not have social power, actors would not be rich and famous. Theatrical ritual also has notable power in America on the playing fields of ritual combat, otherwise known as sports. People collectively re-dream and re-create themselves as they watch. Players provide spectators with fodder for reenvisioning themselves. Movies and sporting events are not just about what happens on the field or the screen. They are also about what goes on in the mind of the viewer. Without that powerful function, there would not be huge professional sports salaries or a contemporary American pantheon of gods and goddesses composed of those who appear in movies. Americans readjusted the relationship of images to reality after 9/11, but they also needed reshaped and positive images more than ever. I wrote that sentence before the Academy Awards ceremony in 2002. Scout's honor: I did not steal it from Tom Cruise.

The feedback between art and life was not going away in post-9/11 America, a fact less escapable than the fact that Americans needed to face the escapist approach to life that they had developed with their media. After 9/11, more Americans might have started concentrating on creating positive real-life stories that the media could reproduce. The media could then have modeled itself on them more than them simply modeling themselves on it. While post-9/11 American media was connected to reality in another way, the change was not quite that radical. The only truly discernible post-9/11 revolution in American culture was in reality TV instead.

At the same time, movie producers, screenwriters, and actors, were all Americans too. Like FBI agents, pilots, and psychiatrists, they all experienced 9/11, and like other Americans did not come at their post-9/11 work situations from a detached point of view. Cruise and Hanks face a future in which the audience, the characters portrayed, and the actors themselves all live in an adjusted configuration.

Movie history post-9/11 started out tough and got easier. Movies lost power for a time, outdone by a reality that topped several movies rolled together. The target that was the target audience had also moved. Arnold Schwarzenegger's terrorist-themed *Collateral Damage* went on hold, opening later to pointed social criticism about its potential impact on reality. The movie on hold became a new American genre, when *Phone Booth* also went on hold, in the wake of the beltway sniper. Harry Potter appeared after 9/11, akin to Mary Poppins, who blew in just when the children needed her most. Americans needed movies to inspire not less than before, but more. The movies took a while to come back, in a recovery that was not as quick as for sports. A reconfigured America needed to tie inspiration from movie images more back into social life, instead of having them left inside individual boxes of American consciousness. Within a year, American imaginations had developed an incredible hunger for sustenance. Many more Americans do their meditative dreaming in theater seats than in church pews, and their demand for the products of the post-9/11 Hollywood dream factory skyrocketed.

By spring 2002, American hunger for positive movie images was prodigious and unabated, and the fare was there. The blockbuster year in which America went back to the movies made the nightly news, and the dream factory had produced just what America wanted. The expressions of the culture's subconscious in films were right on the mental sweet spot. The updated heroes had internal challenges, or were small, unlikely, or socially inept, until they put on the personal transformation the script called for, and tackled evil outright. Spiderman, the leader of the pack, was not just color-coded for patriotism. His movie also united America in practical terms, drawing female and male, and old and young viewers all together, in an unheard of feat of "marketing" that looked more like audience communalism than promoter planning. Spiderman made connections both on and off the screen, and there was a message in that. In the 2002 holiday toy season, Spiderman's doll had to face off Osama bin Laden's doll on the shelves, but by 2003, the *Homeland Defense Journal* was sporting images of Spiderman along with the American eagle.

George Lucas's *Attack of the Clones* read like an allegorical object lesson, in which the "good guys" were not paying enough attention to hold their position against destruction. It was a message that seemed worthy of cultural meditation in post-9/11 America. Movies and baseball were labeled as distractions and escapism, and they were both, but they were also more. By 2003, the movie *Thirteen*, made social connections by billing itself as "cinematherapy," to be used systematically for exploring the social issues and personal experience of an American age group through film. Film had been applied to real life in America before, but the conscious and stated connection was also part of an updated post-9/11 cultural milieu. Violence did not disappear from American movies any more than SUVs did from American roads, but the notion that 9/11 made no impact on American moviemakers or viewer consciousness was also hard to support.

Messages that fed the post-9/11 American consciousness with fallible everyday heroes affected a culture already primed by reality for unlikely heroes. The magic that Cruise was looking for might come from people watching such characters, who might be able to conjure themselves up as local heroes in everyday life afterward, not by saving people from burning buildings or slaying demons, but by bringing strength of character and common courtesy to daily life. The conceptual distance between the hero and the person watching was not as great, making the actor both more and less important at the same time. The tricky part over time would be remembering the importance of the viewer as well as the actor, as American fantasy moved toward reclaiming its traditional cultural place. Fortunately, TV helped take care of that.

Translating screen inspirations out of the ether and into social action could keep the viewer in the social equation, with Spiderman touted as particularly user-friendly for social modeling. If more Americans used what they ingested in theater seats for positive modeling instead of sheer escapism, Hollywood might end up using material from their lives for new movies. Tom Cruise and Tom Hanks cannot achieve that effect, though. It is up to the people watching, which is perhaps what Hanks was working to express.

More than the movies shifted. Twin Towers in video games forthcoming on 9/11 disappeared almost as quickly as the real ones. Media served reality more, drove it less, and was sometimes overcome by it. Television actresses, emotionally moved by program content that honored real people in 9/11 dramas, bore a closer relationship to the people they enacted than before. Like many social distances in America, that distance became shorter.

Celebrities were sometimes humble and sometimes strategic in their revised relationship with the public. Movie actress Jennifer Lopez played the relationship in 2002, when it seemed the movies could do no wrong with the public, regardless of what reviewers said. She said, in an argument well structured in terms of post-9/11 social semantics, that the public and not the experts were the real critics. By the time of the Academy Awards ceremony in 2003, a documentary on the Twin Towers and Michael Moore's *Bowling for Columbine* appeared on stage within minutes of one another, with Moore using his acceptance as a bully pulpit for a crushingly political speech, in a context where most celebrities were walking on political eggshells about what they said in reference to the war in Iraq.

Television moved to comfort, and then cashed in on the new media-reality equation. First, "comfort" TV focused, as real life did, on family and friends. It time-warped, with revivals of shows from a more comfortable period of American experience, making comfort intergenerational. *Friends, I Love Lucy*, and *Laverne and Shirley* all teamed up. Comedy and everyday life trumped even a time-warping sex goddess in the 2001 Super Bowl commercial sweepstakes. Britney Spears, costumed across American decades promoting Pepsi, could not outdo the guy sliding across his satin sheets and out the window. America was as ready for the comic side of unpredictability as he was for his Bud.

The shifting relationship between reality and images of it made "reality" TV look anomalous for a while. Ratings plunged, and the ongoing existence of the genre was in doubt. The first impulse was to get those people out of there, and put them back to work doing something real. Real real. Not staged real. Backbiting individualism in the games did not match well with initial post-9/11 social sensibilities, although later shows documented the direction of post-9/11 file-toothed American anger onto scapegoating of contestants. The foundation for *Survivor*, a social projection of competitive individualism into "exotic" locations, softened for a while, along with the competitive American metaphor for social relations. Then, the decreased American cultural distance between media and reality exploded into a frenzy of new reality shows. The new quasi-celebrities were all just everyday people. Media and reality also continued to mix it up with embedded reporting in the war in Iraq and with the beltway sniper case. The cultural fire wall between media and reality went down and stayed down.

Over the short term, television news became both less entertaining and less entertainment-oriented. Television news was more of a reflection of the medium as public servant and less as entertainment maven. News was pitched to a concerned citizen rather than a self-indulgent consumer. News, now itself more closely integrated with reality, had to be presented carefully. Sensationalism in reporting about anthrax attacks might serve an individual journalist, but the associated disservice to the public was not to be tolerated. There was not just an economic, but also a media code prohibiting individual gain from terrorism. Spreading fear without facts could bring in-house retribution in the form of instant criticism on *Larry King Live*. Everyone had to be a symbolic straight shooter, as the premium on the careful, the responsible, and the clearly corroborated went up, and every reporter conveying information about anthrax became an extension of national security. Since anthrax inaccuracy and alarmism were their own dangers, the reporting situation became trickier yet when the government's information on the subject did not jibe.

Newspaper reporters changed demeanor, and took frameworks for understanding, as well as answers to questions, from the people they were interviewing. Reporters were receptive and vulnerable, as well as powerful. First Lady Laura Bush exhorted members of the National Press Club to use news to harness national energy, sporting an uncommonly cooperative model of relationship between herself and the press. The media also inducted the Bushs to have a social impact on post-9/11 American culture. Peggy Conlon of the National Advertising Council orchestrated a Thanksgiving thank you from them to Americans, for having given of themselves in response to 9/11. Conlon's earlier public service ad "I Am an American," had cleanly framed the importance of appreciating cultural diversity in post-9/11 America. The "product" being sold made no profit, and went beyond a politically correct adversarial model of diversity to one that celebrated humanity as the core of the culture.

Debate over the CBS news documentary drama *9/11*, which aired six months afterward, highlighted the media's adjusted position in the culture. The show aired, but so did criticism from victim's relatives about the choices made in producing it. Having everyday citizens appear on CNN to criticize CBS was a new feature of American culture. The show itself was a kind of media shock therapy. While it may have, as some claimed, helped revive visceral short-term American memory so that long-term American consciousness could keep processing the meaning of 9/11, it was also a mass exercise in revisiting anxiety-provoking images. Some used the debate surrounding the program to aggrandize media by saying that its stimulus was the only way that people would remember. The docudrama itself reminded America that it had been torn apart, and paradoxically put back together at the same time. The tones in fire fighters' voices at Ground Zero were precursors of how the tone of the entire culture would change. Watching the docudrama had ritual status. Families did it together.

Talk shows changed, too. When talk show hosts criticized the FBI, the behavior of the studio participants told a post-9/11 story about the power of everyday people. The regular folks on stage were not buying the arguments from the panel of hosts. They had their own ideas, and were more than ready to overrule the celebrities. The celebrity panel said that people who were not in law enforcement could not actually help the FBI to catch terrorists. The audience participants said otherwise, pointing out in no uncertain terms that the Unabomber was caught in exactly that way. The everyday Americans on stage knew who they were and how they rated. They were happy to convey that celebrity punditry did not impress them.

Later, the new relationship between media and reality would take a macabre twist with the beltway sniper case. With reality and representations of it already more closely tied in American culture, the sniper episode put a terrorist's twist on a shift producing rapid feedback between actual news stories and plots for dramatic television shows. The adjustment to the tightened relationship was not as smooth for the news as it was for drama. There were more than a few tinges of angry desperation evident on screen in newscasters working the sniper story, who clearly demonstrated their frustration with a lack of control over the situation in which they were reporting. While reporters and police chief Charles Moose blamed each other publicly for journalistic and investigative problems, the real source of the problem was the sniper. Everyone else on screen had been handed an unaccustomed role in an American drama that they were forced to be part of, as well as report.

Other media were more grounded in everyday reality in post-9/11 America. At the time of the Grammy awards ceremony in 2003, pop music was being characterized as more honest, earnest, and closer to reality, whether its themes had to do directly with 9/11 or not, but it was back on

TV that the closer relationship between reality and media really took off in a renaissance of reality television.

The television screen reemerged as powerful in America's new normal, but with a twist. It evolved into a cultural halfway house between celebrity and everyday citizenry, as reality and drama became two genres of entertainment increasingly intertwined. The mixing and muddling of recognizable forms in American terrorist crime and a mixed and muddled form of entertainment on the TV screen paralleled one another. American psychodrama remained on screen after *9/11*, but its content shifted to more mundane matters like marriage, inheritance, and restaurant management. The new class of American celebrity consisted of people pulled up from the ranks of everyday life.

Survivor not only survived, but thrived because reality television caught on as an ongoing ritual observance of the importance of everyday people in America. Viewers gained continued comfort and a sense of cultural control from seeing "real" people on TV. As backbiting and brutally humiliating as reality shows could be, they still buffered and symbolically counteracted the darker reality offerings in the news. By 2003, the surfeit of reality TV had become a way to get publicity without becoming a terrorist. Americans flocked to watch and to get into the act. American consciousness consumed displays of American flaws and foibles, as well as graces and strengths. Putting money right in the way of love, and seeing if love could survive the ordeal was a contemporary quest for American character. Risking public humiliation by competing publicly in pursuit of an updated American dream was a media-based Horatio Alger script.

The updated dream involved inversion ritual. Everyday people were promoted, and celebrities were demoted, which some celebrities cheerfully demonstrated by mucking around in the jungle. At the same time, everyday people rose to celebrity by sacrificing their everyday status for the sake of entertaining the public. The human stories that they generated, albeit with pre-twisted plots, created connections with Americans off the screen. Bachelorette Trista Rehn was termed the "spiritual leader" of a group who watched her as a communal experience.[14] Marriage brokering occurred in a strange new form of mass American fictive kinship, in which the television audience chose the spouse. Taking a culture in which social disconnection is endemic and allowing a group of utter strangers to make decisions about one's love life was a striking reversal. While the practice was termed inane, it was also an exercise of a new American cultural fantasy, in which a sense of social connection was intensively pursued.

While family and restaurant business became contrived for the camera, the reality television with the emphasis on reality went beyond the beltway sniper case to embedded reporting on the war on Iraq. War correspondents kept weakening American conceptual distance between movies and reality by describing their assignments as just-like-out-of-action-movies except real, or as trumping Hollywood. Embedded reporting was a media-mediated object lesson in how the relationship between the government and the American public could be constructively bridged with more open communication. Reporters functioned as information brokers with a dual set of loyalties, to the armed forces upon whom they were reporting and also dependent for protection, and to the public they served. The Department of Defense was in the role of trusting the reporters with that sensitive position. Neither the government nor the public lost. Embedded reporting created a non-adversarial win-win situation of more open communication between Americans and their government, and a positive model for future reference.

Much more troubling were the possible implications of the plan for the rapid feedback docudramatized *K Street*, billed as hyperreality TV, in which real politicians and lobbyists would play themselves or caricatures thereof, enacting themes taken from headlines just days before. One of the producers anticipated that viewers would be confused about whether they were looking at news or drama, a dubious public service at best. One of his words of praise for the show was that it was terrifying, making the plan sound like revenge on reality for eclipsing it on 9/11, as well as a plan to retaliate by taking reality over.

SPORTS RITUAL AND RECOVERY

Sports, fields of dreams, no matter the game. It just happened that baseball was up next after 9/11. The Super Bowl and the Olympics came to the plate later, but baseball hit a home run right off the bat. The 2001

World Series helped snap the new American media-reality equation into place. It served up cultural transformation on a fast track, and helped to revive American culture. The seven-game series began and ended in Phoenix, with every game a win for the home team. The national pastime itself was a better fit for the nation than it had been in a long time, but American consciousness had to scramble in order to put its finger on why. Like the aftermath of 9/11 generally, the effects were confusing. The series itself made American heads spin. There was more to it than just seeing happy New Yorkers, as stunning as that development was. As the statistical pundits talked on, baseball flew America back to a place where it was a timeless and mythic expression of American cultural identity, and not just contemporary big business.

There was not a tower in sight, nor was there supposed to be. There was a level playing field that evoked a pre-high-rise and pre-material American Dream, along with an American social history grounded in frontier mentality, egalitarian community, and cooperation. This levelness had not been imposed on America from the outside. It belonged here, and was there to be claimed just when it was needed the most. Suddenly, a level playing field was how America understood itself, even if baseball in America seemed otherwise only faintly to echo its former self. The 2001 World Series was less the escape to innocence it was billed as than a return to foundation. On the baseball field, you have an even chance, no matter who you are. Mythical dynasties are no more or less than their opponents. Who you were yesterday, last season, or who you will be tomorrow does not count. What counts is who you are today. The level playing field is phoenix territory, an environment rich with opportunity for transformation.

There was no place in America in October of 2001 that was metaphorically further from downed Twin Towers than Yankee Stadium. It was there that America had ritual confirmation of itself as a timeless team, and not just a dominant force. The nation got a piece of its heart back. From the point of view of cultural revitalization, it did not matter who won Game 7. The saga swelled hearts either way. As it turned out, Phoenix won, but not until after the nation went through the emotional crucible of Games 4 and 5. Those were Yankee phoenix games, games in which New York provided a mythic comeback story. There was no way for numbers to get the feelings across. America told itself a story about a renewed and old sense of American identity, just when that integration was most in order.

Then the team from Phoenix finished the odyssey with a win that mimicked New York's midseries "miracle." It was as though Arizona had redreamed Game 5 with themselves in the winning role. Maybe they had. The metaphorical phoenix, the sense of rebirth out of defeat, infused the entire series, from the Phoenix Fire Department shirts at the Game 1 flag raising, to the bottom of the ninth in Game 7. Either there would be a victory parade in Phoenix, or the "Yankee Phoenix" juggernaut would finish its ascent in the desert.[15] Either way, there was cultural rebirth written all over both ball fields.[16] Both teams regenerated themselves, modeling self-transformation for the nation, and the American phoenix came along for the ride. Transforming yourself gives you an edge over your opponent. That was the object lesson in the Diamondbacks desert recovery in Games 6 and 7. Diamondback victory in Game 7 was not, as reported, the end of an "aura" for the Yankees, but an expansion of one for the culture. The phoenix was on both sides of the combat. How exquisite.

"Baseball History Made Here," read a sign held up by Yankees fans at Game 5. It was, and a little human history too. The second-game-in-a-row come-from-behind-in-the-bottom-of-the-ninth performance was both for the ages and the record books. Never mind the future. The Yankees, both as actors on a stage of ritual combat and as real people, had taken the Twin Towers hit in their hometown, in their own bodies and emotions. The baseball show still went on, and the Yankees defied augury by turning in a blockbuster symbolic performance. In Game 5, they were the new team version of a tried-and-true American hero myth. They had made a miracle yesterday. They were digging out and down to their last chance. They sacrificed along the way to get back. They did not know when they stepped up to the plate whether the hero in them would manifest or not. Recreating American human being with their guts, the Yankees became a model of people who did not panic. That same message was written large on another banner, "USA Fears Nobody. Play Ball!"

Long Ball. Winged Mercury. Either the throw gets there or it doesn't. You know nothing but your own flight. Chuck Knoblauch is basically a regular guy. What he became in flight that night was anything but. The image he made was not so much about him as an individual. He ran well.

He scored the run. The image was grist for the post-9/11 American mental mill. Roll, fly, it's all movement. First the Yankees, then the Diamondbacks transformed from the boys of October to the phoenixes of November.

Do you believe in magic? It was a strange question to find at the World Series, but it was all over this one. Processing the 2001 series was a little hard without the concept. The series had unprecedented cycles of time. Past the witching hour we go . . . two games in a row. The series went past the traditional bounds of October, and into a newly uncharted November future of the nation and its pastime, past hallows to saints for the pagans or Christians in the crowd. In old time, before midnight, New York was down, the dynasty beleaguered, and almost undone. In new time, after midnight, resurgence and rebirth began in the creation of a cultural myth whose central theme was recovery.

After Game 5, commentators said that the Yankees, like the city they represented, had picked themselves up and come roaring back. That myth was so good that it manifested again in Phoenix, in the bottom of the ninth of Game 7, with the bat in the other hand. The story America told itself about itself repeatedly in the 2001 World Series was about transcending reality. Spines tingled. Rational consciousness gave itself up if it was smart. The connection between story and reality became mysteriously, if not obviously, clear again.

For post-traumatic stressors battling recurrent images of crashing towers emblazoned in their minds, there were replacement images. As American consciousness paused in its recovery from external enemies, new ritual images helped recovery by fighting the internal snapshots of crashing towers. Recreation was not just the diversion or distraction that commentators said it was. It was exactly what it said it was, a re-creation of self. There was food for the subconscious, and physical healing for burned brains. The Diamondbacks won, but some of them were wrong about one thing.

There is magic in baseball. To say so does not take away from the skills of the players. It compliments them further. They are not merely players. While Diamondback pitcher Curt Schilling maintained that "Mystique" was just the name of a stripper, that observation was just for people who like their magic packaged differently. The "midnight magic" in Game 5 was not just about cold statistics on the rarity of World Series games turned around with two outs in the bottom of the ninth, let alone two such games in a row. It was about the human story connected with producing such numbers. That was more than plenty of grounds for "mystique." The Yankees went from being New York victims to comeback kids to defeated dynasty in a whirlwind of sports emotion bigger than any single team.

Game 5 symbolically negated for New York the ceremony of death that had brought down the Twin Towers. The same metaphors were there in the reporting. The Diamondback pitcher had been "victimized." The Yankees' Mike Mussina said the Diamondbacks were said to be thinking, "I can't believe this is happening." New York was dishing out, "I can't believe this is happening," rather than taking it, and posted a powerful survival metaphor on the American scoreboard as well as a winning game. America produced one more answer to the ritual of mass sacrifice in the form of the Yankees. It did not matter what happened the next day. Ritual changes the world, and the world stays changed, regardless of what happens afterward. Rituals are like that. The baseball art of the 2001 World Series did not imitate American life, but reconfirmed it. The phoenix struck back at the jackal on November 1 in New York, choosing a guy running around some bases as a weapon.

By November 8, it was not Chuck Knoblauch, but an image of former Secretary of State Henry Kissinger Americans saw sliding into home plate on the *CBS Evening News,* while Dan Rather talked about multiple miracles. Inspiration was up and running in a metaphor with legs. No purchase of car or truck was required. Kissinger's imitation slide was not elegant, but the point was perfectly clear. The revitalization of consciousness from the World Series was transferable, with the power to catch the consciousness of the nation. Henry's slide into home plate simply showed that the nation had made the catch. Rudy Guiliani showed up a few days later, with flashing lights behind him that said "miracle." It had been a long time since baseball had had it this good.

The magic was not to last. The minute baseball adjourned from the field, economic realities rather than those of communal consciousness hit. Nothing can touch the ritual sanctity of what happens on the field, but the throes of baseball as big business did take a run at sucking the integrity right out of the regenerative reality of the series, with the baseball contraction controversy. One cynical commentator, sure that baseball fans had gone to thinking about the NFL within five minutes, instead of worrying about the impropriety of big business taking center stage so soon after the series, said that the owners could not screw up memories of the series "any more than they could put a hex on Harry Potter." There was a refreshing new brand of American cynicism, cynicism laced with "Do you believe in magic?"

That inexplicable aspect of baseball is not logical. It is not rational. It is not quantifiable. It is not to be messed with. It could teach some people a thing or two about baseball's metaphorical reach beyond dollars. Maybe it did. In the 2002 baseball season, baseball as big business backed off when owners and players second-ranked their own financial concerns in the face of the likely level of public rage at a baseball strike. Little Leaguers were touted as the true boys of summer. The everyday American had a little more clout, and the money metaphor took a back seat to the integrity of the game. That in itself seemed a little magical.

In the meantime, the tie between ritual combat and the revival of post-9/11 American spirit had carried on. At the 2002 Super Bowl, athletes presented themselves as real-life heroes. No longer bowing to people in "real life" as sports heroes had immediately after 9/11, NFL players symbolically associated themselves with everyday people instead. The game was presented as "so much more than football," celebrating not just sport, but freedom. The "indelible spirit of Americans everywhere" was attributed to the players, who also had a commercial spot showing them as more than members of the NFL, showing them also as members of a community dedicated to making a difference in people's lives. Community, not celebrity or status, was the image presented as defining the character of the American sports hero. The New England Patriots, with a name that put the post-9/11 symbolic wind at their backs, chose updated social semantics to go along with it. They were introduced as a team rather than as separate individuals. Then they went out and won the game, and incorporated the symbolic message of social connection into their victory.

The Winter Olympics in Salt Lake City also kept the symbolic linkages between life, sport, and 9/11 going. Favored American athletes who did not win gold medals were pictured instead as being similar to security forces guarding America, in a reflection on moments that had not happened. The "healing games" modeled both nonviolent conflict between cultures and "seamless" security. Spectators walked the streets of Salt Lake City with intense "team" consciousness and the jackets to prove it. If the jacket logos were not from Olympic teams, they were from Bank of America, Gateway, or Visa "teams," a field of symbols that knit ritual combat and economics together. Team consciousness is also a way of thinking about community. American athletes more committed to teammates and family than to winning became heroes. The opening ceremony was long on symbolically knitting generations of American sports heroes together. The theme of "Lighting the Fire Within" imaged using fire to fuel action, and the World Trade Center flag attended.

The regenerative atmosphere created by sports flagged, though, in post-9/11 America. While the 2002 World Series had the drama of unexpected "little guy" victors and commentary about baseball's priceless ability to build a sense of community, and the Super Bowl of 2002 reaffirmed team play and connections of athletes with community, the Super Bowl of 2003 not only lacked that community ethos, but ended with fans who were sore losers raiding the local neighborhood in Oakland. Somewhere between the two Super Bowls, the positive post-9/11 tie between sports and community seemed to have been lost. Baseball had helped heal, and myth hung in with Cinderella Angels, but in a channel surfing culture, the strength of the post-9/11 sports images to promote healing began to fade. Still, in 2003, with the mind of the nation on the war in Iraq, one of the questions emerging from the cultural consciousness was about whether baseball could heal the hearts of Americans.[17]

Other forms of ritual defiance of terrorism besides sports carried on. Some inverted 9/11 to 11/9, and celebrated that date as one that symbolized the power of volunteerism's good deeds to combat the impact of 9/11. Everyone paused for the ambiguities of the rituals of the first "anniversary" of 9/11. Much was muddled in America on that date, including language. "Anniversary" seemed an odd, if necessary, choice of words, as America hovered uneasily between commemoration of tragedy and celebration of a new but uncertain identity. An "anniversary" is normally a celebratory occasion.

The haze had cleared at Ground Zero, but not in American cultural identity. Among other things, the anniversary became a sanctification of American confusion about what fighting terrorism meant for changing American culture. American consciousness was more hazy than clear on that point. The sense of how to take the inspiration from the many rituals that Americans had generated contradicting the meanings of 9/11 and use it to inspire a clearly understood recreated self was elusive. Escapism staged a comeback in American consciousness, now as a salve for dealing with the haze and ongoing sense of vulnerability, as well as for ignoring the pain of other problems in American culture.

CHAPTER 5

CONNECTING THE DOTS

DOTS, DOTS EVERYWHERE

How could the FBI and CIA not have connected the dots before 9/11? The people who had not managed dot connection well were described as incompetent buffoons and idiots. It was much more clear that the FBI needed changes in attitude and accountability, than that similar changes in attitude and behavior were needed throughout the entire culture. People who swore they loved America but indulged in unconditional hatred of the FBI had some of their own rethinking to do. The FBI and other federal bureaucracies share common cultural problems with their critics and with American terrorists. The FBI's issues are just acute and painfully visible. The edge on the anti-FBI invective stemmed from the realization that the rest of America was no better at connecting dots. Even cogent post-9/11 criticism of the FBI also often bore the stamp of the zealous cultural convert. America still is largely a sea of conceptually unconnected dots, even though connecting dots became a stated culture value much more so after 9/11 than before.

The FBI and CIA got caught in the quick cultural shift. The person at FBI headquarters who did not put together the Phoenix memo with urgings from the Minneapolis field office about investigating Zacarias Moussaoui is an utterly typical American. The contradictions in his conduct between loyalty to self and to societal goals are rife throughout the culture. Demonizing him did not just target him as an individual. It also ratcheted up American cultural self-hatred one more notch. To come to grips with the David Frasca in all Americans, on the other hand, would be to make some cultural progress. Americans have cause to criticize him as an individual, but to the degree that they each live their own little piece of the American puzzle without connecting to others or seeing the whole pattern they have no entitlement to criticize him culturally. Replace him with someone else, and you will very likely get the same result.

It is not Frasca as an individual that is the problem. It is Frasca as an expression of a standard pattern, both within the culture of the FBI and more broadly. A February 2002 ad for Americorps asserted: "If the post-September eleventh world tells us anything, it's that we're all connected." If Americans do not believe in such connection, it will become de facto less true over time. Memories of the mental connections that Americans made to the huge dot that was 9/11 will nevertheless remain in American consciousness, with possible future applications.

One of the indicators that conceptual connection of dots took place in American consciousness after 9/11 is that culture as a concept turned up everywhere. Culture became the buzzword for how the whole American social system fit together. It was often applied to government bureaucracies, especially those of intelligence collection. Despite an upgraded use of the concept, what was less clear was whether those who promised culture change knew what culture was, or had a coherent plan for how to go about changing it. The urge to connect dots was there, but the development of a tool kit for doing so was another matter. Many things did come together conceptually in American consciousness after 9/11. Space and time both warped. For a while, New York City was right in the middle of everywhere, and time was all over the map.

COMPLEX TIME

New time was slower. Split-second anything did not have quite the same punch after 9/11 as before. There were more pauses and longer wait times in American cultural rhythms. Fast and instant began to play counterpoint to slow and sustained, instead of being the only beat there was. The supremacy of split-second America was on the run from the moment that people stopped to reflect on what had happened. Airports became central locales of the new syncopation, as well as new temples of community where Americans performed the required sacrifices of their busy, hurried, important selves on the altar of the demand for collective security. Those who did not observe the rituals properly, or failed to recognize pilots or security personnel as undisputed pontiffs, become the newest American miscreants. Many people felt closer bonds to their neighbors in security lines than they did to their neighbors at home.

The land of fast food, instant dating, and breathless lane changes was lectured by President Bush about its patient nature and its long-term view. Never mind the old internal clocks. The war on terrorism was not a war of instant gratification, but a test of endurance and will power. The American public, itself expert at speedy communication, with a write-now-think-later approach to e-mail communication and insta-chat as a shaper of lightning speed consciousness, actually noticed that the news industry drove short-term time frames and consciousness even more than the public did. Trends to instant and disposable communication in America had given face-to-face encounters a nostalgic feel, with a long sitting at a holiday dinner table harder and harder to achieve. But after 9/11, time rhythms revised somewhat into a pattern with more longer cycles offsetting short ones.

With no quick fixes available for terrorism, a slower rhythm began to sink in. A World Trade Center widow asserted that alleged 9/11 terrorist Zacarias Moussaoui should not have the "quick fix" of the death penalty. Quick was out, even if an eternal quick fix was a distinctly mixed time metaphor. While Americans sorted through the new syncopation, with time more legato in some of its paces, the relationship between past, present, and future also went into a different musical phrase. Myopic focus on the present eased. An America that had largely forgotten about history knew again that history mattered, and that it would be part of it. America needed time on its side more than a cultural narcissism that did not care about the past or the future. People started thinking and asking about "years from now."

The distance between generations both stretched and collapsed.

September 11 had divided time. It also created a common experience of crisis between members of generations that had not had much in common before. Pearl Harbor's USS *Arizona* was dubbed an earlier Ground Zero, and new New York widows found solidarity by relating to World War II widows. There were epiphanies of connection between people with little previous sense of commonality.

People reached back for nostalgia, and brought it forward in time for mental reinforcement, along with Norman Rockwell paintings, crock-pot cooking, and flannel sheets. A seventy-five-year-old stated proudly that she had grown up when the values of family and community, now reclaimed, were central in America. She had become a cultural resource, and she knew it. She was not romanticizing the past. She was reintegrating it. Her identity had changed. Junior Americans looked less upon senior Americans as artifacts of a largely irrelevant history. Instead, they became people with experience, people who had survived before. The future still belonged to younger generations, but older Americans were suddenly closer to that future.

Generations X and D had now, themselves, shared a galvanizing experience, and began to look and think more like cohorts and less like assemblages. Governor George Pataki of New York observed that Ground Zero, instead of going away, would be there for generations to come. Longer-term thinking made more sense. People talked about time having been cut in two. Americans cautioned not to think in terms of single events that faded as time went by, acclimated to unaccustomed concepts like lengthy and endurance. The problem with catching Osama bin Laden would be that his capture would make Americans think that something was over. A comprehensive long-term perspective needed to be sustained.

Some people had trouble dealing with their past in new time. On trial, Sara Jane Olson, formerly Kathleen Soliyah of the Symbionese Liberation Army, felt victimized by the fact that things she had said in the cultural context of the 1970s would be judged in post-9/11 America. She cried foul, but there was nobody she could pin the penalty on. Victims of 9/11 would take their traumatic experience into the future, with their social perceptions and citizenship shaped by the crisis. They might tell their great-grandchildren that 9/11 taught them about Pearl Harbor. Generations crossed in casts of performing artists at post-9/11 concerts.

Boomers and Ds and Xs were all in the lineup. People forty years apart in age explained performers to one another. Who is Fred Durst? Who is Paul Simon? What are they doing on the same stage? Things were not just old or new. They were new and old and intertwined.

The 2001 World Series had put America into the therapy of time suspension. The series both took America to the edge of its ability to digest epic action, and clobbered it over the head with timelessness. Baseball does not do well in split-second America. It is clockless, and too slow for instant messagers and instant daters. Dreaming and baseball, including the post-9/11 redreaming that America needed to do of itself, would not happen in split-second increments. Dreaming suspends time. The cultural fields Americans dreamt in after 9/11 had no clocks, or a 1980 U.S. Olympic hockey team would not have meant so much in 2002.

As America redreamt itself after 9/11, the past was not for retreating to, but for use in reconfiguration into forward motion. History was re-examined with new questions about how it could inform current American character.[1] The past intervened at the perturbed juncture between the present and the future. Americans did not just go "back to everyday routines" after 9/11. They went forward to them, with a clearer sense of the past. They went back to an American future. Trying to go instantly back to an unchanged pre-9/11 status quo was a simplistic move in time that did not work well.

PUTTING IT ALL TOGETHER

America had its time sense up in the air, its new rubber meeting the road, and the dots on its cultural map not all that clearly connected. With some things up in the air and others not (notably flights to some vacation destinations), mental fragmentation in America gave some ground. America went back on a track of looking for patterns, consistently understandable realities, and roads with discernible destinations on the other end of them. Thinking long term was itself good practice for incorporating complex patterns into mainstream American consciousness. There was movement toward thinking less about one thing at a time. Solutions to terrorism would be multifaceted. When seamless connections were not there in bureaucracy, Americans wanted to know why, and with a vengeance. They wanted to know why the connections had not been there before 9/11 because their systems thinking was rudimentary. Of course, the connections would not have been there. That was not the culture that was America then.

Americans wanted to know more often about root causes and about how things fit together. But first, they needed a primer on systems thinking. If airline business was down, how could business for private jets be up? If holiday retailing was down, how could Wal-Mart sales be up? Wrapping American minds around varying facts in different parts of the same complex pattern was an unaccustomed exercise. American consciousness both inclined toward and resisted perceiving complex connections. Thinking that there had been no change after 9/11 was not just a matter of claiming the familiar comfort of the old. It was also about the comfort of not thinking about nuances and complexities. That was more mental work than Americans were used to. But in fits and starts, America did try to make mental connections.

Television ads linking drug use to terrorism ran to mixed reviews, but they ran, along with their agenda of showing connections between people's everyday lives and larger social issues. Criticism of the ads labeled them as fear-mongering political propaganda wrongly laying blame for terrorism at the doorstep of teenage drug users. Praise for the ads was based on the value of causing young drug users to face the various consequences of their actions. From the critical perspective, the teenage drug user was powerless, psychologically vulnerable to the government, and a target for manipulation. From the praise perspective, the teenage drug user was a thinking, complex individual with integrity and the capability of making informed moral judgments. The manipulation model of the critics echoes personal disempowerment arguments from the Unabomber or from attorneys suing fast food companies. Models presuming the power and integrity of the individual are more useful in tackling systemic problems in an America that has systemically begun to doubt individual power.

After 9/11, a quick radical shift toward systems thinking moderated with time, but did not disappear. Days afterward, commentator Daniel Schoor emphasized how multifaceted the response to terrorism would need to be, political, economic, diplomatic, intelligence-oriented, military, and investigative.[2] His list of six items sounded right, if unusually long in typically single-focus American news reporting and commentary. His commentary invited a thought style that received few invitations from the American media. Secretary of Defense Donald Rumsfeld presented terrorism as a "subtle, nuanced, shadowy, difficult problem," that was going to demand a long concentration span.[3] Secretary of State Colin Powell declared himself to be not fixing a problem but overhauling a system. An airline pilot staunchly resisted having pilots carry guns as the single simple solution to airline security, emphasizing repeatedly that instead of latching onto one cure-all solution, many options needed to be considered. He held his own on the September airwaves. American tolerance for simplistic fragmentation had gone down.

Trust in the government went up, less because the government had changed than because the world had. Being part of a larger system by supporting government was a conceptual default position in the new and more threatening environment. News commentators said that President Bush would get a good reception for whatever he said to the nation on the night of 9/11. They were right, and the observation was more about the public and the culture than it was about the president. Criticism of the government on civil liberties issues eventually emerged forcefully, but did so slowly.

When critical commentary from Senator Daschle on the conduct of the war on terrorism caused a furor, he had not just a political issue to address, but also the appearance of threatening seamless unity. His political opponents quickly transformed the appearance itself into a political issue. The question of who was in charge of the post-9/11 sense of cultural galvanization was the backdrop for the debate that ensued about unity and dissent in a democracy. The party in power had the concept of system on its side. Protests of military action in Afghanistan also bucked a cultural, as well as a political, tide. To some, they sounded not like the free speech central to the way of life that America sought to protect, but an assault on the sacrosanct post-9/11 sense of American unity. Ted Kaczynski used to have trouble listening to lawnmowers. While dissent is as central to democracy as a lawnmower is to yard care, many people were having trouble listening to their neighbors run their equipment. America had made a shift from relishing fragmentation to demanding seamlessness.

As trust transformed into high levels of expectation for government performance, the government's position became more complicated, with new standards of integrated performance to meet. When the government provided inconsistent information or uncoordinated action, those stories lingered in the news. A story about inconsistent government information on anthrax was a story America deemed worthy of telling itself about itself again and again over a period of weeks. Even "sound-byte" America got into the systems consciousness act. Journalists asked questions with uncharacteristically sweeping scope, questions about how history would view 9/11. People were searching for a sense of system.

A lurid red-covered March 2002 edition of *Time* magazine asked about the next 9/11, in a story about a breach of seamless communication between federal and New York City officials. Even though people practiced in sorting threats had not deemed the threat of a nuclear device "credible," those specialists now also had to deal with the consciousness of other people who were more concerned about the implications of information flow, even if the likelihood of an attack was low. The dynamics of balancing the need for communication and collaboration if the threat were authentic, against the prospect of pandemonium if unconfirmed information reached the public were volatile, but the need for balancing was clear. Fearfulness of fear did not go down well as a rationale for keeping information compartmentalized instead of sharing it. Not informing city authorities did not suit a systemically oriented post-9/11 fear-fighting as well as terrorism-fighting consciousness. America groped toward concepts of integrated consciousness, and how to enact them.

Fragmentary thinking was not about to die in America, but in new American consciousness, fragmentary thinking and relational thinking coexisted. The previous assumption that the person next to you, in line, in class, or on the road, was thinking inside their own box was no longer as safe. People were more likely to watch and be watched, especially on airplanes. The person taking your order over the phone for coffee or pajamas might want to just chat, even if the conversation was being monitored for quality control purposes. Human contact was more important than risking a poor job evaluation. People were grateful for less-than-normal hostility. Social life in America became less predictable. People were less sure of what would come next. There was a little more room to move in a culture that looked less monolithic. The airline pilot who questioned the total efficacy of guns in the cockpit was guarding against oversimplification as much as terrorism. There was a new sense of the power and integrity of the individual human being.

Presuming the integrity of individual humans, and thinking about how individuals fit together into a cultural system was a positive development. To the extent that Americans had given in to a sense of being individually statistically insignificant, it was just the cultural therapy they needed. Thinking in terms of connections in an integrated system was an antidote for "my vote can't possibly make a difference, so why bother?" It made it easier to feel significant. Even if an individual vote did not make a difference in outcome, casting it was still a form of social connection. To the extent that Americans had given in to thinking of themselves as "market share," or passive and powerless in the face of bureaucracy, the cultural therapy provided by America's cognitive and symbolic responses to 9/11 was helpful. Resisting the temptation to think of American selves simply as what they consume is a stroke in the direction of human integrity. So is refusing to allow technology to become a metaphor for humanity. People are not the sum of their component parts. Each one is a system with integrity, which is precisely what makes terrorism so horrifying. Terrorism blasts that integrity.

Enhancing the sense of power that comes from claiming the self as an integral composition helps heal the psyche of the nation. Then, true power can come from the inside out that has nothing to do with bullying clout. Bombing is less likely to be a necessary expression of the self. Thinking of the self as an integral system, and projecting that self positively outward onto society as a whole, is something the jackal would not understand. It uses pain to spread destruction in an attempt to salve a torn-up sense of self by obliterating human integrity. Finding the individual power to project positive social energy outward, instead of creating the self by bringing others down, is phoenix business. The American individual, even when stereotypically regarded as fat and lazy, does not need castigation for America's problems, anymore than the FBI needs a "witch-hunt." What it needs is positive transformation that will generate productive social connections and a truly enhanced sense of self.

Thinking of individuals as integrated systems makes it easier to understand American terrorists. They are not just "nuts." Some are clinically disordered, but there is more than that going on. The American parents who claim that their terrorist or anti-American children are "good" focus on the elements of their offspring's behavior that do not make the news. No human being is reducible to any of their specific behaviors or speech. There is more to them than that. Frank Lindh wanted people to understand the total human being that his son is, and not just the notable mistakes that his son had made. The tendency to compartmentalize people into categories based on their behaviors, though, makes Americans ignore the complex humanity of their own terrorists. Even the tendency to classify terrorists and their acts into separate categories encourages people not to see the overlaps, as when one is dealing with a psychopathological single-issue terrorist or a blend of crime and terror. Tim McVeigh's final victim was Tim McVeigh. He was not just his crime. He was also a brother, a son, and a victim of terrorism in America, by his own hand. The same goes for Ted Kaczynski.

The jackal clan victimizes itself as a starting point for victimizing others. Observers who strip terrorists conceptually of their humanity take a step in the direction of the jackal themselves, and become complicit in the dehumanization inherent to the terrorist dynamic. The assault of a suicide bomber is terrifying because it attacks the very concept of human integrity. The stronger the concept of human integrity, the easier it is to fight off the psychological impact of the terror. Human integrity is facilitated both by cultivating individual identity and fostering the functional social systems that individuals create. Putting things together counteracts terrorism's goal of pulling them apart.

WHERE'S THE CHANGE?

It is difficult to understand your own gestation. Gestation and intellectual reflection generally do not coincide. Cultural gestation is especially hard to think about, since so much of culture lives outside the realm of the conscious mind. As the rules or tenor of a culture shift, the adjustments are easier to sense than to discern. Americans look for their change to happen fast. Right after 9/11, some said America had changed forever. Three months later, some said nothing had changed. Despite the limitations of visible changes to airport security and the amount of red, white, and blue on display, the quick switch to the "no change" posture was not entirely convincing.

The claim that everything had changed was hyperbolic, but the claim that nothing had changed was also hard to support. There were undercurrents of adjustment and a vague sense of reworked reality, but it was all hard to put your finger on. The effect was hazy, but the feeling tone of what was going on in major public arenas from sports to the stock market to the media was not quite the same. Those positive changes in tone have to be thought about and overtly pursued if they are going to be long term. Otherwise, the long-term cultural effects from 9/11 will degenerate into negative ones, and come back from an underground of American consciousness cultivated by the jackal. America is not now paying cultural attention, but its opportunity to revise itself constructively in the wake of tragedy had not yet entirely gone by.

Cultural biases make Americans look for change quickly and on the face of things. If change is not packaged that way, they think that it is not there. In the docudrama *9/11*, James Hanlan of Engine 7, Ladder 1, New York City said: "I look back to last summer, and it doesn't seem like a different time. It seems like a different world." The sentiment coincided with a broader American perception, but one that might be sustained only by those with personal proximity to Ground Zero. While the effects of changed sensibilities might take awhile to surface, some did not think that America could be any different if the new face of the nation looked the same as the old. There had to be visual cultural fallout right away, fewer SUVs, or reconfigured neighborhoods. There were more RVs on the road along with the SUVs, but otherwise, the place looked pretty much the same. There was no instant change to go along with instant messaging. Business was pretty much as usual.

Still, by the first anniversary of 9/11, there was a dominant theme that Americans should expect to see effects to unfold for a long time to come. They did not have closure. Trust in the government was still statistically high, although criticism of the Patriot Act was also pointed. Such changes were complicated rather than simple, and would require complex consciousness to understand. The purely cynical pronouncements that American culture could not change maximized a false comfort factor by allowing the pronouncers to maintain that they still knew their cultural world, but missed the historical fact that the culture has always been foundationed in change, and the fact that contemporary trajectories of American cultural change had become subtle and complicated.

People who said that both everything and nothing had changed were closer to the mark. There was a complex mix. Family was in the plus column, and comfort was definitely in. Couture and cuisine lost ground to company at home and comfort food. The effects of underlying feelings of vulnerability were generally tough to track, except on the odometers of the RVs, until the government posted an orange terrorism alert. Then, the underlying feelings displayed themselves perfectly clearly. Cultural change on most days appeared more as a simmering mindset of uncertainty, an adjustment to the culture in feeling, tone, tenor, and mood. Some people, notably many of the new RV owners, did not fly.

Initial post-9/11 changes in American interpersonal behavior had gone two ways at once, in the direction of both more kindness and more aggression, and the long-term result was difficult to discern. The culture's new complexion had both compassionate rehumanization and increased depersonalized hostility in place. Americans both did and did not trust their government. Americans would either come out of their cocoons, or stay in their fortresses forever. More likely, they would do some of both.

Systemic thinking faded some places in American consciousness, but remained riveted in others. Bureaucracies of American intelligence collection scrambled to create systems consciousness, hampered both by scale and the unaccustomed mode of thought. In the American public, New Year's 2002 news showed glimmers of a consolidation of a stable sense of American self. Risk-taking had dropped in relation to stability, security, and familiarity. Security was wanted, in terms of both safety and a psychological sense of well-being. New Year's resolutions were about social responsibility as much as about self-oriented concerns such as diet and exercise, and it was perhaps not coincidental that many of the socially oriented resolutions came from New York and Oklahoma City, where people had a clear sense that social adaptation could help master terrorism. Still, most Americans seemed to have a sense that there was nothing they could do to help, and a resurgence of the me-ism and now-ism typical of the American 1990s soon papered over feelings of both vulnerability and patriotism.[4] Pronouncements about national unity started sounding progressively more vague.

Americans were more socially connected within families that, prior to 9/11, had seen individual schedules come to take precedence over common experience in families often structured with one parent rather than two.[5] Americans had not been connecting the individual "dots" in their families very well in previous decades. After 9/11, a sudden upsurge in feeling connected to family members was clear. The post-9/11 family had the extreme togetherness of being on vacation, even though they were at home. Families solved lingering neglected problems, or finally got around to breaking apart because of them, but the chances for taking that early sense of enhanced social connections within families and creating an incubator for remodeling American society into one based on closer social connections did not seem good.

While social interdependence made no stunning comeback, there were quiet shifts in consciousness from individual to group thinking. An October 2001 letter from Sally Kanemeyer to the editor of *Newsweek* read: "'Suicide bomber' sounds so isolated . . . Wouldn't it be a more accurate reflection of the new reality to call these murderers 'homicide bombers'?"[6] She wanted to see a shift from self to social relationship reflected in language about terror. Months later, the term "homicide bomber" was all over the news. Either great minds think alike, or they got it from Sally.

Americans identified psychologically with the families of 9/11 victims. On March 11, 2002, George Pataki, New York governor, extolled a new permanent relationship between New York and Pennsylvania, based on their common victimization. The social impulse behind the rhetoric was easy to embrace, even if envisioning the practicalities of a permanent relationship created by parallel hijacked airplanes was not. Keeping dots connected is a tall order in a conceptually fragmented culture, but the new impulse to connect them in the underlying tone of the culture did not entirely disappear.

Many Americans looked only for big dots and obvious connections. Some changes, such as an increased number of applications to the FBI, and changing business priorities among tomorrow's CEOs in training, portended long-term effects. Career paths are durable. The manufacturers making money from the sale of red, white, and blue holiday decorations may have lived in an unchanged mental framework for economic exchange in America, but the emotional driving force behind the motivation to buy in their customers did not evaporate. It just foundered. It was difficult to see the ongoing manifestation of those emotions.

Those motivations may still be, long term, a more significant cultural bottom line than the profit statements, with America still early in its post-9/11 game. While there was truth in criticism that consumerism was the only way Americans knew how to respond to the crisis, the overdriven rhetoric that attributed everything Americans did to greed and indulgence also had its pathology. It echoed the Taliban's criticisms of America, and reflected low cultural self-esteem. Instead of bashing, America's cultural world view needs rebuilding to counteract low self-esteem, and the anxiety that goes with it.

Alexis de Tocqueville observed almost two centuries ago that American individualism promoted the isolation of Americans from society at large by causing them to focus on family and friends. While many social analysts have documented the recent incursion of the isolationist trend in American culture further into key American social environments like the family and the workplace, it does not take a social scientist to observe the effects. Anyone in the culture can report them. On September 10, 2001, my first-year college students said that their lives were much more unpredictable than American lives in the 1960s, when the term "counterculture" implied that there was something coherent that could be countered. Things were not that simple anymore. Their view of American culture was that it was characterized by excessive privacy, isolation, and individualism. They knew little, if anything, about their neighbors. Two doors down might as well have been another universe. Everyone was way too busy; family structure was beleaguered; and the media, computers, and firearms all strongly shaped the culture. If Tim McVeigh had the American equation wrong, how could they get it right?

By September 12, the unpredictability factor had gone up further. By the end of the semester, their conclusion was that individualism was not all it was cracked up to be. That conclusion constituted social progress, unlike for those who had simply "moved on" in their new cars and trucks.

At least now, there was a contingent on the road with a nascent sense of community, and a clear sense that the concept of "normal" was no longer a good description for much of anything about American culture.

A renewed, but largely unshaped new faith in humanity persisted in America a year after 9/11. On the whole, America was still in a post-9/11 haze, with feelings and sensibilities about where America was headed unclear. The second anniversary was much the same as the first. Were Americans now connecting the dots? Some places they were. Some places, they were not. Dots relating to the investigation of terrorism are connected with great zeal. In American minds, Osama bin Laden is connected to Saddam Hussein, and the Bali bombings are connected to Al Qaeda, without or before there is evidence for such connections. Extremely thin connections can form the basis for investigating American citizens as terror suspects. What has not occurred with the same zeal or effectiveness is the pursuit of connections among the "good guys." Americans now connect to catch bad guys, but not to prevent their emergence, or on principle because connection is so sorely needed at many levels in American culture. The phoenix clan is running behind its own game.

CHAPTER 6

REFORGING COMMUNITY

SENSE OF COMMUNITY

The problem for a nation faced both with terrorism and rampant individualism is that societies with alienated citizens are likely to produce terrorists. The already well-bivouacked pre-9/11 American individual now faces the disgruntled worker, social extremist, or troubled youth in an even more challenging cultural context. Terrorism is only one of the problems American society experiences because of its exaggerated focus on the individual and the cultural rule consistently elevating the self over others. The price of extreme individualism is loss of a sense of community, the place where people take individual social dots and connect them into functional social patterns. While attacking social disconnection in the bureaucracies of American intelligence collection can help to catch terrorists, the application is much too narrow. Attacking social disconnection also needs to be a much broader American goal. America can still be "changed forever" by 9/11, but in order to get there it will have to keep up its post-9/11 folk therapy on American consciousness, character, and culture.

A lack of social cohesion puts American society at risk in a number of ways that have been dramatically documented by Robert Putnam in *Bowling Alone: The Collapse and Revival of American Community*, and with situated examples of Americans rebuilding social ties in *Better Together: Restoring the American Community*.[1] Putnam demonstrates how everything from civic and religious participation to voting habits, philanthropy, and entertaining at home has degraded in recent decades in America. He updates the notion of social capital, which is the social power that derives from social connections—the social equivalent of economic capital. Social capital increases with the cumulative effect of social connections. Individuals cannot simply build it alone. It is based in the nature of the system, as well as the behavior of any individual actor.

Putnam details the precipitous decline of social capital in America, and the increased focus on isolated individuals. Those isolated individuals, as he also demonstrates, often sit alone in front of a screen. Putnam maintains that if Americans had more collective social capital, they would be "smarter, healthier, safer, richer, and better able to govern a just and stable democracy."[2] Helping to prevent domestic terrorism by weaving American social fabric more tightly comes under Putnam's "safer" provision. Low social cohesion helps to foster and hide jackals.

Putnam reflects on the relationship between low social capital and increasing rates of depression in America, including depression's milder, subclinical form of "malaise," and its acute deadly outgrowth, suicide. One part of the American pattern of depression is socially isolated, suicidal citizens who make their deaths into desperate, intense final statements of perverted social connection. The social statements made by bombing or shooting others, as American terrorists kill themselves, comprise a cultural tradition for jackal kin to build on. Tim McVeigh was willing to die.[3] Charles Bishop did. So did Eric Harris and Dylan Klebold. An American dream that has begun to run toward killing others and oneself in order to gain fame after death is a dream so starved of social capital that it needs redirection.

David Burgert, head of the right-wing Montana militia "Project 7," arrested in February of 2002 with weapons and plans to assassinate local officials first and then work outward, reportedly established the group after a dispute over a parking ticket. If American social cohesion has become so weak that a parking ticket can become the foundation for a militia movement, there is a great deal of preventive social medicine to be practiced. The parking ticket may have sparked the fire, but the fire was laid in American culture. The process by which it was laid deserves consideration, as well as just what sparked it. With generally low levels of social capital, many Americans are jackal's fires waiting to happen. Hopefully, Putnam is right about the revival of American community.

In the lives of many Americans, even friends and family have now become marginal as social contacts. Disconnected American families that are more aggregations of individual schedules than cohesive social units model radical individualism for their members. Since families are incubators of social consciousness, disconnected families produce individuals without a clear model of social reciprocity, the principle that if you help others without expecting direct help in return, you still benefit from living in an improved social system.[4] People from such highly individuated families, sent into an individualized society will seldom fail to become even more individually oriented. Even spiritual practice in America has developed a focus on the self rather than on community.[5] Some American subcultures, including domestic terrorist organizations, work to counteract the effects of extreme individualism in America by seeking violent radical change. No productive social reciprocity results from that effort. If Americans renewed their pursuit of positive social reciprocity instead, they could reinvigorate American society and make it a less friendly place for jackals.

Putnam pointed out, before 9/11, that Americans had come to trust each other less. September 11 bolstered mutual American trust, but major financial scandals occurring afterward assaulted American trust again, this time in American financial institutions. The blow was not just about money, but also about reinforcement of the post-9/11 sense of instability that had become part of American identity. The intensive self-centeredness of powerful CEOs who shifted from celebrity status to being American antiheroes damaged trust at a central location in the culture, both in direct victims and in everyone who observed. This time, the violence was economic, but new stores of fear and anger built up in the stories that Americans were forced to tell themselves about themselves nonetheless.

Ongoing domestic terrorism did not promote social trust. Fear about everything, from child abductors to ineffective bureaucracies, seemed to loom larger than the belief that post-9/11 social capital could be built.

Individual ethics seemed almost beyond imagining in a culture where even the sacralized concept of property meant little to music downloaders, and ethics education had to be promulgated by lawsuit. With the sheer understanding of social relatedness and social reciprocity both as endangered American mental species, the national psyche can only move in the direction of more fear and anger, unless Americans remodel their social environment. If Americans fall further into individual adversariality instead of enacting social reciprocity, the emotional health of the nation can only become more strained.

Even with general levels of trust in fellow Americans degraded in recent decades and with ongoing post-9/11 challenges to American trust, post-9/11 impulses to trust one another are also replaying in American minds. Undercurrents of a post-9/11 sense of American community remain. While nobody seemed to use the community of Valley Stream, New York as a model for writing the concept of community large in American minds, the national community, with problems of scale that Valley Stream did not have in organizing itself, nevertheless continued to try. In Valley Stream, within commuting distance of New York City, people volunteered after 9/11 to work in the fire department, provide meals for mourners, hold interfaith services, and put on benefit concerts. Valley Stream became an updated version of the historical small town in which the concept of American community was originally based.

More broadly, even among people who could not find their way to a plan for serving the national community, such as joining Citizen Corps, there was still a palpable hunger to find a way for individuals to make a difference. What lacked was not will, but a strategy for putting that impulse meaningfully into action. In a setting where scale is a challenge and social capital is low, it is difficult to imagine building more social capital. Presumptions of individualism quickly outstripped creative thinking about community based on examples like Valley Stream.

Revelations about pre-9/11 dysfunction in the bureaucratic structures of intelligence collection set off a huge federal scramble to restructure and create functional community. People in government seemed acutely aware of the potential power of a future electorate infuriated by security lapses. But building a subcultural community within a general American cultural climate of mistrust is more than a little difficult. If the public is functionally the adversary instead of being on your "side," the foundations of improved social connection cannot be borrowed from American culture as a whole. Instead, with a dappled pattern of loss of trust amid attempts to build trust in post-9/11 America, a sense of confusion reigns. The newly economically disenfranchised, the newly unemployed, the newly security-sensitive, and the government-trusting but wary and anxious population lend a touchy and disgruntled tone to post-9/11 American culture. Whether America possesses an effective level of mutual post-9/11 trust is not at all clear.

Some statistics on the subject are clear, and it is Robert Putnam who has them. Shortly after 9/11, Putnam appeared skeptical about the prospect of culture change emanating from 9/11. Appearing on CNN, he asserted that changes in thinking or images was not what would count. What would count was whether there were changes in behavior. After Pearl Harbor, more people picked up hitchhikers. That constituted a palpable change. Since that appearance, his own data have made a different sort of believer of him.

In a February 2002 article, in which Putnam published comparative results of a survey performed in 2000 and again after 9/11 in 2001, Putnam's evaluation of the potential positive impact of 9/11 on American culture was much more hopeful.[6] Images and patterns of thought now mattered, in his view, as well as behavior.[7] Putnam found "unmistakable evidence of change" in "the implications of the attacks and their aftermath for American civic life." What his data did not demonstrate was whether those changes would make it substantially out of the realm of consciousness and into the realm of behavior. Putnam did continue to observe that unless behavior followed attitudes, the "blossom of civic-mindedness after September 11 may be short-lived."

Putnam's 2001 results showed, in consonance with other survey results, a striking increase in the level of stated trust amongst Americans. Trust in the national government was the runaway leader, with an increase of 44 percent among his respondents. Trust in local governments, of local police, of people of other races, of shop clerks, of neighbors, of people running the community, and of the local news media all went up, by an average of 15.5 percent. Considerably less clear from his survey data, though, was whether Americans would translate those elevated levels of trust into behavior building social capital in America. On questions about working with neighbors, giving blood, volunteering, working on community projects, attending political meetings, reading newspapers, visiting relatives, attending club meetings, attending public meetings, contributing to secular charities, attending church, belonging to organizations, and having friends visit your home, the average increase was only 3.5 percent. What is not clear from these results is whether markedly elevated levels of trust in American consciousness would transform into behaviors strengthening the American social fabric.

What lacks, even in a post-9/11 America with elevated levels of trust, may well be a conceptual model of how to go about enacting that trust into stronger social ties, or the emotional will to do it. Putnam's post-9/11 results also indicated that already-high levels of TV viewing in America had gone up. Perhaps people chose to trust one another while sitting at home alone in their living rooms. Trust with longevity would be better cultivated by bowling together. Americans cannot afford to keep walking as though there is nobody else on the sidewalk, or afford the self-centered sense that people's lives are not intertwined. Those ideas are now out of the range of cultural affordability.

The concept of community, like the concept of culture, took an upswing in post-9/11 America, but the upswing was hard to see or work with. The rhetoric of community, from the Arab-American community in Dearborn, Michigan to communities on the Internet, the sense of national community, the community ethos on airplanes, and the increased community presence of those who had stayed closer to home after 9/11, could all have become the beginning of a long-term revival of a sense of community in America. Degraded American communal consciousness could be revived, if the pattern had enough redundancy to keep community going as a reemerging concept. The American sense of community bears both reforging and reinforcing. It needs to be reborn beyond the conceptual and geographical confines of the American small town. In contemporary America, the idea of community should be robust, even though it is diffuse in its applications.

Community's primary public relations problem in America is the idea that it stands in opposition to the individual, an idea that finds its most common expression in America in the notion that government, whether it is "city hall" or the federal government, is the opponent of the citizen. Elevated trust in government in America may not hold up to long-term wear and tear without a stronger concept of community. Sociologist Amitai Etzioni points out that both individualization and commitment to community are key elements of American experience.[8] He identifies part of the exercise of American social life as maintaining the two so that they are mutually enhancing, rather than antagonistic. Etzioni also defines community as a web of reinforcing relationships characterized by commitment to "shared values, norms, and meanings, and a shared history and identity—in short, to a particular culture."[9] The most problematic value, or cultural rule, in contemporary America is the one that relentlessly prefers the interests of the individual, and it is that aspect of American culture that requires adjustment if American community is to be bolstered.

Some communities are still geographically based, some are electronic, and some are transitory, but face-to-face. A strategy that would reinvigorate social connections and community in America would be for more Americans to both think and act as often as possible in terms of social reciprocity. If Americans carry a sense of community with them, and look for places where they can create community, as well as intersections between types of communities, they can network together both their sense of social possibilities and the level of interconnectedness of American society. Making "mosaics" of communities borrows a metaphor from urban consciousness, to update and augment the traditional small-town sense of American community.

If the governing questions in any social encounter were "What do I have in common with this person?" and "What community memberships do I or could I share with this person?" and appropriate action followed, American social life would begin to look different. Trading in cultic individualism along with its relentless question about benefit to a socially isolated self for a constantly carried concept of community would make America socially strong. Changing patterns of behavior such as volunteering and inviting people over more often would help, but Americans can also make a strong beginning simply by changing the social presumptions and quality of interaction in encounters that already present themselves every day.

A new sense of transitory community would be a special asset, particularly in the context of terrorism response. A transitory community is made up simply of people who are temporarily in the same place. Whoever is next to you in the airport waiting lounge, on the highway, in the stadium, or in line anywhere, is in the same circumstances you are. Such people are often construed purely as competition, or even as objects in the way. With as much time as Americans spend in transit, however, commuter community could be a perfect place for a primer in reorienting social consciousness. People in transitory communities in America are people with common interests, but they seldom think of themselves that way.

The community of here and now in America is the group of people most interdependent in defending against terrorist attack. The highway, the sports stadium, and the road can all be an entry-level practicum for social reciprocity, an applied exercise in Remedial Social Thinking 101. It is not necessary to experience a terrorist attack to begin the social practice that will create more cooperative American consciousness and conduct. In addition to practicing the social cohesion necessary in the face of a direct terrorist attack, elevated levels of social cooperation will allow Americans to take generally less-stressed, fearful, and angry selves into their workplaces and homes. To make a productive social exercise out of transitory commuter communities, however, Americans would first have to get out of their habit of dismissing short-term contacts.

New community will require new consciousness. Living in the moment is fine, but living in the instant can create chaos. Americans have developed a distinct tendency to react to the person or issue in front of them as though they or it will be there only for an instant. People do not just presume that encounters will be transitory; they count on it strategically in order to serve their own interests. The consciousness of channel surfing pervades the American mind set, expressing itself in a channel surfing cultural style of interacting with people, information, or plumbing parts. Social interaction becomes like flipping channels with a remote control. Post-9/11 admonitions about patriotism as something that required daily practice succumbed fairly quickly in the face of rapidly shifting American consciousness. It lacked follow through. Contemporary American patriotism is heartfelt. It just does not have much of an attention span.

When Americans interact, the television consciousness of "watching nothing" translates into an interactive consciousness of "interacting nothing," an ongoing stream of rapid, meaningless encounters in which the reality of the expectation of social support is constantly eroded. "Get this person off my phone line or out of my interaction space, so someone else has to deal with them. I don't care where they end up next, as long it has nothing more to do with me. Put them somewhere else in the bureaucracy." "Get yesterday's information off my desk. I don't care what happens to it, as long as I don't have to think about it anymore. File it, shred it, forward it, but do not ask me to relate it to what hits my desk today."

In a channel surfing mind set, strategizing to come out ahead as an individual in an encounter becomes an art form, but it decimates the cohesion of a social and informational system. Customer anger and frustration build, when every time customers pick up the phone, they have an entirely new social event. The person at one desk may have little sense that you just came from another desk in the same company. Medical personnel treat the wrong patient, or the wrong part of the right patient, because their mental connection to the person they are treating is not strong enough to prevent the error. Everything becomes remote, which is why practicing cooperative connection in transitory communities could constitute a cultural revolution.

"It's not my department" in America turns into departments that never are connected. Self-serving middle managers cannot catch self-serving American terrorists, because the terrorists and the bureaucrats all live in the same chaotic disconnected pattern that works for the terrorists and against the bureaucrats. People tend to serve themselves as individuals at the cost of making social connections. They feel at liberty to discharge negative feelings onto someone they will not see again. It does not matter whether the target deserves it. The target can go and discharge their feelings in turn on somebody else. The dynamic is a negative or inverse social reciprocity, and a social calculus that supports terrorism.

With both social presumptions and behaviors of random aggression tearing the culture further apart, Americans are building not community, but a more dangerous cultural environment by the day. Sports rage, cell phone rage, and road rage are all lesser outgrowths of the same cultural symptoms that led to Oklahoma City and Columbine. Real culture change will involve inverting the negative social assumption that what serves the practical independence and freedom of American individuals is constant adversariality. Post-9/11 impulses toward trust and social connectedness were the right medicine for America, and they need to be applied long term to make less room for jackals. If America digs down, finds the root of the problem within, and applies grit and determination to solving it, it can take off again as a culture in a way that has nothing to do with physical flying. Cultural regeneration for America will begin in the social imagination.

Realizing that the American individual is shaped by community, however closely or loosely knit that community is, and refining the concept of American individualism away from "harsh disconnected individualism" is the proper prescription.[10] Reinvigorating the community will also reinvigorate the individual. Connected individualism knows that it can do something. Conceptually pitting the individual and the community against one another misses the point, if the goal is to connect social and informational dots. When the price of self-concerned individualism becomes too high to pay, the community and the individual need realignment. Post-9/11 American comfort of sweaters, soup, and classic reruns does not also have to rerun social passivity. The social front is a place that Americans should get out of their current comfort zones in order to create authentic mutual comfort. The addictive comfort of self-satisfaction is illusory.

The heroes of 9/11 provided a model for drawing the moral fiber out of a generation of young Americans, but that model also needs to go somewhere for the vast majority of Americans who will not serve in Americorps. Robert Putnam's newest volume *Better Together: Restoring the American Community* indicates that even when contemporary Americans do work to enhance their social ties, they seldom set out specifically to build social capital.[11] Intentionally building social capital, is however, precisely what Americans should be doing, in as many ways as possible.

After 9/11, people temporarily strengthened their social spheres, and made new threads of connection across generations. There was less perceived space between the tops and bottoms of social hierarchies. Bosses, senators, and celebrities were humanized, and the average American was canonized. The blow of Pearl Harbor had come on terms that Americans understood, but this blow was different, and more complex.

Its terms were not clear. It threw the American world view up in the air, leaving Americans with a need to recreate that world view. Americans were caught at the end of a continuum of individualism and fragmentation, and movement was required, even though it was hard to sustain. A constructive legacy for 9/11 would be as the event that catalyzed an already much-needed internal revision of American culture. What the post-9/11 sense of national unity meant is still unclear. People can still use the wave of 9/11 consciousness to heal the fractionated sense of American social life before it completely passes them by. Tighter-knit communities are literally healthier communities, and Americans have a great deal of work to do on their communal health.[12]

Americans can make social differences, becoming more often connectors and less often conceptual dividers. For example, a question that arose after 9/11 was how adults could manage to take care of the postcrisis needs of both children and the elderly. How could they, as stressed individuals, handle that burden? It was a good question, but it was the wrong question. Senior American generations are made up of survivors. They were not only people who needed support, but also people who could lend it. Children needed support, but could also point the way to the postcrisis future with their consciousness. Both groups needed care, but both were also cultural partners. The "individual" in the middle did not have to feel alone or unsupported.

Thinking of connected generations in a web of mutual support, instead of conceptually isolating them, was smarter. Connect the dots. Let the children and seniors help heal each other too. Relational social thinking enhances a sense of social unity and reduces individual burdens. September 11 otherwise became one more obstruction on parallel individualistic social roads. Conceptually and socially together, Americans can help to stunt the growth of the jackal clan. Divided, they are sure to promote it.

September 11 temporarily decreased the sense of social distance in all directions. High and low status came closer together, families came closer together, generations came closer together, and, at least for a while, New York City was right down the road from everywhere else. America was more like a level playing field than a skyscraper. Those sensibilities provided a perfect opportunity to rework American life away from social isolation and disenfranchisement.

Tellingly, those who feel disenfranchised in America include the privileged and intelligent, as well as structurally disenfranchised victims of poverty or racism. College students who are future lawyers, doctors, scientists, and teachers say, with a philosophy not far removed from the Unabomber's, that they do not think they will be able to make a difference in their workplaces. Bureaucracy is too strong for that. For them, what a person says is not "real" unless it is reported in the media. To change one other person's opinion about something is not effective social action. People cannot have an impact on their government. These are "normal" mainstream young American adults, not bombers. But they clearly share with Kaczynski a sense of an interrupted "power process" for the American individual. They have little sense of their individual social efficacy or of having social capital. If upper-middle class pre-professional American students feel disenfranchised, where are the Americans who do not?

One answer to that question is that they are among the families of 9/11 victims. Some widows found it easier to battle their own emotions if they got out of the house and focused on another human life that they could do something to change. Those widows had a prescription for the emotional challenges of the entire country. A New York fire fighter admonished college students after 9/11 to make their lives count. He understood both social reciprocity and the force multiplier effect: "If I reach one person . . . in the long term I didn't just help save one life, but I affected a generation."[13] His social philosophy reached out. Affecting one person's life was not the end of a matter. It was the beginning. Some of America's recently huddled masses, pictured in a September 2001 *Newsweek,* were clearly psychologically downtrodden. The headline was "We Shall Overcome," but clearly, much of what needed to be overcome was not external, but within themselves and the fabric of their own society. The best response to terrorism is to strengthen everything from within, and the principle of social reciprocity is an extremely valuable tool.

NEW NORMAL

"New normal" is what America makes of it. On September 13, 2001, the defining characteristic of new normal appeared to be that anywhere one looked, Americans were coming home to the importance of humanity and human connection as the basis for their culture. That impulse can be fostered as a weapon in the war on terrorism, or the flush of feeling can pass away. A cultural focus on humans, instead of money or technology, can be kept by remembering the importance of symbols, stories, and dreams in inspiring people to generate social action. Reading the meanings out of 9/11 heroism stories and applying their wisdom to daily life keeps the stories alive, since a story retold is a story that continues to inform the life of a culture.

Americans' immediate post-9/11 consciousness told them that they had power as individuals and that they could have an impact on the culture. American ideas changed, and behavior did, too. People volunteered after 9/11 because they had a sense that they could make a difference, and they cared enough to try. New normal could be about taking personal achievement out of overdrive, so that there is time to be part of a community initiative, educate about ethics, or write a letter to a representative. Action can be taken to strengthen the post-9/11 connections of trust between Americans of different classes, genders, ethnicities, or age groups. The work that is always there to be done in knitting America's social fabric together has intensified in importance. A well-lived model of a society in which people can carry both a common national identity and deal with social differences constructively would make the best new normal American export to date.

A symbol about which there was considerable confusion in post-9/11 America was the flag. It was both revered as a symbol of American identity, and resented as a new representative of commercialism and signifier of shallow patriotism. There were as many kinds of flag waving, heartfelt, knee-jerk, proud, angry, and respectful, in America's new normal as there were Americans. Ethnic immigrants who also bore a post-9/11 wave of ethnic discrimination did some of the flag waving. In the national confusion about the varied meanings of the flag, displays of red, white, and blue became problematized in some public contexts. From New York to California, post-9/11 flags and ribbons and signs came down in schools and cities where concerns were raised about their presence offending international students, Americans of some ethnic backgrounds, people who disagreed with military action in Afghanistan, or possibly Native Americans.

The supporting rationale was that the flag symbolized not unity, but social division and exclusion. It was a point of view that was grounded in overblown individualism. Removing a symbol of unity was a weak way to deal with difference. While the flag has flown in the past over both honorable and dishonorable conflict, its status as a symbol of the American quest to create a principled fusion of varying people into a single coherent social organism was lost on some in the midst of roiling post-9/11 emotions.

At a Dakota powwow the weekend following 9/11, there was more red, white, and blue dance regalia than there had been in any year before. Eagle feather staffs and the half-staff American flag were posted side by side. Given what the Dakota have endured from some of those who have carried the American flag against them, if flying it was good enough for them, it was hard to imagine it not being good enough for others in America. That was a post-9/11 contribution to American identity that Dakota-Americans could make. Similar stories came from other powwows around the country. Dakota values of unity and brotherhood in a culture that is now also an interconnected part of the cultural tapestry that makes up America is a vision that could have refreshed and reinforced an American culture whose identity was burdened by fear and hate. The Dakota were perhaps not a place some Americans might have thought to look for inspiration, but not looking would have been a mistake.

The World Trade Center blast was a multiethnic American event, as well as an intercultural event. All Americans lost compatriots of several ethnic origins. Seriously sanctifying the ground there in American new normal would mean making an ongoing commitment to social justice for all of their surviving relatives and their ethnic communities in post-9/11 America. In an America where fear and anger had the upper hand, though, public anxiety turned instead to vitriolic diatribe against people of differing cultural backgrounds or political opinions from one's own. America's culture wars got nastier. In the midst of the hate mongering in a muddled post-9/11 America, there were examples of social bonding to inspire. People who housed college students so the students could protest the same policies against military action in Afghanistan that the hosts themselves supported, showed a level of pro-Americanness in which people of different perspectives can still stand together as members of the same polity.

No flags needed to come down there. The conduct of the hosts balanced conviction with humility, instead of anxiously grasping a narrow unity that demands that everyone join you in your conceptual space. Such narrow concepts of unity are actually projections of an American individualism so extreme that it undermines community, rather than building it. With anxiety as one of America's greatest enemies and social bonding as one of its greatest psychological weapons, the rhetoric of hate in America is a prime social problem.

People from everyday citizens to Brad Pitt talked about the importance of Americans continuing to educate themselves after 9/11. Some of the education was formal, with students intently focused on new subject matter on terrorism in the curricula of colleges and universities. The students who have studied in such courses will have a subsequent impact on American society, wherever the coffee shops they converse in, and whether they realize it or not. Contrary to impressions, there is more to American thought patterns than just what is in the media. Knowing more about both yourself and your opponent is not just good strategy; it is also an exercise that can be practiced in conversational groups. Terrorist attacks are perpetrated by people who pay attention to the weaknesses of their targets, one of which can be a lack of self-knowledge. Extreme individualism fosters social myopia in Americans who tend to equate their culture with their individual perspectives on it. New normal Americans need to catch up on their social study of themselves, as well as of terrorism. Without a clear sense of what is being attacked, psychological self-defense is impossible.

For a while, news became a vehicle of education and deeply interrupted the rhythms of American life. Appetites for knowing became excessive, even obsessive. Post-9/11 American media trancing had a twist, though. Instead of just passively "zoning out," American news watching, even when it provoked exhaustion, was still voracious behavior. Information was like water in the desert or food to the starving. People had to have it in order to continue being themselves. They could not function without it. A milder version of that feeling could be maintained as a form of cultural self-defense. Even when the news is not sensational, thoughtfully processing its content on a daily basis would leave Americans less able to be as completely ambushed by it as they were on 9/11.

Communication changed. Some post-9/11 Internet chat groups discussed more than drivel. The classic American disconnect, epitomized by the structure of the Internet, gave way to a medium whose message on occasion was e-community. Website variation ad infinitum shaded slightly in the direction of communities of conversation, which sorted in turn into subcultures such as "CINCH" (Commander-in-Chief of the House), an Internet support group for families with military spouses on duty abroad. The people, and not the technology, were clearly in charge.

There was also a disturbing new sensibility about the new "normal," that came from the acutely aggressive side of post-9/11 American character. American terrorists are not completely crazy, and American culture is not completely sane. Crime statistics confirmed the hyperarousal and irritability in America's "new normal." Splitting skulls in new normal was perhaps not as big a deal as it might have been before. *Time* magazine reported in February of 2003, as it worked to make journalistic sense of orange alert duct tape hysteria, that the comfort in covering the Texas dentist who had run over and killed her husband with her Mercedes was "a luxurious whiff of normal."[14] That was definitely a new normal in which the sensibility of the jackal rather than the phoenix seemed to have the upper hand.

FROM FREEDOM FROM TO FREEDOM TO

There can be enhanced social connections in America's "new normal," or America can be left in the realm of not just rugged but ruthless individuality. American individuals, when they are radically socially isolated want to be free from participating in democracy, from their compatriots, from the government, and from incursions into their privacy. The well-adjusted post-9/11 American will independently give up some of that freedom from in favor of freedom to break the mold of passive and self-oriented social thinking, to redefine relationships with other Americans constructively, including those in the government, and to act so that their individual social presence has a positive impact on American culture. Exercising "freedom to" can recast the context in which the debate about terrorism and civil liberty goes on.

The post-9/11 social environment, in which a long-term shift to a sense of social connection sorely needs to be achieved, could scarcely be more confounded, conflicted, or confused. Since 9/11, the role structure of American citizens and their government has gone into a state of confusion from both sides. Citizens who want the government to provide perfect seamless protection from terrorism say that it is not doing enough. Many of the same citizens, in addition to their specific concerns about the civil liberties impacts of government action, also regard enhanced government antiterrorist activity as a categorical assault on their freedoms. The government protector is to provide perfect performance at the same time that it is regarded as an enemy of freedom. The social equation makes no sense, and models for solving it are acutely lacking. In the meantime, the sensation of an unhealthy relationship between citizens and government adds to the cultural haze.

On the other "side" is a government equally conflicted in its social modeling. Treatment, in the context of a metaphor of war, of even domestically apprehended U.S. citizens as "enemy combatants" (cf. José Padilla) not entitled to the same civil liberties as other American citizens, and proposals for "administrative subpoenas" have set up a similarly muddled dynamic. The citizens who are to be protected can also effectively be removed from that status upon suspicion of people in the government, without due legal process via the judicial branch. People in the government, fighting terrorism, fear the wrath of citizens terrorized more than they fear the wrath of citizens with compromised civil liberties. Neither the government nor citizens have a clear sense of whether the other is an enemy or a friend. This unresolved role structure creates a citizenry that reasonably fears the government that protects it, and a government that reasonably fears the citizenry it is protecting. There is no clarity of social modeling, only the contradiction and confusion of a society working to tear itself apart internally.

Post-9/11 America has rapidly recycling relationships. There is no way to tell from one moment to the next whether citizens and their government will be mutually cooperative (i.e., tipping authorities to help catch the sniper suspect), mutually antagonistic (i.e., citizens refusing to assist investigations based on the presumption that civil rights-infringing authorities have prejudged them or a neighbor), or a mismatch of the two (i.e., a cooperative citizen with a hostile government agent, or a hostile citizen hoodwinking a government agent who is acting within the constraints of civil liberties and human respect). The complete lack of predictability about what you will get next, the equivalent of Forrest Gump's box of chocolates, promotes anxiety all across the social map. The openness of American society becomes its own enemy, when filtered through the psychological warfare created by terrorism into mutual internal fear. Anxiety "wins" if it becomes a defining characteristic of the American system. The overzealous prosecutor and the threat to the state perceived as inherent in individual rights live at odds, contribute to universal unease, and throw the post-9/11 American individual and community further out of balance with one another, instead of into consonance.

Ambiguity about orange alerts provides a perfect example of the pathology. Alerts have created more hysteria and anger at the government than a sense of a unified, galvanized social force in the face of a threat. A weak sense of community is difficult to muster with an alarm, and a community whose alarm system drives it further apart is poorly adapted to threat. When everyone fears everyone, if not as a terrorist, at least in some way as a threat to the American way of life, the resulting environment is one in which it will be extremely difficult for trust or a sense of community to grow.

The post-9/11 American social environment will involve both cooperative and antagonistic social modeling, which need to occur in some stable relationship with one another. Scattershot modeling will simply tear morale further apart, and hand the 9/11 terrorists an ultimate psychological victory. Overapplication of adversarial modeling, something that Tim McVeigh would have heartily endorsed, is a core problem. The model is common, reflected in language about the war on terror "vs." civil liberties, the government's need to know "vs." privacy, or government expansion "vs." individual autonomy. People observe less often that the conflict model is overused.

Even the concept of working to "balance" the two concerns of fighting terrorism and preserving individual privacy and liberties can move the nation further apart, if it leaves the concept of compromise between opposing forces in place. Anthony Romero, Director of the American Civil Liberties Union has been articulate on the problems inherent in the model of trading off individual freedom for public security, and security expert Bruce Schneier points out both the overdriven counterposing of the two concerns, and the inherent security risks of excessive government power.[15] Wholesale conflict modeling in antiterror initiatives will disserve both the American polity and the American psyche. Asymmetrical "balancing," in which one of the parties (in this case, the public) does not use its voice or has its rights curtailed, is a poor response to an asymmetrical threat.

A better response has two strong partners, citizens and their government both responding dynamically to needed adjustments in their relationship. Social modeling that steps outside the relentlessly hostile dynamics of terrorist threat and into constructive criticism is the solution to the problem of creating a social context in which the particulars of responding to terror can be addressed. Blanket criticism of government information collection need not apply any more than characterizations of civil liberties concerns as hysterical.

Excessive conflict modeling leaves America without "teams." If citizens have both the government and terrorists out against them, do not know and, at best, can only count on their neighbors for benign disregard, then who are their friends? If people in the American government have to remove the civil liberties of citizens in reaction to an entire American citizenry regarded more as a potential source of terrorists than as an ally, and at the same time must depend on a reluctant public to assist in surmounting the threat while also battling growing terror within because of increasing dissatisfactions among citizens, then who are their friends?

Universally applied adversarial modeling leaves post-9/11 America in a social bind, with America's internal social organization a place where the war on terror is not being won. Adversariality between American citizens and their government means that there is no potential victory for the American system as a whole, future terrorism or no. America loses either way. It misses the opportunity to make a vibrantly viable response to terrorism by creatively reworking its understanding of itself. Its cultural self-esteem will depress rather than grow. The alternative to a relentlessly competitive win-lose model is to model the benefits of social bonding and social reciprocity, and to reap the benefits of symbiosis through cooperation and collaboration, while tackling tough tactical antiterror problems. The urge to cooperation in post-9/11 America has not been clearly codified into American social thinking. America now is not more unified because of 9/11. It is less so.

Some proceed from the premise that security and privacy can coexist, and that the model of balancing civil liberties and security should be replaced with one aimed at serving both.[16] Cooperation and competition models need to be structured clearly in relation to one another. I may have to "give up" my sense of having personal privacy while in public places (although proposed legislation as of this writing that could result in the death penalty for my presence at a protest represents an extremely overdriven reaction to creating social connections among "terrorists" and their potential supporters, a reaction which has been partnered by insufficiently strong reactions to creating stronger social connections among those in American government who are combating terrorism), but I should expect to enjoy the protections of an innocent American citizen until I have been judged otherwise in court. Sometimes, I cooperate. Some boundaries I maintain.

In a healthy society, one with the high cultural self-esteem that will protect psychologically from terrorism, the fundamental context in which citizens and their government relate must be one of trust, in which the interests of both are seen to substantially coincide.[17] Within that overall understanding, the devilish details of how best to create security and preserve civil liberties can be worked out by participatory citizens and their responsive government. Such stability in social modeling is critical to civic health in American society and to the emotional health of the national character.

Indulgence in constantly adversarial thinking takes America on the path of the jackal. It provides the "comfort" of a return to pre-9/11 American social modeling, but is a poor adaptation to terrorism. It is a capitulation to fear. Without a non-adversarial social context in which Americans in and out of government can pursue their post-9/11 social relations, security questions can only pull America further apart.

The problems on both sides of this public-government antiterrorist social configuration are prodigious. American citizens can only respond cooperatively to a government seeking more information by projecting reasonable complaints, but not anxieties, onto the government. Americans in government, faced with the prodigious task of preventing terrorism and dependent on cooperation from an anxious public, face their own fears of failure. With the terrorists out against them, the public perceived out against them, and their own anxiety to manage, the easiest course is to fall back into a default cultural pattern of individual power acquisition. What is substantially missing in post-9/11 America is a sense that there are teams at all. "Good guys" and "bad guys" are impossible to distinguish, and the jackal loves social confusion. Domestic terrorism compounds the confusion. The problem is not just with the fact of domestic terrorism, but also with the concept.

The concept of domestic terrorism after 9/11 has further confounded America's "team" structure. The definition of domestic terrorism in the Patriot Act works against social clarity. Acts that are criminal, endanger human life, and "appear to be intended" to use intimidation or coercion to influence the government are defined as domestic terrorism. The post-9/11 key to interpreting that language is to understand that it is post-9/11 American human beings in government who will be doing the perceiving of the appearances. They are people who were traumatized by 9/11, are responsible for preventing a recurrence, and who, themselves, must fight the psychology of fear. That kind of pressure can have an impact on one's perception of appearances. Post-9/11 prosecutors in terrorism cases have subjectively maintained that one knows terrorism "when one sees it."[18] Sanctifying the power of such subjectivity in officials, especially when new laws have diffuse definitions of concepts such as "material support," can be distinctly problematic.

Post-9/11 confusion about antiterrorist role structure in America also relates directly to the question of whether the "cultures" of law enforcement and intelligence collection can be successfully fused. Senator Bob Graham stated his skepticism that such fusion was possible at the FBI. Fusion is possible, but only through clarification of social relationships in the projected culture. The current metaphor for fusing the cultures of law enforcement and intelligence is to break down the "wall" between them, similar to the concept of "breaking down" administrative stovepipes. Destructive metaphors do not always get regenerative jobs done.

The reason the two "cultures" cannot be fused by breaking the wall alone is that doing so will create additional social confusion. The "wall" already in place between criminal investigation and antiterror intelligence collection, from a social organizational point of view, had already artificially segmented investigation of the same human being into two informational and administrative categories, information collected based on suspicion of foreign-inspired terrorist activity, and that collected as part of a criminal investigation. The wall is based on categories of information, not on categories of people. The relevant categories of people are insiders and outsiders to American society.

In post-9/11 America, simply breaking the wall will serve the investigative process, but will further confuse sensibilities about who is an American insider and who is not. The context for confusion is created by an inconsistent post-9/11 pattern of terrorist prosecution, with non-nationals such as Zacarias Moussaoui and Richard Reid tried under the criminal justice system, and American citizens such as José Padilla and Yaser Hamdi treated as enemy combatants under the system of military justice.[19] If investigation and prosecution of terrorism in America proceeds from unclear boundaries about who is an American insider, the composition of "teams" becomes even foggier. Capitalizing on negative stereotypes to prosecute a suspected American terrorist as an outsider may be tempting, but the cost of doing so to American identity is substantial. Simply breaking the wall between criminal investigation and collecting intelligence about foreign-related terrorism can only confound, rather than effectively fuse the preexisting subcultures.

Such confusion is a recipe for new social dysfunction, when fusion that is considered from the point of view of bureaucratic categories but unconsidered from the point of view of human relationships creates new conflict in terms of the larger culture. "Domestic terrorist" ought not become a concept that undermines the integrity of America's sense of itself, or creates confusion about where America stops and any other culture begins. It should be a category that realizes the fact of American perpetration of terror, including the potential for cooperation by Americans with hostile foreign influences, without undermining America's identity or the security of the civil rights of American citizens. Investigative needs and cultural identity needs are in direct conflict post-9/11, and will remain so, unless someone does some clear and creative thinking and applies it to some viable cultural reengineering. Without resolving the muddle created by conceptual fusion of the concepts of domestic criminal and enemy combatant, America's civic self-consciousness can only decline.

The boundary between crime and terrorism has shaded toward terrorism in post-9/11 American culture. The FBI definition of terrorism is: "the unlawful use of force against persons or property to intimidate or coerce a government, the civilian population, or any segment thereof, in furtherance of political or social objectives," FBI Director Robert Mueller, in a speech given in the middle of the sniper's campaign on October 18, 2002, referred to the beltway snipers as "terrorists" before either sniper John Muhammad's anti-American sympathies had become known, or demands for money had been made.[20] Mueller did not choose to reserve judgment about the case being rooted in intimidation. Intent to intimidate loomed large and clear in his consciousness.

To others, later, it appeared that intimidation intended by the sniper was only a byproduct of a money motive. Prosecution in the case proceeded in part under antiterrorism law. Before 9/11, the same sequence of activity would have been culturally classified as crime. In the investigation of a series of sniper shootings in West Virginia in the summer of 2003, theories about the perpetrator's motive varied from drug-related to choosing to echo the beltway sniper crimes, but gravitated toward terror as the investigation went on. The consciousness of terror looms large in post-9/11 American culture.

When people in government equate their own interests as social actors with those of society, another cultural pathology arises. Under the stress of both terrorism threats and a civically passive citizenry, those in government easily forget that they represent members of the culture, rather than defining it solely themselves. Criticism of a proposed second Patriot Act suggested that the government's antiterrorist initiatives had themselves taken on an addictively self-centered quality, with the administrative drive to create extreme vigilance with respect to terrorism requiring countervailing vigilance of citizens with respect to government, before "the fog of war (on terrorism) becomes toxic."[21]

The "war on terror" itself was criticized for having too strong a character in relation to other concerns. A cultural interpretation of that perspective is that President Bush's commitment to antiterrorism is not just as commander-in-chief; but also as the American individual-in-chief, who projects his personal responses to terrorism through maximal reliance on the executive authority of his office. George W. Bush, the cultural individual, as well as George W. Bush, holder of the office of president of the United States, acts. By two years after, the strength of Bush administration responses to terrorism were characterized by some in America as capitalizing on fear, cynical, and symptomatic of an infallibility complex, hardly the rhetoric of an America still unified around its experience of 9/11.

The lack of clarity in post-9/11 American role structure beleaguers the possibility of creating a cooperative American response to terrorism. That possibility is further beleaguered by an acutely felt dearth of effective communication between the public and the government. Elevated terrorism alerts have been attended by public frustration and anger about vagueness of the alert system and the lack of specific information provided, as well as by panic and hysteria regarding the prospect of an attack. Neither unity nor calm could be found in relation to the alerts. State and local authorities, as well as citizens, expressed frustration about poor communication with the federal government, and if information was not flowing well, even in critical up-and-down government "stovepipes," hopes for government creation of meaningful communication outside of those stovepipes also had to be discounted.

The same citizens that felt informationally shut out by the federal government, faced the prospect of the creation of vast government databases compiling information about them. The total picture presupposes much more equanimity on the part of citizens than is reasonable, and anxiety grows, about the government as well as about terrorism. The prospect of information audits within government databases will do little to assuage public fear if there is already a basic lack of trust. Enhancing the effects of social distance and conflict, alerts have not been communicated directly from the government to the public, but to local law enforcement instead, with the assumption that the media would broadcast the information further. That asymmetrical statement of communicative relationships does nothing to enhance American unity. Patterns of noncommunication do not point in the direction of cooperation building between citizens and their government.

In this problematized cultural context, both the public and the government could do more to support a concept of one another as partners and not adversaries. There has been criticism of the government for not doing more to support community volunteer initiatives since 9/11, in order to keep the spirit of cooperation growing in American culture. The criticism is fair, but it is only half the story. There is nothing that prevents "we, the people" from taking the initiative to improve their communities themselves. They are free to do so. The government could temper its perceptual focus on the public as a place from which terrorists emerge, by giving the public a positive role in assisting those efforts.

General Wesley Clark suggested in a 2003 speech that the government set up citizen tip lines geared toward gathering suggestions for how to go about fighting terrorism.[22] Such a tip line would have none of the problematic implications of tip lines geared specifically toward gathering information. Suggestion lines would allow members of the public to envision themselves as something other than passive protectees or potential civil liberties targets of the government. They would also invite people in government to remember that the public they serve is an active, tough, but fundamentally cooperative force in fighting terror. Citizens could meaningfully participate in their democracy to support the efforts of those in the government to keep them safe. People in government could reap creative ideas along with a healthier context of communication. In post-9/11 America, there needs to be an enhanced understanding, both in and out of the government, that Americans cannot always be free from each other. They also need to be free with each other, and because of each other.

The relationship of American citizens to one another in this overall setting of confused social relationships and poor communication is no clearer than is their relationship with their government. The relationship between citizens is complex. It is not simply one of social disregard, or of presumed friendship, or of enmity. The proposed government TIPOFF program for providing tips on fellow citizens did not get the relationship right. The response was anger and cancellation of the program. While the anger of American citizens on behalf of themselves and other Americans upon whom the government might want them to "spy" demonstrated some level of community consciousness, it was a community consciousness that still needed an upgrade.[23]

The same Americans rushed to the phones in the midst of the beltway sniper scare, or tackled Richard Reid with bravado. When people were directly and personally threatened, sharing information with the government was not a taboo. Basing communication with the government only on a sense of personal threat, however, is a sign of a weak community. The safety of the self is connected to the safety of others. Post-9/11 America needs to work out an understanding of how American individuals bear both a moral and a practical obligation to both, at the same time that they do not intrude on the privacy of others.

The relationship between fellow citizens is complex, not dualistically simplistic. There is middle ground between being socially disconnected and spying on each other. FBI agent Coleen Rowley points out that surveillance cameras, for example, can cut two ways at once. In one perspective, they invade individual privacy, even when posted in public. In another perspective, they can help to build community. In a California neighborhood, a surveillance camera posted on one neighbor's house recorded information about the kidnapping of a child from another.[24] Instead of functioning as an intrusion on privacy, the camera helped to save a child. It united, instead of tearing apart, a community of "good guys."

Think about the same scenario without the camera involved, and you will reach the essence of the need to redefine the relationship between fellow American citizens so that they can contribute to one another's security. Whether any given surveillance camera has the effect of bonding or dividing a group is purely a matter of the nature of the social relationships of the people behind and in front of the camera. It is not about the camera. It is about the people.

Neighbors could preempt growing anxiety about both terrorism and privacy in America by organizing neighborhood watch groups in mutual defense, with or without cameras. Such groups would force people to grapple with questions of where helpful cooperation leaves off and where nosiness begins. America can have groups of "good guys" instead of angst-filled lone rangers, with or without government direction. Working cooperatively in small groups would also help Americans model in their minds the possibility of cooperative relationships within larger groups. Americans have already adapted, on behalf of collective safety, to having less privacy when they wish to board an airplane. Now the social dangers of calling in tips on fellow citizens as a matter of self-interest has to be offset with the service rendered to society by calling in a tip in good faith. Americans determine the relative weight of the two options freely, with their own behavior. That ratio is not something that the government controls. The people making the calls do. New American unity must consist of everyone being both respected and suspected, with an upgrade in communal consciousness so that America can deal effectively with both. The matter was not complicated in Times Square on New Year's Eve 2001. People were urged to watch each other carefully. Individuals made community in the process of looking out for themselves, because watching out for yourself also meant watching out for those around you. Americans now struggle with a cultural change in America; freedom from paying attention to the private citizen next to you had become freedom to participate in your own security by paying attention.

Relating to one's fellow citizens is not only about watching for the miscreants among them. The rhetoric of volunteering and community building that emerged after 9/11 still applies. Beyond the service that some Americans give in Americorps or Citizen Corps, there are also less formal alternatives for producing the "culture of national service" called for in early 2002.[25] An everyday sensibility of "volunteering," in addition to joining formal organizations, can bolster both the sense and the reality of social reciprocity. The impulse to volunteer at Ground Zero is transferable to everyday American life.

By two years after 9/11, though, America's challenge was that responses to 9/11 were more in people's minds than in their behavior. Those responding to Internet polls were six times more likely to report that they had changed by becoming more appreciative than that they had become more giving. They were twelve times more likely to report spending the second anniversary by reflecting personally than by getting together with others. Their responses were cerebralized rather than social. A long-term shift in the tone of American social relations was not emerging.

The possibility of fighting fertile ground for terrorism in America by being courteous to the person next to you, whoever it is, or singling out someone in the community with a social need and helping to fill it, was largely unrealized.

Terrorism thrives in America on socially disconnected ground, and Americans are free to improve their position in relation to terrorism by changing that ground, making it more hostile for the jackal. The earnest question that many Americans asked after 9/11 about what they could do to fight terrorism has an answer. The answer is that they can work to change the social environment in which terrorism has to function. They may well not be able to fight terrorism directly. They may choose not to fight by calling in tips to government investigators, but they can still fight. One individual may not achieve much, but every American individual can make a difference. Anyone can take one American problem and tackle a piece of it: homelessness, racism, violence, ethical decline, or abuse in any of its many forms. The problems are not hard to find, and the litany is familiar. Tutor. Mentor. Give. Befriend someone who is socially isolated or in need. People who need support are not hard to find. Do not just think about it. Do it. Making the nation stronger will make it harder to tear apart. That is how everyone can fight terrorism in America.

What FBI Director Mueller calls a "force multiplier," when many people cooperate to help each other simultaneously, works on the same principle as Putnam's social capital, whether it is applied to intelligence collection or service without a snarl. One way to right a cultural ship in which even America's brightest, privileged best feel disempowered is to regard experience as well as expertise as a valid source of knowledge. Citizens will have suggestions about security that government experts will not have thought of. Citizens are experts on the citizen's perspective because they live it.

Without correcting the dynamics of passive and anxious psychology in the American body politic, though, there will be no realistic chance of long-term survival for the renewed post-9/11 sense of national American community. Early post-9/11 exhortations to reach out to families and friends of victims and help the local food shelf have substantially faded into event-related behaviors, instead of being transferred into an ongoing new American identity. Those behaviors will remain event-specific until

Americans start acting more in terms of their freedom to work together than their freedom from one another.

The American people, as well as the FBI, need a change in attitude. Americans asked themselves after 9/11 about whether their renewed patriotism would endure beyond short-term flag waving. Robert Putnam's post-9/11 data suggests that Americans are mentally prepared for the type of patriotism that Amitai Etzioni defines as commitment to be engaged in public and civic life, although the enactment of that commitment is less clear. Etzioni points out that patriotism in its enacted form is fundamentally voluntary.[26] Patriotic Americans can make an antiterrorist difference, but only if they exercise the freedom to volunteer themselves to society by enacting a cooperative vision of American culture in their behavior. Such commitment is necessary to achieving "a social order that is well balanced with socially secured autonomy," what Etzioni calls the New Golden Rule.[27]

Such "balance" cannot be achieved in the realm of civil liberties debates alone. It requires a revitalized American social context within which such debates can be held. The potential for long-standing change in post-9/11 America is in the potential to create that revitalized context. The notion of balance between individual rights and collective security can only have wisdom in a setting where a civic team of both active citizens and their government works to make it. A government that claims additional power in the face of a passive citizenry precludes the possibility of any such balance. Creating a cooperative context for the regeneration of both order and autonomy is the more fundamental issue. Americans who start practicing cooperation with the person next to them on the bus and the neighbors two doors down will be better equipped to bring a consciousness that envisions social stability and unity to the American cultural table.

CHAPTER 7

AMERICAN INTELLIGENCE

FBI: AMERICA'S MOST WANTED SUBCULTURE

Community and the FBI is a tough case, whether the subject is the FBI as an internal community, the FBI as a member of the "intelligence community," or the FBI as part of the national community.[1] The FBI is an American subculture, populated by Americans who behave like Americans. It also has an acute case of organizational individualism. The secretive work of the FBI has spun into a culture of concealment that extends to its identity, as well as its actions. Americans hate it not just because of its misadventures in combination with their dependence on it for safety. They also hate it because it is so much like what they love to hate about the rest of a disconnected America. With 9/11 added to the mix of the FBI's notoriously secretive and inwardly turned bureaucracy and the information-jealous and self-protective strategies of bureaucratic culture generally, the FBI instantly became an intensive focus of everything that America did not like about itself, self-interested inwardness and chaotic organization.

Like the people it pursues, the FBI, from the outside, is a mystery to look at. Forced by its function into social proximity with terrorists and a culture of secrecy, it has evolved an elaborate culture of hierarchical inwardness into a fine art. One of America's premier FBI haters is Ted Kaczynski, but despite his and other bureaucracy-hating perspectives, not even the FBI is faceless, nameless, immovable, or soulless. People in the FBI behave according to general American cultural rules, as well as the rules of their organizational subculture. When the American rule of self-interest conflicts with rules about meeting organizational goals, the organization is unlikely to win out. The real subculture of the FBI bureaucracy cannot be read out of its rule book, its organizational model, its stated goals for cultural change, or even its budget. It has to be read out of what people within the FBI actually know and believe, and what they choose to do. The FBI adaptation to a tough cultural niche was poor before 9/11, and, efforts to the contrary notwithstanding, its cultural problems have only worsened since.

After 9/11, the culture of the FBI was charged with changing. Integrating identities as a prosecution-oriented law enforcement bureau and a prevention-oriented intelligence gathering organization was a daunting challenge, but only scratched the surface of the needed cultural change. Along with significant adjustments to social structure and internal patterns of communication, the bureau also needed to change its public identity and attitude of arrogance. All of this change was called for in a hostile social environment, and in the midst of rapidly shifting demands for practical performance. The order was way too tall, and the move toward culture change at the FBI largely backfired.

The FBI became the conceptual focus for bureaucracies of American intelligence that were not getting pre-9/11 dots of information connected. Public antipathy focused on the FBI's cultural crimes of disconnection came from people who, themselves, lived in a disconnected culture. Hatred of the FBI, in whatever measure justifiably based on the bureau's performance, became itself one more form of American disconnect. Post-9/11 critics of the bureau, often self-righteously and self-indulgently applied new American cultural standards for making connections to a pre-9/11 bureau. The unexamined self-indulgence had the same quality as unexamined American hatred of American terrorists. Some of the FBI's post-9/11 critics forgot that 9/11 had also happened to people in the bureau. The FBI was tried in the court of public opinion, and its trial, like Sara Jane Olson's, took place in a courtroom where American sensibilities had shifted. The FBI had not just the clarity of post-9/11 hindsight to fight, but also its vehemence. The FBI became bureaucratic Ground Zero.

Like American fire fighters, psychiatrists, journalists, and everyone else, people in the FBI experienced a cultural transition, one they had to manage over the long term, and not just as immediate responders. Workload went up. Stigma went up. Scandal emerged. Reorganization plans ensued. The marching orders were endless. Reorient to preventing terrorism. Catch the anthrax perpetrator. Deal with your own fears. Transform internally. Do it fast, and under painful public scrutiny, which goes against your traditional subcultural grain. No other place in America had such an acute focus on the need to perform at the same time that its own and the culture's larger problems came powerfully home to roost.

The new script was to be ridiculed and overburdened while performing miracles. The human beings at the FBI, in the middle of a general cultural shift, suddenly had expectations for their cooperative behavior running way ahead of American cultural practice, and focused like a laser beam on them. Not connecting dots had become one step short of criminal. In an atmosphere where the specter of another terrorist attack ruled, the received expectation was that the American achievement principle would automatically cover the huge gap between the FBI's past and future selves. That level of expectation rapidly devolved into cynicism about the impossibility of the task.

The FBI became a whipping boy for the nation's understanding that significant cultural change in America was not taking place. Suddenly called powerfully to account for its own prodigious but previously shrugged-at sins, and with the nation's anxiety focused squarely on it, the bureau was also forced to face the worst about itself. The situation had overload and retrenchment, rather than effective cultural transformation, written all over it. The near-miraculous transformation expected at the FBI was their problem, and conceptually "not my department" for the rest of America, with the FBI expected to become an effectively connected system within a still-disconnected larger social environment. The task was legendary. The outcome was not.

It is hard to be a hero when you are a scapegoat. Emotional responses to 9/11 created intensive scapegoating, which is the assigning of guilt by association to others in order to assuage one's own pain, across the nation.

Arab-Americans became the ethnic scapegoat of choice. The FBI became the bureaucratic scapegoat of choice in a culture looking for someone to blame for its own trauma, as a check of post-9/11 cartoons will demonstrate. The FBI was not just criticized. It was vilified, living in the mind of the public one step away from the terrorists it had not caught before they acted. People at the FBI were regarded more as faceless quasi-criminals themselves for "allowing" 9/11 to happen, than as among its victims. Adjectives like "evil" and "incompetent" circulated, and Ted Kaczynski must have been delighted to have so much of America agreeing with his assessment of the organization.

The bureau was in a poignant high stress mix of being called on to be cultural innovators by creating a concrete application of a functional new American community, and bearing blame for the tragedy and the equivalent of witchcraft accusations. It was not a situation that was likely to elicit a new openness in a traditionally secretive organization, or promote the honest self-evaluation and broad-based commitment necessary for authentic culture change.

It was in this configuration that Minneapolis FBI Agent Coleen Rowley would emerge, with a different image of the bureau to purvey. The problem with Agent Rowley was that she was much more popular with the public than with the bureau. She fed public hunger for positive images of the FBI. Although she called for change at the FBI based on honest criticism instead of a witch-hunt, the public relations problem was that there already was a witch-hunt on for the bureau as a whole when her original letter to Director Mueller was leaked. Past problems, from Waco to Ruby Ridge, Wen Ho Lee, the Tim McVeigh document snafu, and the Agent Robert Hanssen scandal, had all became a huge bureau tab that was suddenly due with the American public. With 9/11 added, it was not only time to pay the bill, but the total had mushroomed overnight. Americans' greater trust in government after 9/11 was not focused on the FBI. The bureau became instead an icon of an inimical relationship between the American government and the American public.

The FBI was liable to become an icon of renewed mistrust of government. The FBI has symbolic cachet, and mystique is the province of either heroes or villains. Mention that you have any involvement with the FBI. People's jaws drop, eyebrows raise, and the expressions on their faces are full of amazement. The mystique is such that there is sheer disbelief that any regular person could be associated with the FBI. Popular culture representations of FBI agents often depict them as menacing, frightening, emotionless automatons, a force to be avoided almost as devoutly as the criminals they pursue. Part of that image comes from the way the FBI handles information. Information goes in, but seldom comes out. Talking to the FBI is like putting information into a black hole, a situation that demands tremendous trust; trust that is generally in short supply in American culture.

Being in a public mess and the mystique of being a secretive information priesthood do not go well together, especially when you already fit the perfect symbolic profile of what to fear about one's own government. The cloaked identity of the FBI as cold, secretive, and powerful works against the bureau when they depend on everyday Americans to volunteer information. The image, sunglasses and all, becomes a strategic problem that haunts the bureau itself, not just citizens. Being cast as chillingly infallible sets you up for a fall. Peggy Conlon, whose post-9/11 "I am an American" public service ad provided a message of social solidarity of Americans from differing ethnic backgrounds, later produced another ad, but this time the message was one of social division rather than solidarity. The public service ad produced in response to the Patriot Act had a nightmare scenario of a library patron being approached by menacing government agents. The symbolic icon for civil liberties concerns raised by the Patriot Act was a federal agent hostile to the public, in a post-9/11 cultural environment that was no longer focused on social cohesion.

Some Americans think that the FBI should be able to do its job without them. Experts should be able to do their work without bothering private citizens. Speaking to citizens constitutes at least an inconvenience, if not a violation of their civil liberties. A public that does not want to be bothered, or regards the people investigating on their behalf as categorically inimical, does not leave much of a starting point for creating a culture of connected dots. Such a public will be receptive to sensationalized criticism of the bureau, and of little help in solving "needle in a haystack" cases. When FBI personnel hone to the bureau's secretive and arrogant image, either from cultural habit or in self-defense, it promulgates its own stereotype. Cultural relations worsen.

People at the FBI are not their stereotype. They are not emotionless automatons or bumbling idiots. They vary. They live in a troubled subculture, high on attitude and low on effective social connection, but there is equivalent disorganization in neighborhood plumbing stores in America. The problem is not just with the FBI. Its organizational rule book, like other rule books in America, lives through human error, foibles, weaknesses, brilliance, prejudices, strategizing, and unpredictability. The FBI also lives with the general rule in American culture focusing on individual self-interest over organizational mission. The bureau just has a particularly acute case of the pathologies that are generated thereby.

In theory, the chain of command at the FBI creates connected order. In practice, it creates obstacles, with entrenched individual self-interest and organizational chaos working against effectiveness. A subculture where an atmosphere of secrecy has layered itself on secretive activity has allowed even more flourishing of self-interest than in many American bureaucracies. The subcultural character of the FBI is not unlike that of a depressed individual, inwardly focused and disorganized, and socially isolated.

The FBI's three critical cultural problems are: (1) communication (both internally and with the public), (2) social organization (ineffective connections between street agents and superiors or central), and (3) public perception (from leaving disconnected patterns of information or communication between people that can and should be connected). All three of these problems are typical of contemporary American culture, although they have especially intensive and stunning manifestations in the closed culture of the FBI. All have been highlighted by the testimony of Agent Coleen Rowley, by Peter Lance in his book *1000 Days of Revenge: International Terrorism and the FBI: The Untold Story*, and by other sources.[2]

Peter Lance's 2003 volume is a mixed cultural blessing. His work explicates examples of the cultural problems above. The FBI and other law enforcement failed to connect dots before 9/11 because they were thinking in a typically American way about social organization. An American who has apprehended top individuals in a terrorist organization and is generally more likely to perceive a perpetrator as "lone" rather than as part of a connected social organization, is unlikely to further pursue organizations or conspiracies of terrorism. The social consciousness stemming from extreme American individualism will, without the benefit of intensive cultural briefing about highly coordinated perpetrators, obscure the perception of their level of social cooperation. People who are short on social imagination about working together to begin with cannot connect informational dots about potential perpetrators effectively. Connecting informational dots is an activity that is subsidiary to a social consciousness that can envision the human collaboration making the dots into a meaningful pattern.

In the pre-9/11 FBI, individual isolation and extreme social hierarchy trumped pattern consciousness in an extremely predictable American cultural configuration. In an environment created by disjointed social modeling, a cry from a field office about a suspect being involved in a larger plot was easily interpreted by an agent at central as the Minneapolis office becoming "spun up over Moussaoui," instead of as part of a potentially crucial pattern of facts.[3] Individualism ruled. The cognition of social connection, both about the "good guys" and the "bad guys," did not. No matter how much pain may have resulted from that "lapse" in consciousness, it was still utterly typically, culturally American.

Lance's volume also documents the bureau's tendency to disassociate itself with outsiders who might be of service. Lance's focus is on fire fighter Ronnie Bucca. In the anthrax case, the relevant person was scientist Barbara Hatch Rosenberg. There is a pattern there that is worthy of investigation. Lance identifies the wisdom of decentralized action with coordinated control, closing the volume with "the best way to turn the FBI into an effective preemptive force against terror is to give more power to the street agents while providing them with the guidance of veteran agents as mentors."[4] Hierarchy at the bureau has interfered with the breadth of perspective necessary to effectively combat terror. Lance also provides examples of the same type of disconnect between public statements by the bureau and actual facts that was identified by Agent Coleen Rowley in her first letter to Director Mueller, where she challenged his assertion that there had been no indications of 9/11 prior to its occurrence.[5] Such disconnects are deadly opponents of public trust in the bureau. All of these observations on Lance's part are pertinent and productive, but the tenor of his volume is not.

In May of 2002, in discussing FBI reorganization, Director Mueller said, "I want to say that the bureau is only so good as its relationships." That statement boomerangs back onto the bureau, in the form of criticism of untrustworthiness or intransigence in bureau relations with outsiders, but it also indicts Lance. Despite Lance's clear explication of the three main cultural problems at the FBI, he also indulges in a new culture war. This culture war has nothing to do with the political left or right. It is a new, post-9/11 culture war, a dot connection war. The war is based on the righteousness of being "more connected than thou." Lance connects the dots in post-9/11 culture, exploiting new American sensibilities and a heightened atmosphere of criticism of the bureau. The melee ensuing in the press upon the publication of the book had Lance's descriptors "dropped balls" and "bungled," opposing FBI responses of "hearsay" and "innuendo." Lance's overbalancing in the direction of connecting the dots was countered by FBI characterization of the book as gossip, speculation and rehashed stories. There was no common American ground in sight.

The pattern created by the dots is, of course, easier to see after they have already been connected. Lance has hindsight, one thread of investigation among many more than 1,000, adversarial social modeling, and public excitability on his side. He invited the American public to inform itself, which was a good idea, but the casting of relationships between himself and the public on the one side and the bureau on the other as fundamentally inimical was not. A WWF-style face-off between the public and the FBI, with Lance as the public's champion, cannot serve the creation of effective post-9/11 collaboration in American culture, or better relationships with the bureau from any perspective. Individualized adversariality still rules.

POISON

The FBI found itself on the horns of a dilemma after 9/11. Facing the anthrax case, the FBI was caught between its need for help from the public, and the public's impression that the bureau should be able to solve the case themselves. Close interaction with the public was not exactly in the FBI's comfort zone. The bureau was set up to be ambiguous about the public, since accepting help to find the "needle in the haystack" threatened a tarnished self-image and reputation further. Not accepting help made the job harder. An uneasy bureau identity and a lack of resolution of the case both prevailed. The public did not call in to the tip line for the case. Despite an offered one million dollar reward, the call volume was very low. The money was not moving people and neither was anything else, unlike in the Unabomber and beltway sniper cases. By January of 2002, the idea of increasing the amount of money in order to reinvigorate public interest had emerged. The public, both intransigent and a threat to the FBI's beleaguered professional pride, stayed uninvolved, expecting their feared and hated bureau to solve the case quickly and without their help. Failing to solve the puzzle would bring more condemnation.

Psychiatrists have words for relationships that are structured with mutual dependency, dislike, and disassociation, like the one between the public and the FBI. The word is dysfunctional. The same word was used frequently after 9/11 to refer to federal agencies, perhaps most often with reference to the Immigration and Naturalization Service (INS). There was more going on, though, than just dysfunction within the agencies. Their relationships with the public were dysfunctional too. Steven Brill, author of *After,* asked, in reference to the INS, who would care whether the agency was dysfunctional, since it had no effective constituency other than foreigners.[6] The answer to Brill's question of who would care, in a society with a functional relationship between citizens and their government, would be the public. It was not just the agency that was dysfunctioning, but also the cultural context.

While the national psyche may not need psychiatric help, the public and the FBI could definitely use relationship therapy. It was no surprise that FBI Director Mueller had a slip of the tongue when addressing Congress in June 2002. He referred momentarily to 9/11 as "the attack on the FBI," instead of "the attack on the U.S." Stuck between being a lightning rod for criticism and needing to solve the anthrax case expeditiously, and pinned in a national love-hate relationship with the public, the bureau was forced to turn straight into its dysfunctional relationship with the public by asking for help. Small wonder, under the circumstances, that the bureau did not communicate effectively, and it did not. Its appeals for information were characterized as the begging and pleading of a desperate agency. The concept of collaboration and cooperation in post-9/11 American culture seemed not to extend to assisting the FBI. Instead, the anger Americans expressed in letters to the editor, on computer message boards, and elsewhere, was intense. One angry American, who characterized the profile of the anthrax terrorist as a "no-brainer," later realized that her anger was more about expecting that the FBI would make things right in a stressed post-9/11 world, than it was about the profile itself. She needed the bureau to sound convincing and appear to be in command, in order to provide her with a sense of comfort. She was furious when it did not. In general, the ridicule factor, rather than the assistance factor, went up. Given the social distance, the stress levels, and FBI mystique, few Americans thought through their increasingly compromised relationship with the FBI. The dots were just moving further apart.

Senator Patrick Leahy pitched for a sense of connection in mid-October 2001. Standing next to the assistant director of the FBI Washington field office, he attempted to mobilize the public to help with the anthrax case by using post-9/11 social semantics. The anthrax victims were not the intended victims, but hardworking, solid people, just doing their job. Leahy's Norman Rockwell portrait of actual victims invited other Americans to identify with them, as they might not have with famous intended victims such as himself or news anchor Tom Brokaw.

Leahy told the public that good investigative work could only do so much. Regardless of the number of investigators, when looking for a needle in a haystack, every member of a national community who might also be the next unintended victim was needed. He worked to close a gap of consciousness in everyday American citizens between themselves and terrorism, while his political opposition urged Americans to realize that terrorists were after specific people who were symbols in the culture, and not people like them. Later in the month, Director of Homeland Security Tom Ridge characterized local people both as potential victims and potential collaborators with law enforcement.

FBI Director Mueller was less adept than Leahy when he called for public help in solving the case some weeks later. He renewed the call for assistance from a nonresponsive public by linking the FBI's lack of progress in the case to its quiet phone lines, a bad communicative move on his part. He appeared to be assigning responsibility for solving the case to the public rather than to the FBI. He appeared to be asking the public for help less because the public could be helpful than because the FBI was stumped. The schizoid social semantics of being both blamed and marginalized did not go down well. Responses to Mueller's call were wildly derisive, citing desperation, frustration, incompetence, and bafflement on the part of the agency. Negative descriptors for a bureau with an already deeply compromised image were colorful and varied. Most insulted FBI intelligence. The public clearly was not drawn further into the FBI's sphere of social cooperation. Even without awkward expression, Mueller already had the cultural wind against him. Relying on others for social support is a last ditch, not a default American social position, especially if you have a coldly powerful and secretive identity.

By early November, bureau officials had been "forced" to turn to scientific experts for advice on anthrax. Bearing mystique, a bad public relations run, and hit with a high-level crash course in biology, now there was also confession that they were figuring out what they were doing as they went along. But wasn't the FBI supposed to know everything? Few would imagine that the FBI could be intimidated by scientific experts, but now there emerged expert voices on the subject of anthrax, saying that the bureau was stubbornly ignoring what they needed to learn in order to investigate effectively.

Unaccustomed to not being the experts themselves, people in the bureau were vulnerable. The bureau's learning curve on the subject of public relations, while taking its biology course, was slow. The strongest outside voice was that of molecular biologist Barbara Hatch Rosenberg of the Federation of American Scientists, who regarded her ideas as having been discounted by the bureau. Her views were given unflattering characterization by the bureau in a shooting match in the press about who was right. Her advice, even after she had become frustrated, and even if "uninformed" from the perspective of the current disposition of the case, remained informed from the perspective of the scientific community upon which the bureau depended. Shooting back at her in the press only furthered conflict between the FBI and the public.

Another practice that set up a negative dynamic between the bureau and the public was the labeling of solicited advice from informed experts as unsolicited. Public ambiguity about giving help, and FBI ambiguity about receiving it, both evolved into additional ill will in the anthrax case. The bureau was not forthcoming initially in admitting its vulnerabilities in needing expert opinion on the scientific intricacies of anthrax, nor was it gracious in receiving it. Needing help filtered through an already detached social identity to make more relational trouble. The bureau's image of self-protective arrogance rather than an image of effectiveness was reinforced. People said that they loved America but hated the FBI, creating at least one notable breach in America's seamless new war on terror.

Things were no better in the FBI's relationship with Congress. The stone-faced agent who appeared before Senator Diane Feinstein on Thursday, November 8, 2001, in regimented response to her pointed questioning about how many labs there were in the country that could produce anthrax, said he did not know. Her visible anger was enough emotion for both of them. She flared in rage and disbelief, "You don't know!" He continued stoically, "No, we don't know how many." There was no elaboration, no clarification, no enhancement, no damage control, just "We don't know." On Saturday, the tenth, after a visit to the bureau on Friday, Feinstein appeared in the news again, with a large rough number to report and an understanding that there could be basement as well as standard labs. In the interim, angry reaction to FBI stoicism that appeared as arrogance had done nothing to promote an America unified against terrorism.

Thinking through the identity of the anthrax perpetrator is a worthy mental puzzle for mustering America's social imagination about itself. With the FBI's published profile as a tool to shape consciousness, what comes out? The perpetrator is angry. There was little doubt of that. The perpetrator is male. Statistically, one would expect that based on historical patterns, but it was perhaps not a bad place to reserve judgment. The perpetrator clearly had scientific background, but when questions about "ruses" in the writing, being a "lone wolf," or being an "American" arose, things got much more interesting.

While the "ruses" in the letters may have included a clumsy attempt to appear as a Muslim, and an effort to look dumb by spelling penicillin "penacilin," looking dumb is not always so smart. It would be dumb to pretend that someone who can handle anthrax cannot spell a simple related technical term. The misspelling may have been a stupid attempt in someone, otherwise smart, to appear dumb. Clearly, the question of whether the writer is dumb or smart has a complex answer, not a simple one. Perhaps, as the profile projects, the writer does not know how to use abbreviations. But if the writer is playing tricks on the reader, not using abbreviations could be a trick, too. The order in which the person writes dates says little, with many people varying the American and the European orders, depending on what they are writing and to whom. Where any ruses start or stop is not easy to tell.

Is the perpetrator a "lone wolf"? This one is more fun than a barrel of Americans. Alone to what extent? Could a lone wolf have some minimal connections to an organization sharing similar views? Could even a lone wolf be part of a formal conspiracy? Tim McVeigh's case remains a muddle along these lines. What counts as a social connection? What do Americans mean, exactly, when they say that another American is a loner, and how does that term condition responses to profiles? Would members of the public presume that they had had no contact with someone described in a profile as "lone"? Would Ted Kaczynski's Montana librarians have described him as a "lone wolf"? The concept of the "lone" terrorist in America is as stereotypical as it is precise, and "alone" is a common cultural category in America with a great deal more variation to it than the term itself implies.

"Alone" is a sliding scale, with all manner of gradations of degrees of contact between a perpetrator and others. A more sophisticated definition of what "lone" means could be a key to apprehending American perpetrators. It is a concept that profilers fooled themselves with in the Luke Helder case, and that may have confounded investigative thinking prior to 9/11. The confusion about the concept reflects general confusion in America about the relationship between the individual and society. Americans have a poor concept of where being alone stops and where being social starts. Being a loner is significantly different from being a hermit. If the anthrax perpetrator shunned human interaction, in what pattern, and to what extent?

Even Ted Kaczynski and Eric Rudolph both had some level of social contact with others, from stealing food to riding on buses. The application of the concept "lone" makes it difficult to envision the weirded-out neighbors, estranged friends, or distracted coworkers of the anthrax perpetrator, or any other American perpetrator. Dots cannot be connected until they are first found, and the first investigative job in finding the perpetrator is finding the links to the perpetrator. American "loners" who perpetrate terror count on the fact that nobody is paying attention to them, and American weaknesses of social perception play into their hands. Misperception of people who are working together as "loners" is a related problem.

Whether the anthrax perpetrator is an "American," as the profile projects, is a haunting question. Is an "American" someone with citizenship, someone with permanent residency, or someone who is a native speaker of English? Many citizens are not native speakers of English. Many non-citizen residents are. Could the perpetrator be an American who loves the Constitution, but hates the government? The possible variations are endless. The question of whether a perpetrator is "American" or foreign begs a definition of what those words mean. A homegrown citizen may have allegiances elsewhere, and the concept of American ethnicity is itself so diffuse that it is as misleading as it is helpful.

The profile, as a conceptual tool, should not be in charge, and one way for people to command their tools rather than the other way around is to understand the parts that the tools are made up of. One way to hone the process of profiling is to examine the social presumptions encoded into the profile's parts. On the subject of Americanness, for example, America is a composite of social diversity handicapped in its perception of its own members by a facile concept of its unity. The FBI faces one of the most dauntingly complex social equations on earth, the intricate complexity of the American social landscape.

The question of whether the anthrax perpetrator was not just an American, but also a government insider, further thickened the cultural plot in the anthrax case. As of June 2002, after thousands of suspects and interviews, millions of dollars, hundreds of polygraphs, over one hundred databases of information, and prods from scientific experts, a short list of names emerged. People on the list fit criteria of scientific training, knowledge of anthrax, and being male "loners" with a grudge against society. It was terrifying all over again just to think that there was a list of several Americans with that description. Fighting jackals is the domestic equivalent of guerrilla warfare. You cannot just try to find the enemy; you have to know the territory to win. The challenge intensifies again, because culture does not stand still, and cultural innovation gives the edge to the perpetrator. Profiles based on statistical projections from past patterns can point away from or toward the particular human being perpetrating terror today from any unlikely social location, which is all the more reason for the bureau to keep the public on its side.

Restructuring of the FBI was first announced in early December of 2001, with a new division of labor that would allow for a focus on terrorism and cybercrime. A new coordinator who would improve cooperation with local law enforcement would be drawn from local police chiefs. The question that remained was how far one coordinator could go toward creating systemic collaboration. Deficient skills in collaboration were a general problem in the anthrax investigation for a series of federal, state, and local agencies, including the Centers for Disease Control and Prevention but the perceptual focus remained on the FBI. Its public relations problems with experts, Congress, and local law enforcement boiled on, soon to be joined by internal turmoil with the advent of the Phoenix memo and the letter to Director Mueller from Minneapolis agent Coleen Rowley.

The FBI's top-down problems with local law enforcement and the public notwithstanding, some Americans were ready to communicate from the bottom-up anyway. Some everyday Americans beamed with pride at the idea that there might be something they could do to help in response to the anthrax threat, and were able to envision doing so without invading the privacy of fellow citizens. Their post-9/11 consciousness had shifted into a state of being able to make a positive impact on their culture. They were not thinking about citizenship or community membership as spectator sports. They were not thinking that they could afford to indulge themselves in hating the FBI. Although it has received relatively little encouragement, a sense of that kind of power in everyday Americans has emerged since 9/11.

Nobody in Helena, Montana had thought of that mostly isolated man up in the hills who strung trip wire as the Unabomber. The problem with he and other "loner" American terrorists is that they are so close to home that Americans cannot see them right under their own noses. Ask a group of Americans about what is going on next door, and you are likely to get mostly shrugs and vacant looks. They might want to know at least which of their neighbors do not want to be known. Setting out to know more about people around them might cause them to stumble over a terrorist, or maybe just find someone who could use their social support.

Soon, the "little guys" in the public who thought they might be able to have a positive impact on the FBI had a champion inside the bureau in Coleen Rowley. In the meantime, the trouble with the anthrax case, besides anthrax, was that it was an advanced exercise in American social perceptions of connection in a nation where most people needed Remedial Social Thinking 101. Many in the public wanted to know how to actualize their renewed sense of patriotism, and the FBI had to develop a learning curve, not just on anthrax, but also on relating to a public that it both serves and depends on for information. Social affiliation remains an underrated and underused weapon in the domestic war on terror.

MUSE, NOT HERO

The environment of challenge for the FBI intensified again as an FBI voice entered the national scene from within. Minneapolis agent Coleen Rowley conveyed to Robert Mueller what she thought he needed to know about pre- and post-9/11 disconnects in his bureau. From her field office, she fingered complacency, miscommunication, and disconnection at central. The impact of her criticism about neglected requests in the Zacarias Moussaoui case came to rest first at the headquarters desk of the head of the Radical Fundamentalist Unit, David Frasca, who had also received the Phoenix memo from agent Kenneth Williams about the flight school training activities of non-nationals. Then, it delivered charges of lack of organizational integrity directly to the desk of Director Mueller, himself. He not only received the charges. He was subject of some of them.

As a local agent close to a significant case who had the guts to speak truth to power, she had the post-9/11 cultural wind that favored the bravery of everyday Americans at her back. From the point of view of the public, the sunglasses came off. That same wind, though, ran her straight into big bureaucracy's gut reactions drawing it back into its familiarly comfortable secretive identity. The intense scrutiny that her cogent criticism created overloaded an already beleaguered bureau identity. She was too much of a shock to the system.

Her encounter with the media also worked against her cultural effectiveness. As favorably as she was portrayed as the American hero-of-the-day appearing before Congress, media coverage also negated her core message. America's best move with Coleen Rowley was not to make her into a hero, but to keep her as a standard working model for creating meaningful cultural change within the FBI. She risked her own self-interest on behalf of defending organizational goals, and that was American cultural news. She attempted to build communicative bridges between agencies by contacting the CIA, and that was American cultural news, although it violated the FBI's organizational rule book. She was a perfect model of a post-9/11 federal employee who was ready to build an accountable, flexible, collaborative federal culture. Once she became a sound-byte hero, though, she could be perceived as someone whose self-interest had been served. Even more importantly, she was perceived as an individual, someone who could be dismissed from fractionated American consciousness in not much more than a day.

She would have served better as a socially adopted example of a proper pattern of integrity of thought and action. Instead, her fame predestined her to rankle rather than reform. As gut-wrenchingly necessary as her actions were, they broke the first rule of FBI organizational culture: "Don't embarrass the bureau." In an already adversarially minded culture, the dichotomy that her performance drew between the honest down-home agent and the faceless self-consumed middle manager became a story of sensationalized conquest, instead of the morality tale of unification it was meant to be. She went to Washington and took it by storm, but her story in the American hero mold did nothing to create bureaucratic seamlessness. Having surmounted the disincentives to step forward did not translate into cultural leadership at the bureau.

Congress was enamored of the ethos of character her story generated, but commentary on FBI defensiveness, unwillingness to admit mistakes, and arrogance would not earn her points in the bureau, unless it was a bureau truly ready to face itself. Marginalized at headquarters in a culture of adversariality, her message was so dead on target that she rendered anyone without similarly superb aim into an enemy. Even though her arrow quivered right in the middle of the social target, many people entirely missed her point. Nor was there any time for her point to sink in. She was yesterday's news even before it was yesterday. Her bravura performance as a "little guy" illuminating a crippling, rather than enabling, bureaucratic structure was culturally upstaged on the same day by the biggest bureaucracy possible, the announcement of the plan for the Department of Homeland Security (DHS) by the president of the United States.

Was Coleen Rowley's story one of madness or integrity? Some styled her as a Cassandra, a mad prophetess doomed to be ignored, speaking unbearable truths in a culture with its own compromised sanity. Rowley's value as a model and a muse was in her message about integrity. If that message were mad, where was sanity in the culture that made it madness? Integrity was what post-9/11 America had told itself it was about, integrity in systems, integral seamless protection, and the moral fiber that would help deliver it. Integrity, whether in an individual human being or in a social system, is about fitting things together. It is about connections, results, and accountability, but America was unsure about the muse bearing the post-9/11 message.

One of Rowley's complaints was about the integrity of documents. An affidavit with multiple unattributed authors robs the depersonalized bureaucracy that creates it of a paper trail with informational integrity. No one person is identifiable as being responsible for the document. It becomes the product of a diffuse network, rather than of an integral human perspective. Extreme American individualism had allowed the work of one individual to completely subsume that of another through modification of affidavits, with the result that the work of both people was robbed of its integrity. Human dots cannot be connected, if they cannot be told apart in the first place. Informational dots cannot be connected, if the integrity of both the information and the human beings who provided it is not respected in movement across multiple desks of middle managers.

The House Select Committee on Intelligence, Subcommittee on Terrorism and Homeland Security phrased, in July of 2002, the need at the FBI to be one of ensuring adequate information sharing. The committee was right, but their focus was misleading. The core issue was ensuring adequate social connection of the human beings who generate information and move it, so that the information could be effectively shared. Intelligence systems need to be rooted in a cultural understanding that every human being in a bureaucracy is an integral information-processing system, interpreting and moving—or not moving—information according to how they see themselves as members of the culture. Coleen Rowley provided a case study of human integrity, which to some, looked like madness.

The seeress faded, some missing the point that Rowley was a loyal insider, and labeling her instead as a bureaucracy-buster in the mold of Erin Brockovich. In an individualistic, adversarial, and media-minded culture, the distinction between a critical loyal insider and an external adversary was too fine for some people to make. Making such a distinction would involve going back to Remedial Social Thinking 101, where Rowley would have to be appointed as a tough teacher and a muse of poetic social action, even if not a successful cultural innovator.

While Rowley, Mueller, and the entire bureau were eclipsed by the sheer size and centralization of President Bush's plan for the DHS, her internal FBI wake-up call still echoed the social clarion call that went up in post-9/11 American culture. Individual people count. They make a difference one way or the other, whether they choose to remain silent or stand up and speak. They cannot be ignored if bureaucratic structures are going to work. They have to be able to make a difference in bureaucracies, as long as individual terrorists have the power to make a difference. In the almost-obsessive focus on Rowley as an individual heroine created by a public and a Congress both starved for continuing stories of heroic character in post-9/11 America, she was immediately forgotten as a social heroine. The hundreds of e-mails and phone calls she had received from other FBI agents with stories similar to hers rapidly became a footnote in public consciousness, and apparently in bureau consciousness, as well.

Rowley did not, however, just go back to her quiet corner of the bureau. She warned again, in March of 2003, in tones that sounded more strained, that the bureau was not adapting to the new need to collect intelligence that could prevent future terrorist attacks. It remained highly focused on the prosecution of Zacarias Moussaoui and Richard Reid, instead of also regarding them as potential informants, a situation that left the country at increased risk from attacks that could come in retaliation to the war in Iraq. Perhaps what Rowley refers to as "Organized Crime/ Terrorism 101" bears a curricular relationship to "Remedial Social Thinking 101." A spokesperson for Director Mueller, while not addressing the specific content of her second letter, said in response that several steps had been taken to make the bureau more flexible and responsive. Mueller spoke of the bureau continuing to evolve, and Rowley talked about its cultural survival. They were both talking about culture, but it was a little hard to tell if they were talking about the same one.

August of 2002 brought both former U.S. Army bioweapons expert Steven Hatfill's denials that he was the anthrax perpetrator, and contradictory rhetoric from FBI agents about the bureau both being cooperative and having a closed culture. September of 2002 brought news of an outdated case management system, which had left the author of the Phoenix memo unaware of earlier reports about terrorist groups seeking aviation training. November of 2002 added a chapter to the Rowley saga, in the form of a bureaucratic shoe bomb on the other foot. Director Mueller, still expressing confidence that the bureau was reinventing itself, also had field offices that were not committing resources to headquarters' new goal of fighting terrorism. Field offices that had been ignored by headquarters were returning the favor. By February of 2003, the FBI was still one of the most wanted subcultures for bureaucratic change. Field offices were still not cooperating. Talking the talk of cultural change at the top, and walking the walk throughout the bureau were different.

Along with Rowley's reprise in March came more revelations and contradictions. An incredulous *60 Minutes* journalist Ed Bradley queried an FBI internal affairs agent about whether the wake-up call of 9/11 and Mueller's move to change the culture of the bureau had not had an effect. He received a resigned shrug about an intransigent culture in which incompetence was promoted, a double standard of discipline biasing against lower ranks still applied, and in which egregious misconduct negating organizational effectiveness, such as destroying completed work in order to make it appear that more staff needed to be hired, was still being reported by whistle blowers.

Part of the post-9/11 haze that remained in America in 2003 was created by the disconnect between such reporting and a renewed statement by Director Mueller that the FBI was working to understand every piece of information as part of a larger puzzle. The part of the larger puzzle of how to put the information together that involved improved social relations and communication within the bureau was apparently still substantially missing.

STOVEPIPES TO SEAMLESSNESS: A MYTH OF CULTURE CHANGE

A myth is not necessarily untrue. A myth is a story that informs a culture about what it is. It can come true, or not. There is a post-9/11 myth in America about creating seamless antiterrorist integration in federal bureaucracy. The reality will depend on whether people effectively enact the myth. Attorney General John Ashcroft said to the House Select Committee on Intelligence in July of 2002 that the government had created a "culture of compartmentalization" by separating intelligence gathering and law enforcement activities, and that it was time to get rid of the old cultural myth that foreign and domestic threats were meaningfully different. The new cultural myth with which he replaced the old one was that former divisions would be replaced with a bureaucratic "culture of cooperation," characterized by collaboration, with the DHS as the "institutionalization of the cooperation and coordination that is essential to our nation's security." Institutionalized cooperation and coordination would, in turn, produce a "culture of justice."

Asked in June of 2002 how effective the DHS would be in filtering intelligence and eliminating turf battles, President Bush responded that if the cultures of the agencies needed changing, we'd change them. That was a lot of culture, and a lot of cultural change. Effective change would have to be anchored in more than just myth. It would have to be actualized through taking human beings, their technology, social organization, and information handling, and drawing them all together in an integrated package, to produce true coordination. Creating collaboration between subcultures of already internally disjointed and "dysfunctional" individual agencies into a seamless overall structure would take much more than lip service to the concept of culture.

Confidence that the promised cultural change would consist of more than rhetoric was hard to find. With "dysfunctional," the American adjective of choice for intelligence bureaucracy, and communal impulses in the culture rapidly fading, the government became a focus for cynicism and as well as new levels of trust. Where the myth of collaboration would go under such circumstances was hard to know. When FBI Director Mueller said that FBI culture must change, the response in national news commentary was to ask how you go about changing culture. If the DHS's culture of collaborative seamlessness was to be built of units themselves in dysfunctional disarray, how, as a practical matter, could such titanic changes be achieved? The myth's expression in reality was doubtful.

Until radical individualism is addressed, even the notion of accountability cannot get to the heart of the matter of creating collaborative culture in America. American individuals employed in government bureaucracy will still be encouraged by the basic tenet of American culture directing them to focus excessively on themselves. The new megadepartment has to have a compelling cultural plan to rescript the consciousness of its members, realign the interests of individuals with updated cultural goals, and remotivate individual American workers within its ranks in new ways. It remains to be seen whether the myth of seamless bureaucracy in America will be realized, or the DHS will become the newest form of essentially aggregate, rather than collaborative, American government. As the example of the FBI illustrates, dictating cultural change from the top of an organization is not, by itself, necessarily effective.

If cultural change within one federal agency is difficult to achieve, change will be that much more difficult when the "top" is the entire federal government, and the "bottom" is citizens and local and state governments. In a May 2002 statement, Senator Bob Graham of the Senate Intelligence Committee asserted, as does the charter of the DHS itself, that the war on terrorism is going to involve the citizens of America. What cultural movements will be made, and by whom, to incorporate the public into a cultural concept of a seamless America that does not simply enrich the currently schizophrenic role of the citizen as passive victim or angry voter? In a culture where the citizens and the government are both averse to addressing each other directly, the question may be difficult to answer. The current specter of "threat fatigue" has to do in part with the quality of information provided in alerts, but in even greater measure with the brittle communicative relationship between the public and the government.

A public apprehensive both about terrorism and a lack of forthright communication; a neglected, disconnected, and psychologically threat-stressed public will not be part of a collaborative America united against terrorism.[7] Polls recorded a drop in the public's attention to the issue of terrorism within a year of 9/11, and unaddressed, the conceptual polarization between American citizens and the government will only increase, regardless of any level of collaboration that the government may achieve internally. Increased polarization will be good news for militia movements and bad news for workload at the FBI. On July 11, 2002, the power and prestige of American government reverberated as Secretaries Rumsfeld, O'Neill, and Powell, and Attorney General Ashcroft appeared in front of the House Select Committee on Intelligence, but the scene remained essentially reactive. Terrorists were still calling the atmospheric shots.

A key to sorting out the confusion surrounding the development of "seamless" antiterrorist social organization within the government is the concept "tribal." "Tribal" is a slang term in American government for localized small-scale organization, but the formal definition of the word is much more useful. The existing models of centralization vs. "tribalism" work against collaboration, and mistake the true nature of tribalism. The isolation of units of American government is a problem. The levels of coordination and trust between police and fire fighters responding to the World Trade Center on 9/11 were not optimal. The degree to which they did not successfully function as parallel structures requiring integration gives a flavor of the challenge America faces in changing its culture at any level.

A WorldCom executive described similar social organization in explaining the demise of CEO Scott Sullivan. He said that no single operating unit in the organization knew what was going on in the rest of the organization. The only place it all came together was at Sullivan's level. Central control of otherwise-isolated units does not produce robust communication. Central is too busy for that. But none of that is how tribal structure works. In tribal structure, local units communicate with each other.

On the other end of the continuum from isolated units that do not communicate is the model of strongly centralized control creating coordination. Centralized control does not necessarily create coordination, although that is the model that is the basis for the DHS. Flexibility and agility are actually more likely to be generated by connected decentralized units, as they are in cultures with tribal structure. When "tribal" is not American slang, it refers to organizations in which local units do communicate with each other. "Tribal" as a code word for isolated individual units has no capacity to help change American culture, and the "antitribalism" of strong central control is unlikely to change it either.

Instead of posing local and central as structural adversaries, with greater coordination resulting from central exerting more control and locals enjoined from communicating with each other, the answer to creating truly collaborative culture in American bureaucracy is to create centralization with a decentralized difference. Decentralization, on the individualistic model of the independent local unit doing what it likes and ignoring central will not work. In true tribal structure, communicative connections between units are robust, and a sense of autonomy in local units is balanced with a clear knowledge of their dependence on other units. Rebalanced relationships between the individual and the group is what American culture needs in general, and rebalanced relationships between constituent units and centralized control is what the structure of federal bureaucracy needs if is to become truly more collaborative in nature. Otherwise, the rule of the American individual will just keep taking over.

Models for true tribal structure are readily available. One of the cultures with tribal structure, in a poignantly relevant model for application in this case, are the Pashtun, an Afghani ethnic group, who are the majority ethnic group making up the Taliban. American sources too, such as the Brookings Institute and the Markle Foundation, have urged local autonomy and decentralization in the construction of antiterrorist American bureaucracy.[8] Connected decentralized units have a power that a centralized but constricted pattern of few connections and little communication cannot match. Even working on the scale of the U.S. federal government, you can still learn from an opponent who understands the power of decentralized flexibility, and should, when it is that opponent who has just beaten you. To cope effectively with an opponent who uses flexible tribal structure against you, you will want to take a cue and a clue from them. Tribal does not mean isolated. It means connected. Know your enemy. Know yourself.

Reorganization of units of federal culture, or "chair-shuffling" alone on any scale will not create cultural change. A different configuration of units made up of people using the same cultural presumptions as before will simply generate again America's traditional problems with communication and interaction patterns. Changing the size of the budget or the nature of the technology will not create changes in social modeling or behavior. Changes in social organization by themselves do not have the power to change culture. Nor is changing culture simply a question of how information is handled, even if information handling is a culture's central concern. Changes in culture are generated by what human beings think and do, in the context that is created for them by their tools, their resources, and their patterns of social structure.

Attempts to apply the myth of seamless bureaucracy to the culture of American intelligence based in traditional notions of individual self-service and strongly centralized control, rather than in cultural values rewritten to support communication and connection, will leave the myth a myth. American cultural rules must be taken into account in designing bureaucracies that are subcultures of American culture. Decentralizing, as well as centrally coordinating communication patterns by remotivating American workers toward the goal of decentralized coordination, would help to realize the myth.

Designing cultures where rules and social organization and information and technology are all integrated conceptually into a coherent, fluid entity by strategic human beings, instead of making changes in those subsystems in a piecemeal and stop-gap manner, would produce a cultural result that would move in the direction of effective integration. Without such thinking, the only predictable cultural result will be the continued application of the American rule of individual self-interest, and popcornlike results. Authentic tribal structure is very simple.

It capitalizes on individual initiative to create robust connections between units of social organization. It has eminent applicability to the current need for American cultural change, but America's cultural rules and existing subcultures work against it. It only has the myth in its favor.

Even recent decentralized managerial models of American corporate culture, designed to be "nimble" and "flexible," with corporate adversaries in mind, may not manifest themselves in a government application that can best address the elusive shifting threat of terror. Corporate America, even when it solves its own problems with individualism, does not face an opponent with a shifting and secretively elusive face. Another corporation is an opponent that you can always see coming. Any concept of culture identified with economics will also tend to pull American consciousness toward adversarial social modeling, and away from a strong departure into the realm of valuing the social connection, instead of regarding that connection more as a threat.

Fighting terrorism effectively will take strong cultural adaptation. The cultural response has to match the power of the diffuseness of the terrorist threat. The social organization of a culture of "collaboration" that focused on the power of each human actor within it to create social connection would most effectively outsmart and outmaneuver any scenario that terrorism could counter with. The level of flexibility required has to be enacted by people in a culture that does not just allow but encourages creative connection.

Individual initiative can create flexibility instead of chaos. Knowing when it is better to do things by the book, and when the book needs revision, is an art. Management cannot mandate the flexibility created by initiative, but can create a fertile environment for it. The career interests of individuals within the system have to be served by working creatively to connect dots, instead of leaving them unconnected, in a culture characterized by social passivity and a lack of information flow. Where unmitigated American self-interest rules, served by social isolation, American bureaucracies cannot achieve social cohesion, regardless of stated goals. The single most powerful rule, that the American self looks out for No. 1, is the No. 1 enemy. That rule is more monolithic than the DHS, and works against the initiative that will make it collaborative.

The rule creates bureaucracies in which chain of command pulls apart, instead of putting together. Translation up, or even down, the chain becomes impossible to achieve, as layers become blockades instead of conduits. A sense of obligation may only run upward, instead of also downward, as it should. In the Moussaoui case, the field agents who were closest to the situation, and who had integrity of experience with it, were disregarded. If central and the field have cracks between them, terrorists will easily get into those cracks.

If people like David Frasca do not perceive patterns in information that hits their desk three weeks apart, as with the Phoenix memo and the Moussaoui request, the terrorists will get into those cracks, too. The chain of command does not serve group needs when the unstated rule operating at each link is to serve the individual. Tightening discipline in the chain will help, but not reach the heart of the problem of achieving true collaboration, because selfish bureaucrats cannot catch either selfish American terrorists or well-organized decentralized non-American ones. Collaborative American bureaucratic culture can only be created by realigning the interests of American individuals to bring them more in accord with organizational goals.

Cultural reform rooted in executive authority is a model of cultural reform based essentially on the individual, rather than on social connection. When things are in doubt in an individualistic culture, the reflex is to move all of the responsibility to top and center. President Bush admonished Congress not to micro-manage his security initiatives in establishing the DHS by exerting any influence on the biggest reorganization of the federal government in over half a century.

In the super-sized microenvironment that President Bush created, he also took on the job of reorganizing structures characterized by distance and conflict, not simply cobbling together the cultures of separate agencies, but unifying them. But exclusive central control that leaves fiefdoms and turf untransformed, or attempts to eliminate them merely by brute force, will fail to create manifestations of a culture of collaboration and cooperation. The underlying social presumptions will remain individualistic, and the results will be individualistic.

An extremely centralized approach to culture change discourages effective collaboration by drawing emphasis away from the benefits of socially complex connections. Executive dictation of a culture of collaboration may not be an oxymoron, but it does put a premium on the existence of a clear plan for culture change, if the myth is to manifest. Security expert Bruce Schneier highlights the benefits of creativity and system resiliency in a decentralized social structure: "Security works better if it is centrally coordinated but implemented in a distributed manner."[9] Central cannot effectively dictate cultures of flexibility; it must instead serve to facilitate them, and if central does not model processes of collaboration and cooperation, the prospects for generating a culture of social connectedness are not good.

The primary mission of the Department of Homeland Security is to prevent terrorist attacks within the United States. One of its four divisions is "Information Analysis and Infrastructure Protection," and the department's stated goal is to "mobilize and focus" federal, state, and local governments, the private sector, and the American people to accomplish its goal. The integration of twenty-two agencies "containing over 100 bureaus, branches, subagencies, and sections—each with its own distinct culture," is a gargantuan task of cultural engineering.[10] That task, despite the rhetoric of cultural change, appears to have been largely unattended to.

The Brookings Institute has projected that the plan for the DHS is overly ambitious, possibly creating more problems than it solves, opining that agencies would be too proud to cooperate in an atmosphere created by employees trained for compartmentalization rather than sharing, and that joinings of the organizations would be volatile and jagged. The only operating model found by this author in personal contacts with employees of several federal agencies for the integration of organizational cultures as diverse as the Agriculture Department, the Coast Guard, the Department of Defense, FEMA, and the Department of Justice, was the pull of centralized authority over time. Not everyone was sure that even that model would work.

Comptroller General David M. Walker stated publicly that resistance to cooperation could take the government's counterterrorism capabilities backward. Members of Congress expressed concern about harmonizing different workplace cultures, at the same time they expressed hope that newly collaborative American bureaucratic culture would create responsive, agile, nimble, and cohesive bureaucracy to replace an outdated and calcified system. Although some government-sponsored conferences on homeland security take place in Las Vegas, there are no bets being placed on whether a culture of collaboration will be achieved.

It is time to go back to the subject of plumbing in America, this time not the installation of a simple bathroom faucet, but the wrenching of the biggest reorganization of the federal government in over a half a century. "Plumbing" is the metaphor of choice in government circles for discussing structural reorganization of bureaucracy. Bureaucratic plumbing has two dimensions, horizontal ("in and out"), and vertical ("up and down"). While social structure (or "plumbing") is only one element of culture, for those less skeptical than Senator Ted Kennedy, who criticized the move to establish the DHS by reducing it to the equivalent of rearranging deck chairs on the *Titanic*, the goal is to use reorganization to get from Type B to Type A bureaucratic cultures (see Table 1).

TABLE 1

CONTRAST TERMINOLOGY FOR BUREAUCRACIES OF TERRORISM PREVENTION*

CULTURAL TYPE A	CULTURAL TYPE B
collaboration	compartmentalization
cooperation	competition
communication	isolation
"outside the box"	"in the box"
"connect the dots"	turf
break down, go around, bridge	stovepipe (smokestack, silo)
flexible	entrenched
nimble, agile	calcified, ossified
interoperable	inward, secretive

* Terms apply variably to both social structure and information flow.

Source: Conference participants from government symposia and convention on Information Sharing and Homeland Security and Emerging

Technologies, Philadelphia (August 2002), Las Vegas (January 2003), and Philadelphia (June-July 2003), hosted jointly by the U.S. Intelligence Community, the Law Enforcement Community, the Department of Defense, Federal, State, and Local Agencies, and the Department of Homeland Security.

The two types emerge as clear concepts in the post-9/11 discourse of government conferees from the intelligence community, state and local antiterrorist concerns, the Department of Defense, the DHS, and similar organizations. The goal of collaborative integration is applied to improving interchange both horizontally and vertically.

According to the new cultural myth, along with the structural reorganization of the Department of Homeland Security, a cultural shift will also take place from Type B to Type A. While the concept of Type A culture is clear, it is used loosely, just as the concept of "community" is applied loosely within the American public (including its application to the "intelligence community"). What is unclear is how cultural movement from Type B to Type A is going to be achieved. How do you change culture? Some say, by force, but that will not work. Nor will changed social organization alone produce a cultural shift in America, where the skills of individual actors and individual bureaucracies at compartmentalization are legendary and entrenched. Opposed, those skills will simply recreate themselves in relationship to any new organizational structure.

Reorientation of cultural values, as well as structural redesign, is what is necessary to achieve real change. A bureaucratic culture of intelligence that can generate stories from as recently as 1999, about representatives of the FBI and the CIA who were unaware of so much as the existence of U.S. Army intelligence is a culture of prodigious compartmentalization facing a prodigious need for culture change.[11]

Larry Castro of the National Security Agency (NSA) observes correctly that even when an organizational basis for communicative collaboration is achieved, that does not mean that the trust or sense of community that will bring about communication are there.[12] Culture goes beyond plumbing, as well as beyond received ideology. In 2003, representatives of the FBI and of state terrorism task forces still gave an unqualified representation of the culture of Washington as one of competition and refusing to share information. They did not see any culture change occurring.

One FBI agent paid lip service to the idea of interagency collaboration at the same time that he claimed that the FBI was a "closed" culture, without even noticing the disconnect in his own speech. Some government insiders observed that achieving a cooperative culture in a single agency remained a significant challenge, let alone achieving the breadth of interagency cooperation intended for the DHS. The effective fusion of twenty-two component agencies into the DHS will clearly take time, but real questions also remain about the quality of the eventual result. Will bureaucratic relationships be characterized by flexible collaboration within the DHS and between it and its working partners, or will the effect be something more akin to separated territoriality?

While improved communication is easy to adopt as a new cultural ideal, it battles the prodigious weight of traditional turf consciousness and the perceived service to individual and organizational self-interest in not sharing information. The general behavioral response to information at the FBI and in law enforcement generally is to hold it, as though it were something with economic value—not to share it.[13] That impulse will be difficult to overcome. More than two years after 9/11, new reports indicated that the impulse still had not been overcome at the FBI. The inclination to withhold information also stems from a lack of trust in relationships, and differences in organizational cultures.[14]

Trust within American bureaucracies is no more elevated than elsewhere in American culture. Directives of central authority to collaborate cannot wipe away adversarial social modeling. Since sharing and competition do not coincide, the powerful American cultural rule about individual self-interest will have to be addressed before behavior will change. Until the competition model is exchanged for one that rewards social connection, isolated protectionism will remain a subcultural norm, regardless of rhetoric or reorganization. Getting from isolated social boxes to connected dots means not winning turf battles, but eliminating them as a concept with an operating model of cooperation. Organizational "stovepipes," a metaphor borrowed from the competitive world of business, are a federal bureaucratic plumbing fashion that is out, but there is no clear model of what is in.[15] Stovepipes can be broken down or gone around, but with what result?

In an individualistic culture, simply "breaking" stovepipes down will raise resistance unless other adjustments occur at the same time. Instead of being "broken," stovepipes should be reconfigured in ways that make communication between them attractive to their occupants. Without new patterns of communication viewed as beneficial, behavior will retrench, even within new structure. Culture will not change. Like American individualism, stovepipes are not going away, but they could be recreated of more porous material, with more connections between them, if an effective model for culture change is used in the retooling. The best idea is to build bridges between them.[16] Those bridges, themselves, should be flexible and shifting, based on shifting strategic advantages for members of the bureaucratic community and the public with changes in the terrorist threat. A model of flexible, movable bridges between units that serve the people who create them, as well as the goals of the group as a whole, is available from the Pashtun.

It is not only tribal people who understand the power of decentralized social organization. The Markle Foundation Report, *Protecting America's Freedom in the Information Age*, couples its focus on humans rather than technology as the core element in terrorism prevention with a clear recommendation that a flexible organization of local units, with its "front lines outside of Washington," should be empowered to provide local expertise to a responsive central.[17] As threats emerge from previously unidentified sources, a decentralized structure with symmetrical patterns of cooperation and communication between central and constituent units will have more power to flex. The report cautions that the DHS-based counterterrorism plan is too centered on Washington, recommending that intelligence analysts rotate between agencies as a way to promote flexible bridges between separate agencies.[18] The authors of the report view the key to effective decentralized structure as teamwork, so that "separate fiefdoms" do not fight over "limited turf, money, and power," or information.[19] Generating that level of cultural change will require tremendous social integration.

The American public has not found the pace of that integration thus far very hopeful. While the technological coordination of databases necessary to coordinate twelve terrorism watch lists held by nine different agencies is complex, members of Congress, the public, and the Brookings Institute all called for more speed two years after 9/11. At the same time, a question about data base coordination at a government conference on terrorism was met with the response that an integrator would have to do that job someday. Thinking about technological integration, much less the social integration that would support its creation, seemed not to be a foremost concern. The answer to the question was individualized, and the time frame invoked was later.

The centrality of the position of the DHS, working in effective horizontal cooperation with the "intelligence community" is also not a foregone conclusion. An observation in the June 2002 *Newsweek* was that the planners of the Department of Homeland Security had not consulted with significant players in the intelligence community while planning. That lack of modeling of collaborative culture may have elicited distinctly non-collaborative responses. Commentary, a year later from government insiders, was that members of the intelligence community regarded DHS people as lacking knowledge about intelligence, a view that was hardly a foundation for cooperative relations. If intelligence agencies play, in relation to the DHS's central, a role similar to the one independent FBI field offices play with respect to FBI central, the cultural dynamic created by the DHS will not become flexible, centralized responsiveness.

The DHS will become instead more like a conductor trying to run an orchestra with a pit full of reluctant musicians. Even with intelligence agencies eventually "absorbed" into the DHS, questions about the quality of collaborative relationships within it will remain. The DHS can become effectively central or ineffective, if ignored by its constituent agencies. New architecture and more resources do not guarantee a more effective response to terrorism. The quality of relationships, as well as the quantity of resources, is part of the overall puzzle to be solved.

While it may be difficult for many Americans to mount an image of the FBI or CIA as the "little guy," the DHS will also have to take into account the human dimensions of interacting with "little guys," like the FBI. Human behavior can still trump the models of bureaucracy in which it is generated. Big little guys can ignore central just like small ones can.

Post-9/11 American culture told Americans about the power of the "little guy" to be a hero, and found in those stories a revitalization of national identity in the wake of the attack. Whether that revitalization will be incorporated into crafting the government response to terrorism is doubtful, and some of the little guys in government are pretty big.

Up and down relationships in which the DHS is superordinate have also not been characterized by the robust sense of human connectedness that flooded the nation after 9/11. Some officials at top levels of government work mightily to diffuse information downward, but an "asymmetrical threat" still cannot be effectively met by a fundamentally asymmetrical information flow, with an extreme imbalance between information going up the chain from local and state agencies to federal bureaucracy and what comes back down. Collaboration is a two-way street. Representatives of over a half million police officers, while proud to point out that Tim McVeigh and Eric Rudolph were apprehended from among their ranks, feel as though they rank themselves as an afterthought in federal discussions of homeland security.[20] Even the tracking of panels in the structure of government conferences on homeland security keeps law enforcement and central federal bureaucracy apart. Police officers do not sit on the same panels with DHS personnel.

Three stories about the relationship of the "little guy" to the DHS give a flavor of how up and down relationships continue to function mostly in a downward rather than a collaborative fashion. They are not stories that Americans are telling themselves about themselves that affirm the power of everyday humanity.

The first story is about the intensive debate in Congress over the status of 170,000 federal workers who would become employees of the DHS. The position interpreting their individual worker's rights as a potential threat to bureaucratic flexibility prevailed. President Bush won on the point of subsuming the individual rights of workers to the flexibility needed in pursuing the national mission of homeland security, but the lingering question in the story was with what impact on their self-image and their performance as workers in relationship to organizational goals. The DHS is not a desirable place for Americans who have an acutely felt sense of their individual powerless. While the government has more flexibility in dealing with them, they may well not become the American work force that is motivated toward collaboration and creative, innovative, assertive ideas. The tradition of cultural passivity in the American individual might be reenacted right in the center of the nation's response to terrorism, instead of the DHS being a culture from which nimble flexibility emerges.

The second story is about air marshals. In the view of some, they provide a first line of defense against terrorist attack. Less than a year after 9/11, though, there were reports of air marshals with long hours, low pay, and prohibition against unionization. By October of 2002, air marshals shared headlines on the same day with the beltway sniper, in two different themes on American alienation. Morale problems among the marshals were more serious than had been acknowledged by the Department of Transportation. Some were reportedly calling in sick in order to get a day off.[21] The frenzy of antiterrorist sentiment at higher levels in the bureaucracy had not allowed for sufficiently humane treatment of employees situated on the front lines to help keep them effective in their work, not a good sign for security, the marshals, or the nation. Personally, I like the doctors who treat me to be rested, happy, and healthy. I like my air marshals the same way.

By July of 2003, the Transportation Security Agency was proposing to cut back this human resource-based program, for relatively insignificant economic gains in relation to expenditures for technological resources. Rapidly on the heels of the proposed cut came new warnings from the government about possible hijackings, and then anxious responses from the public about mixed messages from the government. Amidst Congressional outcry, the DHS stepped in and said that the program would not be cut back. There still would be, though, delays in the training of future marshals, as a budget balancing measure. Maintaining and shepherding human resources was clearly not a strong focus in the overall context of fighting terrorism.

The third story is about orange alerts. In theory, they pull America together in the face of terrorism. The story seems to have more to do with pulling it apart. Besides commentary on the adverse psychological effects of alerts that do not provide specific information, orange alerts also brought disconnects in the up and down dimension of homeland security into clear relief.[22] When state and local agencies do not receive enough specific information to make intelligent responses from their situated perspectives and with their limited resources, there are adverse effects on the overall "enterprise architecture" of homeland security. That architecture becomes less, rather than more collaborative in nature. Without the funds necessary to support full-fledged responses to the alerts, locals were left in a position where their practical option was to cultivate disconnection. Federal directives were not based on sufficiently collaboratively thinking to appreciate the human effects of long or double shifts on local workers. Effective collaboration requires being able to appreciate the other person's point of view.

The police chief of Phoenix, Harold Hurtt, prominently quoted in the July 2, 2003 issue of *USA Today*, said that in response to the first high alert he had gone "full bore," putting people on long shifts and canceling time off.[23] He concluded later that he could not respond fully to alerts just because Washington said so, unless there were a direct threat to Phoenix itself. He and other chiefs were frustrated by the lack of specific information in the alerts. Other city and state officials were also frustrated and fatigued. Some would work to develop regional warning systems. The problem from a tribal organizational perspective with such initiatives was that independently generated regional systems would be neither part of the formal architecture nor linked to one another. There would be no centralization and no decentralized coordination, only localization.

Even if Hurtt and others made a curtailed response to a federal alert, going to a "lighter shade of orange," the frustrations of insufficiently precise information to assess local threat still built, along with the frustrations of the public. Frustration built. Collaborative culture did not. Federal cards were held too close to the vest for the effective social incorporation of either the American public or first responders in the field, and certainly too close to support an ethos of more open communication. A culture of information sharing continued to be trumped by a culture of information holding.

There was talk among police chiefs, in the absence of realistic plans for tailoring responses to existing resources, about not responding to orange alerts. While director of Homeland Security Tom Ridge was hopeful that states would "think twice about not doing something" in response to alerts, that low level of response on his part offered scant hope for enacting cultural change. By August of 2003, some very high-level locals, a group of state governors, tasked Ridge on the subject of the overly generalized nature of the warnings. His response was to decentralize information by expanding by five the number of people in each state who could receive information, a quantitative response to a qualitative problem.

SO WHAT?

The "So What?" test in America's intelligence community is a test of whether information is important enough to pay attention to. The "So What?" test for the American public is whether establishing the DHS will make enough difference in the government response to terrorism for them to pay attention to. That question is part of a larger question about whether America can respond collaboratively within itself to the challenges of terrorism. The public is not enacting its new levels of social trust. Up and down, or in and out, the creation of collaboration in the government remains in doubt. The concept of creating a cultural system in which America meaningfully enhances patterns of connections between people is so big conceptually that it is hard to get one's mind around it, even when it applies only to the government. Add the public, and the idea dwarfs the DHS, which is actually just one small piece of the overall puzzle. American national character is supposed to respond well to big challenges. It has never been tested at this level of magnitude before.

Bill Gertz is right in asserting that it is "crucial that the American people understand . . . detecting pieces of a terrorist plot is extremely difficult."[24] Intelligence agencies are by definition out of control of situations from the outset. Finding out about plots and gaining control is an extremely high-level task. Understanding that difficulty can help the public retain a sense of connection to people in their government who are trying to solve the mythically huge problem of terrorism prevention. Mythically huge problems evoke cultural myths, and the American myth of post-9/11 cooperation needs to be pursued. A sense of "interoperability" between citizens and government will prevent movement of the public to extremes of critical hostility or cynical despair. Interoperability is the concept that reflects the ability of different agencies to communicate with one another, a key factor in producing a coordinated response. It is a term with a transferable meaning.

The difficulty of the task at hand is also a reason that those in the government should involve citizens in antiterrorism for criticism, suggestions, and social solidarity, as well as for information. Citing the difficulty of the task should not be a shield to hide behind, but an occasion to build collaboration. Without a vision of the whole cultural cloth, the pattern in which officials seek terrorists, citizens experience anxiety, and some Americans choose to become terrorists—the problems of relating the parts of the whole will remain intransigent. Detecting the pieces of a terrorist plot is difficult, and detecting the nature of the cultural context in which America fights terrorism may be even more difficult yet.

Have the post-9/11 symbolic shifts in America's identity survived in any meaningful way in creating the new bureaucracies of antiterrorism? (1) Has faith in technology been supplanted by faith in people? (2) Is trust in community running ahead of trust in financial resources? (3) Has post-9/11 American culture changed in ways that will be maintained, or did America mislead itself after 9/11 that something of cultural significance had happened? Let's look.

Technology and humanity. Despite compelling work on the importance of the human factor in security and the post-9/11 renaissance of faith in the human being, expectations about reorganizing federal bureaucracy have moved inexorably back toward defining technology as closer to the core of a cultural system than people. America's technological needs in fighting terrorism are prodigious, but also misleading. The emerging assumption in government circles is that the coherence necessary to fight terrorism will come from technological coordination. The focus of spending on research is on technology rather than people. People receive homage as an important part of the overall system, but not concentrated attention. Only 20 per cent of the presentations slated for a 2003 conference on government knowledge management touch significantly on the place of human users in relation to "netcentricity," emerging technology, and "agile data," and one of them focuses on the fragility of the human communities that relate to and through a high-tech environment.

Technological and informational coordination, like changed social organization, is only one piece of solving the larger cultural puzzle. Dependence on technology produces a consciousness that excludes the role of humans in promoting solutions. People need to be brought together, as well as their computers. For example, biometric identification is optimized when technologically generated results are also checked by a human observer.[25] Security system specialist Bruce Schneier cautions against the idea of technology as a cure all, noting that the American tendency to regard it as a "magic bullet" does not create effective security systems: "The trick is to remember that technology can't save you . . . You always build the (security) system around people."[26]

The most telling commentary on America's cultural focus on technology at recent government conferences on homeland security came from views from outside America, from India, Israel, and the UK. Non-American police personnel repeatedly stated that it is people to people connections that win the war on terror. The UK's Special Branch creates a human, not a technical, link between national databases and local communities of citizens and first responders. The countering cultural mythology in America to that solution says that the scale of the U.S. system is so great that technology must substitute for humans in making linkages. That myth battles against, and helps prevent the realization of America's new cultural myth of seamless collaboration. Machines alone cannot produce cooperation, and thinking that they do can rob you of it.

The most convincing plea for retaining a sense of humanity at the core of the war on terrorism came from Israeli representatives. Nobody would have a finer-tuned sense of the intimate connection between humanity and terrorism than Israeli security personnel. Rafi Ron, former director of security at Ben Gurion airport in Tel Aviv, and director of security at Boston's Logan airport, admonished in January of 2003 that what was at the bottom of antiterrorism was the human factor. Technology was important, but the human factor was basic. Yaakov Preger, deputy head of the Jerusalem bomb squad, briefed his American colleagues in July of 2003, first on the historical and technical details of suicide bombing, and then on his antiterrorist focus: "Technology is good. Technology is nice, but technology is supposed to assist you. It's about people."[27] Those on his staff personally responsible for defusing suicide bombers would doubtless echo his sentiment.

Terrorism degrades humanity, and its primary combatant is human beings, equipped, of course, with the appropriate tools. Right after 9/11, Americans and the culture they generated were close enough to the human truth of terrorism to realize that. Now, they are forgetting that a culture with people at the core of its structure is most effective in solving a human problem.

Money and community. The maintenance of a sense of community, in relation to thinking in terms of money, is even less apparent than a focus on people. With the framework for thinking about value in government circles often being how much money is spent on something, in an America where people are often valued in relation to the size of their paycheck rather than their character, it is not just that Americans put their money where their mouth is. The cultural effect is stronger than that. Where American money is, is where the American sense of value is bestowed, creating a steep uphill battle for building a consciousness of community in a materialistically oriented culture. When the interests of community are at odds with the economic values of company profit, America comes down on the side of money. There is no new cultural process in place that will allow the interests of national security to outrank those of a company producing security-related products. Such a company, facing an opposing product with clearly superior technical specifications, will not think about community. Their move instead will be to launch a disinformation campaign about the other product, in self-interest. Nobody in the "losing" company can withdraw the inferior product and survive. They still have to fight for the government contract. The system does not have a provision for serving community.

While the prospects of collaborative cooperation in American bureaucracies are thin, the prospects for common interest making any inroads into private concerns related to security issues are thinner yet. The post-9/11 symbolic shifts in America from technology and money to humanity and community are in a distinctly fast fade in government responses to terrorism, instead of America having been changed forever on those trajectories.

The concept of culture, a concept that was everywhere right after 9/11, including in reference to government reorganization, is also fading. Culture wars carry on, and culture remains indispensable at Ground Zero, but many in government have discerned that their concept of culture is vague and begun to drift away from it. Some express overt discomfort with the term. As powerful as the idea of culture is, without a grip on the concept and its usefulness, it has begun to be sidelined. While people from the FBI, the NSA, and the DHS still invoke the concept of culture and the need to change it, that does not imply that they can define it or specify how they think it should change. Appearance of the word "culture" in a conference track or a panel title does not mean that the subject receives any systematic consideration. It just sounds good.

The Brookings Institute made a semantic slide away from culture in its seminars for the executive education of senior government officials. A training program scheduled for May of 2003, "Managing the DHS Merger" had several straightforward topics, including explorations of political challenges, organization change, and agency reform. The topic involving culture in organizations "Working with Culture: The Way the Job Gets Done in Public Organizations," was the only one presented in quotation marks, creating a kind of question mark around the solidity of the subject. By summer of 2003, executive education at the institute dealt with culture, but only in historical and contextual terms. The American past, and the larger context of American culture were still on the agenda, but the concept of organizational culture had disappeared.[28] Similarly, "culture" was a concept defining a track in a government conference on homeland security in 2002. By 2003, it was gone.

Without definition or operationalization into action for change, the concept of culture began again to become mysterious, but it did retain its power as a fetish. A fetish is something people believe to have magical power to protect and aid its owner. Belief in fetishes is not rational, but it is potent. In post-9/11 American government culture, the fetish was not an object but a concept—culture. It was used, but not rationally defined. Its use instead became a ritual invocation that made people feel better. They did not have to understand it. They did not have to define it, even if they were making a presentation about it. They did not have to develop a plan for doing anything to change it, as they would with social organization or technological needs. Using the word, though, made them feel like they were discussing an integrated human system. Beyond invocation, culture was apparently to be depended on to take care of itself. The concept of culture provided one more form of post-9/11 solace. It became the conceptual equivalent of comfort food.

In a fetishized form, even when people talk about culture, they do not really believe that they can change it. Senator Bob Graham did not know whether cultures of law enforcement and intelligence collection could be blended. They could, with a clear model of how to integrate them, but Senator Graham's tentativeness was as much rooted in an unclear concept of culture as it was in the two subcultures. Culture, since knowledge of it is mostly rote, works against intentional change unless it is excavated cognitively and engineered consciously. Contemporary American culture cannot be built on a ritual object. A more rational approach, in which culture is defined, examined, and consciously adjusted, with its principles applied to human relationships, is required.

When culture was not being worshipped in government circles, it was being busted. High-level DHS officials spoke about culture taking a long time to "break down," supposedly along with the stovepipes. The metaphor was wrong. Traditional American bureaucratic culture is not going to go away or break down. It needs to be modified instead. Without transformation, it will simply recreate itself in variations on its traditional form. Ideas about destroying or eliminating subcultures are overdrawn, themselves mired in adversarial thinking. Working with an existing culture to change it will have much better results that trying to break it.

Indications from members of the emerging culture of the DHS in 2003 did not point in the direction of achievement of a Type A cultural environment. They said either that the DHS had no culture, or, in perfect postmodern style, that the culture of the DHS was different for everyone who was in it. Radical differentiation of thought is exactly what is supposed to be avoided in cultures of collaboration. An official from the new DHS gave a presentation in which people were cast as part of a material structure, rather than central to the enterprise at hand. People were identified as the first element of "infrastructure," ahead of buildings and networks of financial resources.[29] Technology and information were what was at the heart of things. While the person doing the defining was perhaps simply higher in the infrastructural social hierarchy of the new culture than the ones to whom she referred, the dehumanization inherent in relegating people, and not just their communication patterns or their social organization, to being a component of infrastructure did not bode well for a future of collaborative communication. In anthropology, the concept of culture is holistic and centered on people. It includes their resources, their technology and material culture (including infrastructure in the more narrow sense of physical resources), their social organization, their economic and political power relations, their beliefs and symbols, and their patterns of communication. It incorporates their rules for behavior and their actions, which sometimes do and sometimes do not conform to those rules. All of culture, though, belongs to them. They are not part of a material metaphor. They are in command of the entire system. Everything listed above has to be understood as a whole pattern in order to apprehend the nature of a culture.

After 9/11, it was holism that Americans sought, and the culture concept provided it, but it can only keep providing it if culture is understood and crafted, and not simply invoked as an object of worship. The concept of culture can help Americans keep a focus on building durable trust in human relationships, but only if they use it with intention and discipline, and not as a magical belief. There is magic in American culture, including the magic in baseball, but magic is a poor basis for construction of the federal government.

There are some whiffs of authentic cultural change in post-9/11 government. Those who observe that information sharing, a central value in evolving bureaucratic culture, has technical, organizational, and behavioral components are barking up the right tree. They are connecting the dots that make up a culture. Put together the human focus with the technical and the structural, and you are on the way to having a concept of culture you can work with to create change. American self-interest is not going away at the behest of a central authority with the power to bust culture and break stovepipes. It has to be tempered into producing new behaviors, in the context of modified reward and motivational structures that encourage social connection. To achieve that, though, workable formulas for improving social connections and trust within the government will have to be developed and applied.

Such formulas will have to not only be developed, by also successfully deployed, if American government is to create a culture of trust and model it to the American public. The government has excessive individualism within the Americans who comprise it to battle, along with terrorists. The public, too, needs to be participating in the development of its own internal social connections. A public that quickly perceptually separated surviving relatives of victims of 9/11 into a new American minority group still needs work on its consciousness of American community and its practices of social connection. If both developments transpire, restructuring individualism and enhancing social connection in both the public and the government, then the groundwork will have been laid for long-term increased trust between them. Then, America will have been changed forever by 9/11.

One of the social connections between the government and the public is that the public watches. The government is not just in a position of authority. It is also in a position of cultural leadership. Modeling social cohesion and authentic culture change, the government could help discourage the dynamics that support terrorism in American hearts and minds. Tim McVeigh reminded America, quoting Justice Brandeis, that the government is an "omnipresent teacher" of the American people.[30] Justice Brandeis was right. A teacher with a positive model to present will have fewer problem pupils like Tim McVeigh. The government as teacher freely chooses its own curriculum. It can send messages that little people do not count and big bureaucracy does, or it can send messages that continue to revitalize the post-9/11 positive sense of the American self with true cultural reform. America's culture of conflict needs modification into at least the beginnings of an American culture of cooperation, if there is to be progress on the elusive attacks of terror on America's heart. If "So What?" levels remain prohibitively high, both in responses to patterns of information in the American intelligence community, and in America's perceptions of its ability to adapt culturally to crisis, the jackal will continue to have the upper hand.

CONCLUSION

REGENERATION

PHOENIX GAMES

Culture of concealment, culture of despair, culture of extremism, culture of selfishness, culture of violence; people have noticed that American culture has problems. They want them replaced with a culture of alertness, a culture of collaboration, a culture of justice, a culture of responsibility, a culture of service, and a culture of vigilance. Culture change can regenerate America. Culture wars, as typically American as they are, cannot. Culture wars do not get to the root of America's cultural problems. America is full of culture. There is media culture, popular culture, minority cultures, academic culture, regional culture, political culture, occupational culture, and other cultures, all of which play a role in shaping the generalities of American culture. At the core of American culture, though, is the individual. Solving problems created by extreme individualism by continuing to use America's initial responses to 9/11 can take culture change from rhetoric to reality, creating constructive transformations in America. America needs desperately to secure not just its borders, but also its sense of identity.

Culture is what you chose to cultivate. While some think that a successful response to 9/11 has already been made, with a resilient nation now stronger and more unified, the story is not over, and the picture is not that pretty. If America is to become independent of fear and the extreme individualism that feeds American extremism, and more unified in the face of terrorism, it still has a turnaround to achieve. America has a course of therapy for anxiety to finish. The images of the culture, changed after 9/11 to focus on humanity, in defense of a cultural world view that had been attacked, have to be kept. They have to be combined with changed assumptions about the nature of American reality, that it knits together over time, and that dots can be connected into meaningful mental and social systems. Those images and changed assumptions then have to be activated with modified cultural rules for behavior, rules that relieve an extreme focus on individual self-interest and replace it with values that reinforce constructive social connections that serve the other as well as the self.

American freedom and independence must be made to work for instead of against American culture. Practically speaking, they make it vulnerable to terrorism. American citizens and government have to work to square openness and vulnerability with a sense of security, a new American cultural configuration. Draconian laws combined with complacent citizens cannot achieve the needed change. Instead, American independence to recognize American weaknesses must be used to fight the psychological war on terror, by cultivating American social strength on a daily basis. Americans face more than terrorists. They face a loss of confidence in the moral and social integrity of their culture, and in themselves as effective individuals within it.

If America retains its renewed focus on the power of humanity, it can build something stronger out of injury. To achieve that growth, denial of America's cultural problems must be replaced with a commitment to fight terror indirectly, as well as directly, by changing the American social environment. Fighting domestic terrorism from the social ground up is as good a place as any to start addressing America's cultural problems, the disillusionment, complacency, and violence that work to tear it apart from the inside out. If 9/11 cannot become a touchstone for transforming American culture, it is difficult to imagine what will. Terrorists may not have won in America, but they also have not lost.

Going through a "gate of fire" purifies body, spirit, and soul. UN Secretary General Kofi Annan's reference to 9/11 in a statement that the third millennium had been entered through that gate applied to humanity as a whole, but the fires of that flame burned brightest in America. Both the phoenix and the jackal have been at work in America since 9/11. The jackal has anthrax, snipers, scandal, and fear in its service. The phoenix has a renewed faith in the power of collective humanity.

The phoenix seldom makes the news, but it has been there symbolically in the World Series, in the 2001 New York City Halloween parade, in a restructured Pentagon, in painfully rejuvenating FBI memos, and in the bounce-back toy craze of the 2001 holiday season, the dropper popper. If ever a toy was made for a fledgling phoenix, it was the rebounding resilient repeating popper. It bounced higher than it was dropped, every time. Americans should do more than catch elusive glimpses of phoenix plumage in the cultural environment. They should see it everywhere. They need to move themselves to counteract terror in the heart of the culture, and heal America into a reinforced vision of itself that will insulate it from the psychological impact of future terror. People who live in cocoons and fortresses are not free, even if their cultural ideology tells them that they are.

Literal regrouping is what it will take to combat domestic terror in America. American consciousness regrouped after 9/11, with a search for updated American identity in mental time travel and long-term thinking. Once upon a cultural story, America gained independence. It took that independence, and a couple of centuries, and ran freedom straight to an extremist conclusion of hyperindividualism. Blasted out of that position, there is only one intelligent way to move—to use independence to chose interdependence, and to connect time, people, dots of information, and America's understanding of itself as both weak and strong. The visceral impact of 9/11 brought America screaming back from a technologized, bureaucratized, and cerebralized sense of itself—to a grounded, pained, and embodied one.

Like Ground Zero, that sense of America is a place to linger. Americans started looking for depth and comprehensive understanding instead of disconnected sound-bytes that did not fit together into a discernible pattern. Even as the American news screen continued to shift with traumatic images of murder, corruption, terror, and predation, together with their collective seduction back into a fragmented consciousness of despair, America also began to mentally recover. Cultural tectonic plates shifted, but toward an unknown future configuration. Stravinsky's *Rite of*

Spring would have been fine accompaniment for early 2002. Even as the public lost its sense of active involvement in antiterrorism, and some in government culturally overcorrected by connecting potential terrorist dots so tightly that American civil liberties came in question, the FBI Phoenix memo emerged along with Agent Coleen Rowley's painful truth-telling performance and the biggest of possible bureaucratic reforms in the shape of the Department of Homeland Security.

The cultural marching orders for regeneratively inclined Americans are to keep a sense of connected consciousness, and not go back to the indulgence of treating issues or individuals as radically separate from one another. The consciousness of connection that exploded in America right after the Twin Towers came down can continue to heal America. America just has to keep it. Citizens need to start feeling what needs to be done in America and doing it, instead of depending on their government to tell them to do it. The government needs the citizenry as an active force as it faces prodigious threat, both as a support and as a counterbalance.

Everyone has the ball in their possession. Individuals can revive their sense of being able to do something in America by doing it. Support a problematic classmate, and perhaps prevent the next domestic jackal from emerging. The classmate will have support either way. Take any American horror story on the news, and do what can be done to prevent something like it from happening in your neighborhood. Insist that positive stories also appear on the American news. Educate children about safety. Offer help to someone who is mentally or socially troubled. Instruct tomorrow's leaders about ethics. Make your social surroundings into a neighborhood. A sense of community will begin to emerge from any of these acts.

Work to combat the alienation that produces American terrorists and other American pathologies, and watching the news will be less traumatizing afterward. No matter its content, it will not create the same feeling of helplessness. Anxiety will be held at bay, in the face of post-traumatic growth. Stop accepting the idea that more Americans will try to bomb or shoot their way out of utter frustration, and work to prevent it instead. The answer to the question of how 9/11 fit into the rest of American experience was that it did not. The question is better posed the other way around. How is the rest of American life to be redefined because of 9/11? While the hyperbole of "changed forever" misled, it did point in the right direction. Americans can move culturally in the direction of the jackal or the phoenix. They are free to choose.

CULTURAL RECOVERY

Recovery. Restoration. Rejuvenation. Regeneration. They all sound good, but where can America get some? None of it can just be ordered up. It has to be made. Using adversity to become better than you were before you took a hit is not easy. In this case, a culture of individualism has to go through a painful crucible of self-examination, reorient its ideas about freedom and independence, and have its members find the will to change their behavior. Keeping a post-9/11 grounded, connected, and integrated sense of American culture is the antithesis of addictive tendencies to American terrorism and pathologies of extreme individualism. Celebrating American strength alone will not develop regenerated consciousness, address America's cultural weaknesses, or guide it to a cultural destination where it is changed forever by having confronted the terror within and done something about it.

After the Unabomber caused an explosion in my life, I had to turn him on his head, and come to grips with myself in order to heal. Both of those steps were necessary. I had to make my encounter with him into a story that did not blow up my consciousness about my own culture. A story is, after all, a nontechnological human tool for recreating ourselves. I was soon left with a haunting portrait of the essence of a culture composed of the Unabomber, the American bomber I had known, myself, and the three hundred million potential terrorists and victims around me. The story still unfolds. Americans can use 9/11 to keep healing their culture with stories that focus on the positive power of human beings, or they can keep making pathological connections with one another.

Positive stories can vanquish the spirit, as well as the fact, of terrorism, by beating it back from its goal of producing fear. Such stories will not be just about catching bad guys. They will also be about creating a social environment in which "good guys" are less likely to go bad, and in which their violence is less of a cultural expectation. The Unabomber, privileged, isolated, and tortured by his own gifts into violence, is still too apt an icon for American culture. The culture needs a different formula for describing itself. American national character needs an adjusted profile.

Unity requires being able to think about union, to understand how a system fits together, and that every human being is a unified system with integrity. Fellow Americans are not their component parts, faceless bureaucrats, obstructions in front of us in line or on the road, "nuts" to be dismissed, or celebrities to be deified. They are multifaceted human beings, each working from their own American configuration. Recognizing human integrity on a daily basis begins to counter the dehumanization that infuses the spirit of terrorism. It also provides the building blocks for thinking about complex social systems. People who recognize the multifaceted power of people working in complex systems do not have to bomb. They can envision multiple forms and pathways of human causality. Bombing is only necessary when human sacrifice fulfills a need to make one overriding violent social connection.

Throwing the American cultural system into the complex connectedness of myriad acts of social affiliation every day can shrink the habitat for the jackal clan. Creating positive connections in American culture is phoenix business. It promotes healing. Put your feet in a line, your money in a tower, or your faith in people standing alone instead of together, and you are much easier to knock down. Widen the stance, diversify the thinking, and broaden the base, and you are harder to topple. Budget lines and new bureaucracies of whatever size can only do the cultural job called for in America in a cultural context where human integrity is the "bottom line" of any human system. America's most underutilized cultural resource remains the social consciousness and will of American people. Americans do have much more power to change American culture than nineteen men with box cutters. They just have to use it, finding a strategic plan for social change in order to make the change happen.

In 1997, in the aftermath of the Unabomber case, I developed a lesson plan and tool kit for American culture at the millennium. Both are holding up well. Top on the lesson plan is an assignment in restructuring American individualism, and looking for innovative Americans in unlikely places. After 9/11, the entire country became an unlikely place. Unlikely new heroes and villains emerged, and extreme individualism became a greater threat than ever. The first tool in the kit is to keep people conceptually in charge of their technology, and not the other way around, maintaining the idea that the cultural system is anchored in human resources, no matter how sophisticated their machines. The second tool is to be informed about other people, both for community building and for self-defense.

The third tool is to think in complex systems, and not be blinded by individual perspectives into making a habit of leaving "dots" unconnected. The fourth tool is to learn from hits to the culture, instead of just taking them. Later, Luke Helder said exactly the same thing. Coleen Rowley also encourages both the government and American citizens to learn from their mistakes.[1] Do not just recover, transcend into regeneration. Some Americans dropped their learning mode right away after 9/11, but freeze-frame consciousness has no power to put American cultural identity on a roll. The assignment in restructuring individualism, and the four tools to complete it, still say it all.

Terrorism blows up buildings, hearts, and minds. The counterattack is to strengthen everything, putting things together so intensively that it will be harder to tear them apart in the future. Putting buildings back together and closing gaps in border security are not enough. Passivity, isolation, and complacency all work for the jackal. Thinking and acting in concert works for the phoenix. Keeping the post-9/11 sensibility that a culture is first and foremost about human beings, and that technology, money, and media all serve them, can help make America into a culture that knows itself well enough to admit its own pattern of terrorism. America's capacity to dream should go beyond the movies. Even if the American social imagination is honed in theater seats, it should go back to work in daily life. Domestic terror could strike your community. Imagine it. Then work to counteract it. FBI agent John Douglas said that FBI agents "even in their dreams . . . could hardly have imagined the life story of the Harvard hermit in the woods."[2] Imagine it, and other stories just as unlikely. They will happen, and the stories will have parts for the rest of us. We are free to choose our parts, instead of letting the jackal do the casting.

PSEUDOREGENERATION

You can't keep the jackals and the phoenixes straight without a scorecard. As usual, Ted Kaczynski needs to have his thunder stolen. He is no phoenix, but a jackal who fancies himself as one. The real phoenixes need to feed off of his fire. In 1966, during graduate study at the University of Michigan, Kaczynski sought help from a psychiatrist. The day of his appointment was heavy on personal transformations. He was considering a sex change operation, but fear got the better of him. While still in the waiting room, he transformed his intentions. In session, he changed the subject to depression and anxiety about the draft. After coming out, he transformed again—into a jackal. Angry at both himself and the psychiatrist, in a moment he later described as a major turning point in his life, he reports: "Like a Phoenix, I burst from the ashes of my despair to a glorious new hope. I thought I wanted to kill that psychiatrist because the future looked utterly empty to me. I felt I wouldn't care if I died. And so I said to myself, why not really kill the psychiatrist and anyone else whom I hate . . . What was entirely new was the fact that I really felt I could kill some one. My very hopelessness had liberated me because I no longer cared about death."[3]

Kaczynski's words are those of a fake phoenix, free and independent of any sense of social responsibility, inured to death, with his liberty in killing. Using hatred to destroy does not regenerate. Kaczynski did care about death; he cared about causing it. His impact on his own culture was to cultivate fear and spread a sense of hopelessness by killing, but a phoenix does not seek or celebrate death. His self-identification as a phoenix is just one more barometer of the hold of the jackal clan on an American consciousness where hate and destruction can masquerade as regeneration. Kaczynski's destructive transformation of American culture was the only form of transformation he could see, and his self-indulgence in killing as a personal form of anger management was an extreme reflection of a culture that increasingly handles its fear by hating.

Americans now have a pantheon of American terrorist antiheroes whose legacies reinforce public rituals of terror and death. Americans jackals put their ultimate expressions of individual ill will onto the cultural stage, making themselves members of a dark American priesthood whose officiants are willing to terrorize for the sake of their own temporary epitaphs of destructive potential. Human sacrifice, including of oneself, is worth a chance to get a convoluted message across to the culture. In a culture that reveres all things big, the prospect of making a big destructive statement is one of the sweet sick draws into the poison smoke of the

American terror cult. Americans can keep being poisoned by that smoke, or transform it. Clearing the cultural air, including clearing it of the haze of confusion about American identity left after 9/11, would encourage more Americans to gag on such smoke, instead of savoring it. Combating the roots of terror demands valuing and caring for life every day, and not just on the days that there are funerals for those lost to its ravages. The combat requires practicing patriotism constantly, in ways that reach beyond protest of the Patriot Act. Survivors of 9/11 used helping others to manage their own grief, and there was social, as well as individual, wisdom in that. It was not just themselves that they healed in the process. They became part of a rear-guard action fighting America's cultural dark side, and they need all the help they can get. The worse the news, the easier it becomes to live in a self-oriented American trance, but fear, frustration, and despair all call for replacement of that trance with a sense of what people can do.

Rehabilitation is never easy. It takes step-by-step, inch-by-inch gritty determination, and guts. It comes from being socially supported by other people. American rehabilitation is about recreating America in the wake of American perpetrators, as well as catching them. It is about clearing a cultural atmosphere that is currently as much of a threat to collective American mental health as was the air at Ground Zero to the physical health of recovery workers, so that the phoenix can fly. It is about going to ground with the national character, transforming, and coming back up into a different atmosphere. The phoenix has to tame the jackal that lives within itself.

Bursting the confines of America's problems with wings beating, will take doing—but America really needs to fly. Envision the power of a bureaucracy rooted in exchanging wisdom with its local units, and the public that those local units directly serve. Educate. Give. Discuss. Vote. Volunteer. Resolve conflicts before they grow. The philosophy is not pie in the sky. It is phoenix in the sky. It is therapy for a challenged culture. America can turn its human power to the task of curtailing seedbeds of terrorism at home, and the number of Americans willing to choose the path of the jackal. Nobel laureates pointed America down this path after 9/11, by giving it the "twin goals" of stability and social justice to pursue, goals that are excellent replacements for the Twin Towers.[4]

AMERICA BEYOND TERROR

One hundred days after 9/11, "A Salute to America," a montage of images that Hollywood had been creating for decades, was playing before movie features. The music was Copland's *Fanfare for the Common Man*, which seemed to be precisely the point. Creator Chuck Workman showcased Julia Roberts's portrayal of Erin Brockovich when talking about his work. He picked a contemporary working class hero, a creator of social connection and a crafter of culture, to represent his piece. He cited the virtues of courage, heroism, and patriotism in everyday American life.

A one-hundred-day reunion of a World Trade Center survivor with her rescuer seemed to go down another cultural road. It was both touching and hauntingly vacuous. The rescuers looked awkward and wooden, appearing not to know whether their 9/11 human interest story would be anything more than new nostalgia for old normal. The rest of their day, besides their visit to her, was not part of the story. Would they go on rescuing America, one wondered, or were they done? Ambiguity about what 9/11 meant to the long-term American future had already set in. That ambiguity had developed fully by the time of the first "anniversary." Would 9/11 freeze in social time, or be an ongoing inspiration?

Americans made connections, treating pieces of shrapnel as holy relics, carefully connecting them to both the living and the dead. New York fire fighter Joseph Higgins delivered a piece of one of the airplanes flown into the World Trade Center into to the hands of U.S. military in Afghanistan. That small piece of destroyed technology represented the substance of the people who died because of it. Entrusting it to soldiers in Afghanistan was a symbol of healing, of ritually putting back together what had been blown apart. A shard of technology became a symbol for America's lost ability to fragment itself. A scrap of technology represented people. It did not supersede them or work against them, and the shrapnel was being pulled out of America's heart.

The nation's response to a 2002 trial for a summer 2001 beating death of a Massachusetts youth hockey coach was not just sensationalized; it was also reflective. The death was characterized as a wake-up call, signaling time to do something about a culture of violence in America and in youth sports. A community was shown being torn apart in the news. While that was standard fare, the calls for change in the culture of youth sports in America were not.

People talked about culture change as though they actually believed it could happen. That was new. That was bigger news than the incident. The voices of extreme individualism also came forward, people who could see nothing in youth sports but an addiction to winning. Still, "new normal" responses to the case were somehow different from old normal. The pre-9/11 fatalistic response of a sigh, a shrug, a shake of the head, and resignation about the culture's incremental move toward more everyday violence was replaced with a sense that it was not just defendant Thomas Junta, but everyone, who had been arrested. Cell phone rage, road rage, air rage, and sideline rage were all named as new cultural targets. September 11 clearly had made an intervention in American cultural consciousness.

The human truth at Ground Zero is that America lost people. Compatriots became ancestors collectively, not just as the sum of their individual losses. It was a group that was lost, and a group that lost them, as America processed national grief and collective bereavement. Carrying the spirit of a single lost family member was a daunting task for survivors of individual victims, but there were also three hundred million Americans carrying all three thousand victims of 9/11. Memorializing those new cultural ancestors demands demonstration of a unity in life that they had little choice about demonstrating in death. The ones who did choose, and chose to put the community over self, sealed a model of American character for America to keep.

Memorialization carries whoever was lost into the future. It is not simply about physical tributes of stone or steel. It is also about behavioral tributes of social action and connection. The urgency that Americans felt about recovering bodies and seeing donations go directly to victims remains transferable, but simply saying that America is stronger afterward does not make it true. The site of the former World Trade Center is hallowed not just because it stands for the common fate of the victims, but also because it stands for the common fate of those who mourn them. America's path is different now. The attack targeted America's sense of identity as a culture, and that identity has to keep on bouncing back. Not being soft on terrorism is only half the battle. The other half is America not being soft on itself.

Tim McVeigh's pathology in quoting Thomas Jefferson, "From time to time the tree of liberty must be refreshed with the blood of patriots," was that he took it upon himself to exact the sacrifice. The sacrifice on 9/11 was not exacted by American hands, but the blood fell on American soil and on the American soul. It is a sacrifice that can be used or neglected. A tree that has been nourished with such priceless sustenance should be tended with supreme care. Reaching back to America's roots and reviving an America in which freedom and independence serve something larger than the self is how to do it. The tree has scars, including one from 9/11, as well as the surpassing beauty created by its pattern of differing patriots. A metaphor for the post-9/11 American tree of liberty reaching down to its roots and growing new branches was a gift from a Pashtun/Pakistani-American woman—her phoenix to McVeigh's jackal.

Two years after, America remained in a hazy blur of confused cultural change, lingering in a post-trauma comfort zone, and clinging to the false security of extreme individualism. On September 11, 2003 the front page of *The New York Times* had a phoenix reference. Some, it reported, had found a sense of mission out of the ashes of 9/11. Three remarkable stories about individual Americans followed, but the core concept around which the article was based remained the individual, not social cooperation.

America developed little cultural sense in those two years of how to put itself into the mind frame of domestic terrorists. The pattern of American terror was evolving, and intertwining more closely with American culture, but the idea of domestic terror was still not even on most American "radar screens." The stories America told itself about itself were more often about fear than new social strength. The symbols focusing America on its human identity, with the exception of reality television, were rapidly fading. In the midst of elevated levels of trust of the government, citizens still had passive, conflicted, and dysfunctioning relationships with it. Culture was a languishing buzzword. There was more hope that it might change than plan or commitment, and the tremendous positive potential and problems simmering below the American cultural surface themselves would not lead America out of its cultural haze.

Refining America from within, instead of allowing terror to continue to bolster a mood of anxiety and depression in American character and foment social separation, remains the warrior's move. The human spirit is one of terrorism's theaters of operation. The war on terror is in the soul of American culture, not just in Afghanistan or the Supermax prison in Colorado. Terrorists deliver the message that comes from both Margaret Mead and Ted Kaczynski, that a small group of committed people with determination can change the world. High technology and big bureaucracy are not necessary. One of the lessons in that is that changing America into a very large small group of three hundred million committed citizens with social reciprocity in mind could make America into a global antiterrorist player with real cultural, as well as military and economic power. Attacks on dehumanization and anger in a culture where hate increasingly both happens and sells counter terror.

Not allowing the relationship between the American people and their government to move in the direction of the foregone hostile conclusion that it was for Tim McVeigh will counter terror. Having people, not just new databases or deconstructed stovepipes at the core of America's antiterrorist enterprise will counter terror. America cannot just call its own terrorists crazy or wrong. It has to prove them wrong by making them wrong, and that will take a trip down to America's cultural roots. It will take grit and a lot of American cultural fresh air. It will take a sustained focus on humanity, and on the positive social power, rather than the introversion and pathology, of the American individual. Even if the jackals seem to be ahead, the phoenixes are far from dead. Culture is still on a lot of lips. Let's make some, from Ground Zero up.

> The labyrinth is thoroughly known. We have only to follow the thread of the hero path, and where we had thought to find an abomination, we shall find a god. And where we had thought to slay another, we shall slay ourselves. Where we had thought to travel outward, we will come to the center of our own existence. And where we had thought to be alone, we will be with all the world.
>
> —Joseph Campbell, *The Power of Myth*

NOTES

PREFACE AND INTRODUCTION

1. Margaret Mead, *And Keep Your Powder Dry* (New York: William Morrow and Co., 1975), xii.

2. The standard classifications of terrorists often crosscut one another in situated cases, for example, when religious and political terrorism overlap, or psychopathological and single-issue terrorism overlap.

3. While FBI Director Robert Mueller identified the beltway snipers as terrorists, presumably on the basis of interpreting the motivation being at least in part to intimidate the public (see Chapter 6, Footnote 20 and text material referenced), and Bruce Schneier in *Beyond Fear* (New York: Copernicus Books, 2003), 69-70 identifies a sniper who chooses victims at random as not being a terrorist, Schneier's perspective looks aside from the random selection of victims itself as a form of political or cultural statement. Similarly, Schneier characterizes Luke Helder's bombings as "craziness, certainly, but not terrorism," looking aside from the content of written statements Helder made in association with his attacks.

4. Robert J. Bunker, "Street Gangs—Future Paramilitary Groups?" *Annual Editions-Violence and Terrorism*, Bernard Schechterman and Martin Slann, eds. (Guilford, CN: Dushkin/McGraw-Hill, 1999), 112-13.

5. Bruce Schneier in *Beyond Fear* (New York: Copernicus Books, 2003), 170, discusses mitigation as an aspect of an overall security response focusing on the defender rather than the attacker. America can mitigate terrorist attacks

through changes to American culture that will render it more resilient in the face of terrorism.

6. Minnesota Public Radio, September 11, 2003.

7. A discussion of current civil liberties concerns in relation to the war on terrorism follows in Chapter 6.

8. Recent works by Ann Coulter, Michael Moore, and Michael Savage come to mind as an index of the vehemence of contemporary American critiques of other Americans, cf. Ann Coulter, *Treason* (New York: Crown Forum, 2003), Michael Moore, *Stupid White Men* (New York: Regan Books, 2001), and Michael Savage, *The Savage Nation* (Nashville: WND Books, 2002).

9. Immanuel Wallerstein, "America and the World: The Twin Towers as Metaphor," in Craig Calhoun, Paul Price, and Ashley Timmer, eds., *Understanding September 11* (New York: The New Press, 2002), 349.

10. Simon Reeve, *The New Jackals* (Boston: Northeastern University Press, 1999).

11. That interaction is facilitated, in part, by the Internet. While Willard Gaylin in *Hatred* (New York: Public Affairs Press, 2003), 195, makes a distinction between a "culture of hatred" and a "culture of haters," identifying the former as a "natural community . . . or its subculture," and the latter as an "artificial community" created by the alliance of people who share a common hatred, in practice his two terms intersect, since subcultures of "natural" communities are sometimes formed on the basis of hatred, and the notion that community usually has "a shared locale" no longer effectively applies. Regional cultures of terrorism bear the cultural stamp of the regions within which they emerge and have their primary operations. They are also, like other cultures in the contemporary world, influenced by the cultures around them. One of the "subcultures" of global culture is not ethnic or national, but a culture of terrorism, which in turn has its own regional subcultures. Likewise, the Ku Klux Klan and neo-Nazis in America are best viewed as American subcultures, rather than a categorically different type of cultural entity, because hate is a central premise of both the subculture and, to a lesser extent, the larger culture. Hate is natural.

12. Sun Tzu, *The Art of War* (New York: Delacorte Press, 1983).

13. The stereotypical criticism of the American academy in the post-9/11 American Council of Trustees and Alumni (ACTA) report *Defending Civilization: How Our Universities Are Failing America*, is based on the perception that American academics "blame America first." This academic author regards her views on

cultural self-examination and healthy criticism as a means to strengthening the character of the culture. Any view that America has no problems is untenable.

CHAPTER 1 PATTERNS OF TERROR

[1.] Robert Bellah et al, *Habits of the Heart: Individualism and Commitment in American Life* (Berkeley: University of California Press, 1985).

[2.] See, John Hewitt, *The Myth of Self-Esteem: Finding Happiness and Solving Problems in America* (New York: St. Martin's Press, 1998), 132, for commentary on both the relationship between the concept of self-esteem and social disconnection in American culture, and on the relationship of American culture and disorders of identity.

[3.] Jessica Stern, *The Ultimate Terrorists*, (Cambridge: Harvard University Press), 46.

[4.] If McVeigh himself is included in his victim count as a final casualty of the bombing, the number is 169. His trial attorney, Stephen Jones and others have forwarded the notion that another bomber was killed in the blast in *Others Unknown; Timothy McVeigh and the Oklahoma Bombing Conspiracy* (New York: Public Affairs Press, 1998) and elsewhere. While McVeigh clearly did not act entirely on his own, the extent to which there was or was not a larger conspiracy, and if so, whether that conspiracy was domestic or international in nature, is not conclusively resolved. While McVeigh's accomplice Terry Nichols's travels to the Philippines and the fact of his having met Ramzi Yousef there does raise the possibility of the passage of information with respect to bomb building, that possibility does not necessarily imply, as Peter Lance does in *1000 Years for Revenge: International Terrorism and the FBI: The Untold Story* (New York: Regan Books, 2003) that Yousef had the essential "authorship" of a bomb otherwise planned by Tim McVeigh. Reports of McVeigh's early experiments with explosives leading up to that bomb conflict in terms of their success. Lance indicates that "a growing body of evidence now suggests that . . . Yousef may well have . . . also designed," the Oklahoma City bomb (page 23), referring his readers to another page in his volume, where the material presented is neither new nor developing. Lance also asks (page 372) why, if Steven Gale, terrorism specialist at the University of Pennsylvania had warned that terrorists might crash "planes into the World Trade Center:" "If a scholar could connect the dots, why couldn't the Bureau?" (cf. the FBI). In fact, the prospect of a possible attack on the World Trade Center by terrorists had also been forwarded elsewhere in the academic community. The cover of Harvey W. Kushner's *Terrorism in America: A Structured Approach to Understanding the Terrorist Threat* (Springfield, IL: Charles C. Thomas, 1998) pictures the Twin Towers with a huge bull's-eye superimposed on them. The spectacular notion of planes being flown into buildings in New York actually emerged diffusely in a number of places in American culture prior to 9/11.

5. Letter from Timothy McVeigh, *Union-Sun and Journal*, February 11, 1992.

6. For an account of the linguistic analysis that was presented and challenged in court, see Don Foster, *Author Unknown: On the Trail of Anonymous* (New York: Henry Holt, 2000).

7. Stephen Gould, *Full House*, (New York: Harmony Books, 1996).

8. Rod Probst, senior operations analyst with ANSER Institute for Homeland Security, a non-profit research organization, and Joe Myers, risk engineer at Coast Guard Headquarters, Washington, DC. Citation from *Terrorism Open Source Intelligence Report*, September 4, 2003, 14-15.

9. Unabomber Manifesto, reprinted in John Douglas and Mark Olshaker, *Unabomber: On the Trail of America's Most-Wanted Serial Killer* (New York: Pocket Books, 1996).

10. Matt Reichel, "The Lure of Data: Is it Addictive?" *The New York Times*, July 6, 2003, 3Aff.

11. Sally C. Johnson, *Forensic Evaluation: Kaczynski, Theodore John*, http://www.courttv.com/trials/unabomber/documents/psychological.html, 1998.

12. Ibid.

13. John Douglas and Mark Olshaker, *Unabomber: On the Trail of America's Most-Wanted Serial Killer* (New York: Pocket Books, 1996), 146. The authors also refer to Kaczynski as delusional.

14. Stephen J. Dubner, "'I Don't Want to Live Long. I Would Rather Get the Death Penalty Than Spend the Rest of My Life in Prison'," *Time*, October 18, 1999, 44-49.

15. Unabomber Manifesto, reprinted in John Douglas and Mark Olshaker, *Unabomber: On the Trail of America's Most-Wanted Serial Killer* (New York: Pocket Books, 1996).

16. Rex A. Hudson, *Who Becomes a Terrorist and Why: The 1999 Government Report on Profiling Terrorists* (Guilford, Connecticut: The Lyons Press, 1999), 47.

17. Ibid., 91.

18. Unabomber Manifesto, reprinted in John Douglas and Mark Olshaker, *Unabomber: On the Trail of America's Most-Wanted Serial Killer* (New York: Pocket Books, 1996).

CHAPTER 2 CAN'T KEEP TRACK

1. Lou Michel and Dan Herbeck, *American Terrorist: Timothy McVeigh and the Oklahoma City Bombing*, (New York: Regan Books, 2001), 364.

2. Brigette L. Nacos, *Terrorism and the Media From the Iran Hostage Crisis to the Oklahoma City Bombing*, (New York, Columbia University Press, 1994), xx-xxi.

3. Lou Michel and Dan Herbeck, *American Terrorist: Timothy McVeigh and the Oklahoma City Bombing*, (New York: Regan Books, 2001), 362.

4. Stephen J. Dubner, "'I Don't Want to Live Long. I Would Rather Get the Death Penalty Than Spend the Rest of My Life In Prison'," *Time*, October 18, 1999, 44-49.

5. Judge Garland E. Burrell, quoted in Henry Weinstein, "Retrial Rejected for Unabomber," *Los Angeles Times*, February 13, 2001, A3.

6. Stephen J. Dubner, "'I Don't Want to Live Long. I Would Rather Get the Death Penalty Than Spend the Rest of My Life in Prison'," *Time*, October 18, 1999, 44-49.

7. Unabomber Manifesto, reprinted in John Douglas and Mark Olshaker, *Unabomber: On the Trail of America's Most-Wanted Serial Killer* (New York: Pocket Books, 1996).

8. Stephen J. Dubner, "'I Don't Want to Live Long. I Would Rather Get the Death Penalty Than Spend the Rest of My Life in Prison'," *Time*, October 18, 1999, 44-49.

9. Theodore Kaczynski, "Hit Where it Hurts," *Green Anarchy*, Spring 2002, 18.

10. Syl Jones, "A Familiar Melancholy; Thank Goodness Melville Never Went to New Bedford High," *Minneapolis Star Tribune*, November 30, 2001, 33A.

11. Angie Cannon and the Staff of *U.S. News and World Report*, *The Compelling True Story of the Hunt and Capture of the Beltway Snipers* (New York: Pocket Books, 2003), 116, Sheriff Ronald Knight.

12. Ibid.

13. Ibid., 155.

14. Ibid., 256.

15. Walter Kirn, "Bring It All Back Home," *The New York Times Magazine*, November 17, 2002, 17-18.

CHAPTER 3 PSYCHOLOGICAL GROUND ZERO

1. Barry Glassner, *The Culture of Fear: Why Americans are Afraid of the Wrong Things* (New York: Basic Books, 1999).

2. Bruce Schneier, *Beyond Fear* (New York: Copernicus Books, 2003), 26-31.

3. Post-traumatic stress disorder is a broad diagnostic category adopted into the diagnostic manual of the American Psychiatric Association in 1980, encompassing a wide array of problems from combat exhaustion to situational anxiety. The characteristic symptoms are reexperiencing the event, avoiding stimuli associated with the trauma, emotional numbing, and behavioral arousal. Associated problems can be a feeling of estrangement from others and outbursts of anger.

4. William E. Schlenger et al, "Psychological Reactions to Terrorist Attacks: Findings from the National Study of Americans' Reactions to September 11," *Journal of the American Medical Association*, 288:5, August 7, 2002, 581-588.

5. Antonius C.G.M. Robben and Marcelo M. Suárez-Orozco, eds., *Cultures Under Siege: Collective Violence and Trauma* (New York: Cambridge University Press, 2000).

6. David Gates, "Living a New Normal," *Newsweek*, October 8, 2001, 54-56.

7. Antonius C.G.M. Robben and Marcelo M. Suárez-Orozco, eds., *Cultures Under Siege: Collective Violence and Trauma* (New York: Cambridge University Press, 2000).

8. Kai Erickson, "Notes on Trauma and Community," in Cathy Caruth, ed., *Trauma: Explorations in Memory*, (Baltimore: John Hopkins University Press, 1995), as reported in Robben and Suárez-Orozco and cited in Edward T. Linenthal, *The Unfinished Bombing: Oklahoma City in American Memory* (New York: Oxford University Press, 2001), 82.

9. Robert Millman of Cornell Medical School, "Acquired Situational Narcissism," *The New York Times Magazine,* December 9, 2001, 50.

10. Randall Marshall, Director of Trauma Studies and Services at the New York State Psychiatric Institute, quoted in Eric Goode and Emily Eakin, "Mental Health: The Profession Tests Its Limits, *The New York Times*, September 11, 2002, A1ff.

11. USA Today/CNN Gallup Poll, conducted between September 2nd and 4th, 2002, and reported in *USA Today*, September 11, 2002, 2A, and Kenneth A. Rasinski et al, "America Recovers: A Follow-Up to a National Study of Public Response to the September 11th Terrorist Attacks," National Opinion Research Center (Chicago), August 7, 2002.

12. Kenneth A. Rasinski et al, "America Recovers: A Follow-Up to a National Study of Public Response to the September 11th Terrorist Attacks," National Opinion Research Center (Chicago), August 7, 2002.

13. Ibid., 21.

14. Ibid., 26.

15. "America Enduring," *The New York Times*, September 11, 2002, A34.

16. Tom Pyszczynski et al, *In the Wake of 9/11: The Psychology of Terror* (Washington, DC: American Psychological Association, 2003), 9 and 17.

17. Ibid., 27.

18. Ibid., 38.

19. Tom W. Smith et al, "America Rebounds: A National Study of Public Response to the September 11th Terrorist Attacks," National Opinion Research Center (Chicago), October 25, 2001, 20.

20. Stewart Wolf and John G. Bruhn, *The Power of Clan: The Influences of Human Relationships on Heart Disease* (New Brunswick: Transaction Publishers, 1993).

21. Arthur M. Kleinman, quoted in "Anthropologist/Psychiatrist Decries Government's Alerts," American Anthropological Association Media Advisory, August, 2002.

22. John Hewitt, *The Myth of Self-Esteem: Finding Happiness and Solving Problems in America* (New York: St. Martin's Press, 1998).

23. Reported in David Perlman, "Terror Attacks Stressed out 9 in 10 Americans, Study Says," *The San Francisco Chronicle*, November 15, 2001, A14, and published in the *New England Journal of Medicine*.

24. Aaron T. Beck and Gary Emery, with Ruth L. Greenberg, *Anxiety Disorders and Phobias: A Cognitive Perspective* (New York: Harper Collins, 1985).

25. Jonathan Alter, "Six Months On, The Fog of War," *Newsweek*, March 18, 2002, 20-21.

26. Terence Monmaney, "Response to Terror; The Emotional Toll; For Most Trauma Victims, Life is More Meaningful," *Los Angeles Times*, October 7, 2001, A9.

27. Sandra Bloom, *Creating Sanctuary: Toward an Evolution of Sane Societies* (New York: Routledge, 1997), 211.

28. Terence Monmaney, "Response to Terror; The Emotional Toll; For Most Trauma Victims, Life is More Meaningful," *Los Angeles Times*, October 7, 2001, A9.

29. Aaron T. Beck and Gary Emery, with Ruth L. Greenberg, *Anxiety Disorders and Phobias: A Cognitive Perspective* (New York: Harper Collins, 1985).

30. Abdel A. Thabet and Panos Vostanis, "Post Traumatic Stress Disorder Reactions in Children of War: A Longitudinal Study," *Child Abuse and Neglect*, 24:2 (2000), 291-298.

31. William E. Schlenger et al, "Psychological Reactions to Terrorist Attacks: Findings from the Nation Study of Americans' Reactions to September 11," *Journal of the American Medical Association*, 288:5, August 7, 2002, 581-588.

CHAPTER 4 SYMBOL SHIFTS

1. David I. Kertzer, *Ritual, Politics, and Power* (New Haven: Yale University Press, 1988).

2. See also Jean Baudrillard, *The Spirit of Terrorism* (London, Verso, 2002), for an analysis of terrorism as a symbolic strategy involving sacrificial death, and Tom Pyszczynski's analysis that the destruction of cherished American symbols on 9/11 undermined the integrity of the psychological shield provided for Americans by their cultural world view, in Tom Pyszczynski et al, *In the Wake of 9/11: The Psychology of Terror* (Washington, DC: American Psychological Association, 2003), 94.

3. September 20, 2001, and December 7, 2001.

4. Edward T. Linenthal, *The Unfinished Bombing: Oklahoma City in American Memory* (New York: Oxford University Press, 2001), 234 and 241.

5. Cathleen McGuigan, "Daniel Libeskind Takes Home the Prize," *Newsweek*, March 10, 2003, 58-60.

6. Clifford Geertz, "Notes on the Balinese Cockfight," *Interpretation of Cultures* (New York: Basic Books, 1973), 448.

7. "Tribute of Light" was substituted for "Towers of Light."

8. Report of Aris A. Pappas and James M. Simon, Jr. from the CIA journal, *Studies in Intelligence,* referred to in Bill Gertz, *Breakdown: How America's Intelligence Failures Led to September 11* (Washington, DC: Regnery, 2002), 157.

9. Charles C. Mann, "Homeland Insecurity," *Atlantic Monthly*, September 2002, 81-102, on the work of security expert Bruce Schneier.

10. Kenneth A. Rasinski et al, "America Recovers: A Follow-Up to a National Study of Public Response to the September 11th Terrorist Attacks," National Opinion Research Center (Chicago), 2002, 3.

11. September 20, 2001.

12. November 8, 2001.

13. Philip Nobel, "The Downtown Culture Derby Begins . . . ," *The New York Times*, August 31, 2003, AR20, and Minnesota Public Radio Midmorning, September 11, 2003.

14. James Poniewozik, "Why Reality TV is Good for Us," *Time*, February 17, 2003, 64-67.

15. *CBS Evening News,* November 2, 2001.

16. This volume was entitled and subtitled in September of 2001.

17. CNN, April 1, 2003.

CHAPTER 5 CONNECTING THE DOTS

1. Walter Kirn, "Lewis and Clark: The Journey that Changed America Forever," *Time*, July 8, 2002, 41.

2. Daniel Schoor, Public Radio, September 20, 2001.

3. Donald Rumsfeld, Public Radio, September 25, 2001.

4. Historian Hanes Johnson, Public Radio, January 2, 2002.

5. Robert Bellah et al, *Habits of the Heart: Individualism and Commitment in American Life* (Berkeley: University of California Press, 1985).

6. Sally Kanemeyer, Richmond, VA, Letter to the Editor, *Newsweek*, October 1, 2001, 13.

CHAPTER 6 COMMUNITY REFORGED

1. Robert D. Putnam, *Bowling Alone: The Collapse and Revival of American Community* (New York: Touchstone, 2000), and Robert D. Putnam and Lewis

M. Feldstein with Don Cohen, *Better Together: Restoring the American Community* (New York: Simon and Schuster, 2003).

2. Robert D. Putnam, *Bowling Alone: The Collapse and Revival of American Community* (New York: Touchstone, 2000), 290.

3. McVeigh is reported by various sources, including his attorney Stephen Jones and his biographers Lou Michel and Dan Herbeck, as having experienced mental health problems or having been at risk for them at different times in his life.

4. Robert Putnam's analysis is that social capital is built on the principle of "generalized reciprocity." Anthropologists apply the concept of "generalized reciprocity" to many small-scale societies in order to understand economic behavior. Sharing of material wealth in such societies is done freely, and without expectation of a direct return. The term social capital is also closely aligned with an economic metaphor for social relations, so the term "social reciprocity" allows the conceptual focus of reciprocity to be more clearly in the social arena.

5. Robert Bellah et al, *Habits of the Heart: Individualism and Commitment in American Life* (Berkeley: University of California Press, 1985).

6. Robert Putnam "Bowling Together," *The American Prospect*, 13:3 (February 11, 2002).

7. "Images matter." Ibid.

8. Amitai Etzioni, *The New Golden Rule: Community and Morality in a Democratic Society* (New York: Basic Books, 1996), 37.

9. Ibid., 127.

10. Robert Bellah et al, *Habits of the Heart: Individualism and Commitment in American Life* (Berkeley: University of California Press, 1985).

11. Robert Putnam, "Bowling Together," *The American Prospect* 13:3 (February 11, 2002), and Robert D. Putnam and Lewis M. Feldstein with Don Cohen, *Better Together: Restoring the American Community* (New York: Simon and Schuster, 2003).

12. Stewart Wolf and John G. Bruhn, *The Power of Clan: The Influence of Human Relationships on Heart Disease* (New Brunswick: Transaction Publishers, 1993).

13. John Picaralo, "The Hope of 9/11," April 10, 2002.

14. Nancy Gibbs, "A Nation on Edge," *Time*, February 24, 2003, 20-23.

15. The Markle Foundation, *Protecting America's Freedom in the Information Age* (October 2002).

16. Steven Brill, *After* (New York: Simon and Schuster, 2003), 484, and Bruce Schneier, *Beyond Fear* (New York: Copernicus Books, 2003), 244.

17. David Wise, "If Bush is Lying, He's Not the First," *Washington Post*, June 15, 2003, BO1.

18. Adam Liptak, "Defending Those Who Defend Terrorists," *The New York Times*, July 27, 2003, WK4.

19. While the appeals court ruling on Hamdi deferred, rather than making a ruling contrary to that of the government, on the basis of his having been apprehended in Afghanistan, in Padilla's case, where an American citizen was apprehended on American soil, the assertion of executive authority to invoke military justice remains more problematic at a national social structural level.

20. Robert Mueller, the Jackson H. Ralston Lecture in International Law, given to the Stanford Law School, October 18, 2002.

21. Matt Welch, "Get Ready for PATRIOT II," Alternet.org, April 2, 2003, http:// www.alternet.org/story/.html?StoryID=1554.

22. Wesley Clark, "Strategic Leadership in the Information Age," Speech at 2nd Annual Government Symposium on Information Sharing and Homeland Security, "Preventing, Pre-Empting, and Disrupting Terrorist Threats," (Philadelphia), June 30, 2003.

23. Bill Gertz, *Breakdown: How America's Intelligence Failures Led to September 11* (Washington, DC: Regnery), 145.

24. Coleen Rowley, "Civil Liberties vs. the Need for Effective Investigation," presentation at the Milton Eisenhower Foundation, July 1, 2002, and the Chautauqua Institution, July 24, 2003.

25. Daniel Schoor, Public Radio, December 31, 2001.

26. Amitai Etzioni, *The New Golden Rule: Community and Morality in a Democratic Society* (New York: Basic Books, 1996), 257.

27. Ibid.

CHAPTER 7 AMERICAN INTELLIGENCE

1. The intelligence community includes the CIA, FBI, NSA, NRO, etc.

2. Peter Lance, *1000 Years for Revenge: International Terrorism and the FBI: The Untold Story* (New York: Regan Books, 2003).

3. Ibid., Timeline 30.

4. Ibid., 455.

5. Ibid., reference material regarding Dale Watson.

6. Steven Brill, *After* (New York: Simon and Schuster, 2003), 159.

7. Arthur M. Kleinman, quoted in "Anthropologist/Psychiatrist Decries Government's Alerts," American Anthropological Association Media Advisory, August 2002.

8. Fredrik Barth, *Political Leadership Among Swat Pathans* (London: The Athlone Press, 1959), 12, and Ivo Daalder et al, "Protecting the American Homeland: One Year On," The Brookings Institution, Washington, DC, January 2003, 22. The Brookings Institution report recommends developing "a more decentralized architecture" in order to facilitate information exchange between the federal government and local actors, as well as between local units. Barth's anthropological classic discusses how a local leader creates "wider obligations and dependence which he can then draw upon in the form of personal political support." In other words, creating ties between social units works to the advantage of the individual, and is therefore something that individuals pursue.

9. Bruce Schneier, *Beyond Fear* (New York: Copernicus Books, 2003), 251.

10. Ivo Daalder et al, "Protecting the American Homeland: One Year On," The Brookings Institution, Washington, DC, January 2003, 14.

11. Congressman Curt Weldon, Government Symposium on Information Sharing and Homeland Security, August 19, 2002, and June 30, 2003.

12. Larry Castro, Government Symposium on Information Sharing and Homeland Security, August 20, 2002.

13. The Markle Foundation, *Protecting America's Freedom in the Information Age* (October 2002), 115.

14. Memorandum Re: Intergovernmental Dimensions of Domestic Preparedness, from: The Executive Session of Domestic Preparedness, John F. Kennedy School of Government, Harvard University, to: The Honorable Tom Ridge, Office of Homeland Security, November 2, 2001.

15. Bill Gertz, *Breakdown: How America's Intelligence Failures Led to September 11* (Washington, DC: Regnery, 2002), 111.

16. General Wesley Clark, "Strategic Leadership in the Information Age," Government Symposium on Information Sharing and Homeland Security, June 30, 2003.

17. The Markle Foundation, *Protecting America's Freedom in the Information Age* (October 2002), 10.

18. Ibid., 73.

19. Ibid., 74.

20. Edward Norris, Government Symposium on Information Sharing and Homeland Security, July 1, 2003.

21. Blake Morrison, "Air Marshals' Low Morale Spelled Out," *USA Today*, October 24, 2002, 1A.

22. Arthur M. Kleinman, quoted in "Anthropologist/Psychiatrist Decries Government's Alerts," American Anthropological Association Media Advisory, August 2002.

23. Kevin Johnson, "In Orange Terror Alerts, Wary Cities Hold Back," *USA Today*, July 2, 2003, 1A-2A.

24. Bill Gertz, *Breakdown: How America's Intelligence Failures Led to September 11* (Washington, DC: Regnery, 2002), 147.

25. The Markle Foundation, *Protecting America's Freedom in the Information Age* (October 2002), 29.

26. Charles C. Mann, "Homeland Insecurity," *Atlantic Monthly*, September 2002, 81-102, quoting security expert Bruce Schneier, 101. See also Bruce Schneier, *Beyond Fear* (New York: Copernicus Books, 2003), 133, 144-146, 245.

27. Rafi Ron, Government Convention on Emerging Technologies, January 9, 2003, and Yaakov Preger, "Stopping the Suicide Bomber," Government Symposium on Information Sharing and Homeland Security, July 2, 2003.

28. http://www.brookings.edu/execed/open/exec_leadership.htm

29. Maureen McCarthy, "Department of Homeland Security: One Agency, One Goal, Many Accomplishments," Government Symposium on Information Sharing and Homeland Security, July 1, 2003.

30. Richard A. Serrano, *One of Ours* (New York: Norton, 1998), 320.

CONCLUSION

1. "Speaking of Faith," Minnesota Public Radio, August 31, 2003.

2. John Douglas, *Mad Genius* (New York: Warner Books, 1996), 12.

3. Sally C. Johnson, *Forensic Evaluation: Kaczynski, Theodore John*, http://www.courttv.com/trials/unabomber/documents/psychological.html, 1998.

4. Zhohres I. Alferov et al, "Our Best Point the Way: On the 100th Anniversary of the Nobel Prize, 100 Nobel Laureates Warn that Our Security Hangs on Environmental and Social Reform," *Toronto Globe and Mail*, December 7, 2001.

INDEX

A Beautiful Mind, 160
abortion clinics, 54, 90
  and anthrax, 55, 94, 137
  bombings, 23, 42, 54, 94, 112
Academy Awards, 147, 160, 162, 165
ACLU (American Civil Liberties Union), 210
ACTA (American Council of Trustees and Alumni), 280
addiction, 55, 58, 76-77, 108, 120, 275
  to the individual, 57-58, 131-32, 154
Afghanistan, 133, 277, 289
  and military action, 145, 148, 183, 204, 205
  and tribal culture, 44
  and U.S. military, 192
African-Americans, 108, 127, 160
Agriculture Department, 248
Air Force One, 141
Air Force, U.S., 122
air marshals, 255
Akbar, Asan, 110-11
Al Qaeda, 104, 142, 191
Alger, Horatio, 168

Allegheny College, 51
American cultural personality
  (*see also* American national character, American national psyche), 16, 28, 118
American dream, 60, 150-53, 168, 170, 181, 193
American eagle, 40, 163
American flag, 11, 22
  and cultural warning, 98, 121
  post-9/11 confusion regarding, 204-06
  post-9/11 display, 29, 125, 126, 128, 157, 220
  at post-9/11 sporting events, 41, 171, 175
American national character
  (*see also* American national psyche), 30, 36, 168, 181, 257, 269, 273
  as addictive, 154
  and anger, 43, 115
  and anxiety, 43, 109, 209, 277
  and depression, 131, 139
  as passive, 30, 246

and post-traumatic stress, 135
and social fragmentation, 27,
31, 55, 83, 121, 190
strengthening, 43, 277
through healthy self-
criticism, 281
with human connections,
63, 164, 203, 211, 254
with resilience and initiative, 27, 31, 40, 131, 134
and terrorism, 16, 30, 31, 44,
46, 56, 90
American national identity (*see
also* cultural identity), 28,
31, 62, 66, 204, 213
post-9/11, 26, 145, 153, 157,
171, 194, 204, 254
uncertainty about post-9/11,
219, 267, 273
American national psyche (*see
also* American national
character), 83, 115, 126,
139, 185, 210, 229
and anger, 115-16, 123, 195
and anxiety, 85, 106, 117
challenged, 85, 93, 126-31
concept of, 16, 120
and depression, 72, 83-85, 116
and fear, 115, 117, 119, 123,
195
folk therapy for, 133-36
movement of, 37, 42, 60, 115-
16, 132
and post-traumatic growth,
135
and post-traumatic stress, 113
and terrorism, 24-25, 46, 48,
121
American Psychiatric
Association, 284
American Psychological
Association, 118

Americorps, 178, 201, 218
Angels (Anaheim), 175
anger, 45, 70, 106, 152
at government, 209, 215-17,
230, 232
and mental health, 123, 284
in national psyche, 115, 117,
130, 195
in post-9/11 America, 57,
124, 128-29, 131, 133, 165,
194, 205
and terrorism, 43, 62, 109-12,
135, 272, 277
anger, cultural atmosphere of
and individualism, 28, 62,
125
need to decrease, 41, 43
social disconnection, 44, 57,
200
animal rights groups, 23, 54, 91,
94
Annan, Kofi, 266
anniversary of 9/11, 175-76
first, 175, 187, 274
second, 110, 191, 218
anthrax, 57, 96, 129, 133, 137,
147, 267
and FBI, 39, 63-64, 100, 227-
36
and fear, 40, 94, 118, 137
hoaxers, 55, 94, 137
and media, 166, 184
perpetrator, 63, 96, 100, 104,
223, 232-35, 240
profile, 64, 232-35
anthropology, 15, 16, 64
culture concept, 31, 263
and Unabomber Manifesto,
65, 72, 77
anxiety (*see also* fear), 80, 88,
272
and depression, 78, 83, 115,
129, 277

diagnoses, 78, 123, 284
and government, 131, 212,
    215, 223
individual, 120, 133
post-9/11, 63, 116, 133, 137-
    38, 167
and self-esteem, 128, 190
and terrorism, 43, 67, 79, 85,
    103, 205, 258
anxiety, cultural atmosphere of,
    43, 47, 84, 106-09, 117-20,
    123, 127, 209, 277
combating, 133-34, 138, 190,
    217, 266, 268
Apocalypse, 52
Arab-Americans, 197, 224
Arabia, 40
Arizona, state of, 171
Arizona, USS, 180
Armageddon, 52
Army, U.S., 111, 150, 240, 250
Aruba, 137
Ashcroft, John, 147-48, 241, 243
Atlanta, Georgia, 112, 151
ATT (American Telephone and
    Telegraph), 148
Attack of the Clones, 163
attention deficit disorder, 115
Aztec, 141

baby boomers, 181
Bali, 191
Bank of America, 175
Barth, Fredrik, 290
baseball, 34, 263
post-9/11, 163, 169-75, 181
Baudrillard, Jean, 286
Beamer, Lisa, 145
Bellah, Robert, 55
beltway sniper (*see also* Malvo,
    Lee, and Muhammad,
    John), 12, 23, 103-13, 208,
    247, 267

and fear, 62, 99
investigation, 70, 71, 229
and media, 108-09, 255
profile, 104, 107-08
as terrorist, 24, 105, 106, 214,
    279
Ben Gurion airport, 259
Berkeley, California, 15-16, 64-
    65, 66, 68, 72, 82
bin Laden, Osama, 38
American reactions to, 26,
    128, 180, 191
and Bishop, 25, 95, 122
doll, 163
and Muhammad, 24
Bishop, Charles, 25, 94, 95, 121-
    23, 193
Bloom, Sandra, 135
Boston, Massachusetts, 259
Bowling for Columbine, 165
Boy Scouts, 38
Bradley, Ed, 240
Brandeis, Louis, 264
Brill, Steven, 229
Brockovich, Erin, 239, 274
Brokaw, Tom, 147, 230
Brookings Institute, 244, 248,
    253, 261, 290
Bucca, Ronnie, 227
Bunker, Robert, 25
Burger King, 159
Burgert, David, 193
Burt, Leo, 65
Bush, George W., 166, 215
and culture change, 138, 241
and the DHS, 239, 241, 247,
    254
as an individual, 215
post-9/11 speeches, 125, 135,
    138, 142, 148, 151, 179, 182
Bush, Laura, 166

California, state of, 25, 66, 70, 113, 204, 217
Campbell, Joseph, 277
Cancun, Mexico, 137
Cantor-Fitzgerald, 156-57
Carlos the Jackal, 38
Cassandra, 238
Castro, Larry, 250
CBS (see also CBS Evening News), 166
CBS Evening News, 40, 125, 148, 173, 287
CDC (Centers for Disease Control and Prevention), 235
Celexa, 85
CEOs, 155-56, 158, 189, 194, 243
Cessna, 25, 95, 121
channel surfing, 34, 175, 199, 200
China, 40
CIA (Central Intelligence Agency), 253, 289
    and human intelligence, 75
    and unconnected dots, 177, 237, 250
Citizen Corps, 195, 218
civil liberties
    in a context of social connection, 56, 211, 220
    and criticism of government, 48, 138, 183, 210
    and fighting terrorism, 207-09, 216, 225, 268
Clark, Wesley, 216
Clinton, Bill, 148
CNN, 118, 166, 196
Coast Guard, 248
Cobain, Kurt, 100
cocoon, 53, 137, 153, 188, 267
Cold Spring, Minnesota, 114

Cole, Kenneth, 150
collaboration, 49, 227-28, 237, 243, 258
    bureaucratic, 48, 105, 184, 235, 241-57, 259-63
    and communication, 58, 184, 250
    and cooperation, 211, 230
    culture of, 105, 246-49, 262
    myth of, 241-57, 259
collateral damage, 43, 58, 86, 155
Collateral Damage, 39, 163
Colorado, state of 38, 78, 277
Columbine High School, 25, 76, 94-95, 117, 165, 200
    as act of terror, 25, 42, 91, 109
    cultural impact, 91-92, 112
    and mental health, 83
combat stress (see post-traumatic stress)
combat trauma (see post-traumatic stress)
community, 26, 58, 95, 112, 126, 275, 280
    building, 130, 152, 192-220, 268, 271
    and FBI, 221, 224, 230, 231, 235
    historical sense of, 58, 170
    and individual, 63, 192, 194, 201, 206, 209, 218, 275
    intelligence, 59, 148, 250, 253, 257, 264, 287
    as post-9/11 concept, 142-47, 151-59, 174-75, 180, 195, 197, 260
    post-9/11, 58-59, 138, 179, 191, 195, 218-19, 258, 264
    and terrorism, 25, 29, 60, 271
    and trauma, 121, 140
Condit, Gary, 119

Congress, U.S., 128, 133, 147,
    151
    and DHS, 247-48, 253-55
    and FBI, 229, 232, 235, 237,
        239
Conlon, Peggy, 166, 225
Constitution, U.S., 234
Cooper, Cynthia, 12
cooperation, 213, 220, 260, 276
    in American government, 48,
        248-49, 259
        DHS, 241, 247-48, 251-53
        FBI, 227, 230-31, 235
    of American public with
        government, 48, 211-12, 216,
        230-31, 257
    within American public, 199,
        211, 217
    in American social history,
        170
    culture of, 241, 247, 264
    and current American culture,
        49, 199
Copland, Aaron (*Fanfare for the
    Common Man*), 142, 274
copycat, 25, 45
Coulter, Ann, 280
Coyote, Peter, 152-53
Cruise, Tom, 160-64
cultural context, 33, 97, 258, 270
    changing, 49, 180
    problematic, 92, 192, 216,
        229
cultural identity (*see also* Ameri-
    can national identity), 33,
    43, 55, 170, 214
    changes to, 30, 58, 133, 136,
        176, 271
cultural problems, 61, 71, 73,
    106, 149, 265
    with anxiety, 117, 120
    of FBI, 177, 222, 226, 228

and terrorism, 22, 97, 266
cultural puzzle, 34, 36, 106, 110,
    134, 259
cultural rules, 31, 81, 133, 139,
    186, 222, 237, 263, 266
    of serving self-interest, 28, 34-
        35, 69, 128, 152-55, 192, 198
    of serving self-interest vs.
        organizational rules, 222, 226,
        246, 251
culture (*see also* subculture)
    academic, 16, 265
    bureaucratic, 221, 247-50,
        262-63
    channel surfing, 34, 175, 199
    and collaboration, 49, 228,
        230, 237, 241-56, 259-63
    concept, 16, 31-32, 197, 242,
        246, 260-63
    counter, 64, 190
    and hate, 280
    media, 265
    minority, 265
    norms, 57, 80-81, 84, 198,
        251
    occupational, 265
    organizational, 35, 237, 248,
        251, 261
    political, 33, 265
    popular, 77, 109, 145, 225,
        265
    regional, 265, 280
    shift, 177, 186, 223, 250
    wars, 30, 205, 228, 260, 265
culture change, 63, 196, 222
    lack of clarity about, post-
        9/11, 32, 46, 63, 178, 258,
        266, 275
    myth of, post-9/11, 241-57
    positive potential of, 134,
        200-01, 224, 264-65
culture of

adversariality, 238
alertness, 138, 265
collaboration, 247, 249, 265
compartmentalization, 241
concealment, 221, 265
despair, 265
extremism, 265
justice, 241, 265
national service, 218
responsibility, 265
secrecy, 221
selfishness, 265
service, 265
terrorism, 38, 280
trust, 263
vigilance, 16, 138, 265
violence, 265, 274
Cuomo, Andrew, 151
Curry, Dayna, 161

Daalder, Ivo, 290
Dakota culture, 154, 158, 205
DARPA (Defense Advance
    Research Projects Agency),
    158
Daschle, Tom, 47, 183
Dearborn, Michigan, 197
dehumanization
    in American culture, 34, 99,
    111, 113, 262
    and cultural self-esteem, 143
    and technology, 74
    and terrorism, 36, 57, 99, 106,
    186
denial, 22, 92-93, 119-20, 240,
    266
    and mental health, 88, 115-22
depression, 72, 92
    in America, 16, 72, 78, 83-85,
    115-17, 129, 131, 134, 193
    and Bishop, 122-23
    and Flores, 110

and Helder, 100-01
and Kaczynski, 65-66, 78, 81-
    85, 88, 123, 272
and social isolation, 139, 193
DHS (Department of Homeland
    Security), 45, 116, 241,
    246, 250, 253, 257, 268
    and centralization, 244, 252-
    53
    culture of, 241-42, 250-51,
    253, 255, 261-62
    establishment of, 247
    and hierarchy, 254-55
    plan for, 238-39, 242, 248-49,
    253
Diamondbacks (Arizona), 171-73
Disney, 161
docudrama 9/11, 129, 134, 187
DOD (Department of Defense),
    19, 169, 248, 250, 253
DOJ (Department of Justice), 248
DOS (Department of State), 21
DOT (Department of
    Transportation), 255
dots, 96, 124-25, 177-78, 181,
    189, 191, 225, 266, 271
    and FBI, 177-78, 202-23,
    226, 228, 230, 238, 281
    and government, 237, 246,
    249, 250-51, 263, 268
    informational, 201, 227, 238,
    267
    social, 116, 192, 201-02
Douglas, John, 82, 271
dreams, 39, 102, 122, 204, 271
    and Hollywood, 163, 271
    after 9/11, 132, 181
    and sports, 162, 169, 171, 181
dropper popper, 267
Dulin, Danny, 111
Durst, Fred, 181

eagle, 205
Eagle-Pilcher, 149
ELF (Earth Liberation Front), 113
Elohim City, 62
Enron, 12, 151, 155
environmental rights groups, 91
Etzioni, Amitai, 198, 220
experts, 136, 165, 219, 240
    and FBI, 78, 225, 231-32,
    234-35
    and Helder, 100
    and Kaczynski, 66, 72-73,
    76-84
    psychiatric/psychological
    (see also experts and
    Kaczynski), 100, 119, 128,
    133
    scientific, 231, 234
    security and terrorism, 104,
    149, 210, 219, 248

family, 38, 68, 78
    of Bishop, 122
    of Helder, 96-98
    of Kaczynski, 81
    of 9/11 victims, 129, 156-57,
    189, 203, 219, 275
    in post-9/11 America, 24, 53,
    57, 124, 157, 167, 169, 207
    in pre-9/11 America, 28, 35,
    190, 194
    stronger in post-9/11
    America, 158, 165, 175, 180,
    188, 189, 202
Fanfare for the Common Man,
    142, 274
FBI (Federal Bureau of
    Investigation) (see also
    Douglas, John, Mueller,
    Robert, and Rowley,
    Coleen), 185, 217, 219,
    243, 267, 289

and anthrax, 39, 63-64, 100,
    227-36
attitude, 46, 177, 220
    as bureaucracy, 250-51, 253
    and "closed" culture, 240,
    251
    and culture, 16, 56, 97, 177,
    212, 221-28, 242, 261
    and dots, 177-78, 202-03,
    226, 228, 230, 238, 281
    and Helder, 98-102
    and Kaczynski, 15, 64-72,
    78-79, 82, 222, 271
    and McVeigh, 61-62, 89
    and Moussaoui, 177, 227,
    236, 246-47
    and Muhammad, 67, 105-06,
    279
    post-9/11, 41, 154-55, 167,
    177, 189
    terrorism definition, 21, 214,
    279
fear (see also anxiety), 11-12, 79,
    160, 166
    in American culture, 43, 113,
    115-19, 121-31, 135-39, 194-
    95, 272-73
    and anthrax, 40, 94, 118, 137
    and FBI, 223, 225, 229
    and Helder, 96, 99
    and Kaczynski, 80, 89, 102,
    272
    and Muhammad, 62, 99, 107
    in post-9/11 America, 37, 41,
    171, 182, 184, 194-95, 276
    and psychological warfare,
    129, 209
    and social cooperation, 199,
    205, 211
    and terrorism, 22-24, 37-38,
    129, 184, 208, 212, 215, 266-
    72

Fears, Daniel, 110
Federation of American
     Scientists, 231
Feinstein, Diane, 232
FEMA (Federal Emergency
     Management Agency),
     248
fetish, 32, 261-62
Fireman Santa, 53
Firestone, 149
flag (*see* American flag)
Florence, Colorado, 86
Flores, Robert, 12, 109-10
Florida, state of, 95, 211
football, 55, 125, 174
Foster, Don, 282
Frasca, David, 178, 236, 247
freedom, 68, 141, 174, 207-20
     and Bishop, 123
     and Helder, 102
     and independence, 28-30, 33,
        35-36, 201, 266-67, 269, 276
     and Kaczynski, 112-13
     and Lovett, 112-13
Friends, 165

Gale, Steven, 281
Gateway, 175
Gaylin, Willard, 280
Geertz, Clifford, 144
General Motors, 152-53
generation D, 181
generation X, 181
Georgia, state of, 64
Gertz, Bill, 257
Glassner, Barry, 117
Graham, Bob, 212, 242, 262
Grammy Awards, 167
Ground Zero, 41, 156-57, 167,
     180, 187, 218, 217, 267,
     275
     bureaucratic, 223

consecration of, 142-43
and culture, 176, 260, 273,
     277
effects emanating from, 123,
     143, 156-57
permanence, 180
psychological, 115-40
rebuilding, 159-60
Guiliani, Rudi, 40, 148, 156, 173
Gulf War, 12, 110, 124

Halloween, 267
Hamdi, Yaser, 213, 289
Hanks, Tom, 160-64
Hanlan, James, 187
Hanssen, Robert, 224
Harris, Eric, 76, 83, 91, 94-96,
     122
     diary, 94-95
     as icon of terror, 45, 193
     psyche, 123
Harvard University, 271
Hatfill, Stephen, 240
Healy, Bernadine, 155
Helder, Cameron, 98, 113
Helder, Luke, 94, 95-103
     and other terrorism, 25, 99-
        100, 103-04, 110, 123
     profile, 95, 99-102, 104, 107,
        233
     psyche, 61, 96-97, 99-100,
        123
     as terrorist, 98-99, 106, 279
     writings, 96, 99-103, 104,
        109, 271
Helena, Montana, 64, 235
Herbeck, Dan, 288
Hewitt, John, 281
Higgins, Joseph, 274
Hiroshima, 15-16
hoax, 55, 94, 130, 137
hoaxer, 45, 67, 70, 131

hockey, 181, 274
Hollywood, California, 161,
163, 164, 169
Home Depot, 158
Homeland Defense Journal, 163
House Select Committee on
Intelligence, 239, 241,
243
human sacrifice, 141, 270, 272
Hurtt, Harold, 256
Hussein, Saddam, 111, 191
hysteria, 207, 209, 215

I Love Lucy, 165
independence, 266-67
and freedom, 28-30, 33, 35-
36, 201, 266-67, 269, 276
and Helder, 102
India, 259
individualism
and addiction, 275
in American culture, 26, 30,
58-59, 112, 138, 165, 190,
195, 246
combating, 194, 265
culture of, 22, 53, 127, 152,
169
excessive, 34, 128, 151, 205,
263
extreme, 34, 125, 127, 151,
192, 206, 266, 269, 276
hyper-, 46, 61, 267
organizational, 35, 221, 227,
238, 252
paradox of, 39, 48
radical, 55-56, 194, 242
restructuring, 36, 190, 194,
264, 270-71
and social isolation, 55, 192,
198, 201-02, 206, 227
and terrorism, 30, 34-35, 44,
48, 54, 58, 92, 94, 97

INS (Immigration and
Naturalization Service), 56,
229
integrity, 41, 173-74, 186, 236,
266
cultural, 41, 120, 213, 286
of individuals, 131, 182, 185-
86, 270
and Kaczynski, 71, 87, 89
and Rowley, 12-14, 237-39
Internet, 63, 68, 74, 207, 218, 280
and community, 58, 197
interoperability, 257
inversion, 123, 168
Iowa, state of, 99
Iraq
U.S. military in, 110
war in, 11, 131, 165, 169,
175, 240
Israel, 259
Israeli security, 259

jackal
within America, 42, 44-46,
62, 90, 91, 95, 187, 273
and Bishop, 122
combating, 201, 219, 235,
268, 271
and complacency, 129, 271
and confusion/disconnec-
tion, 193-94, 212
and Helder, 97, 103
and integrity, 185
and Kaczynski, 89
and McVeigh, 61, 89, 276
and Muhammad, 104, 106-07
path of the, 49, 92-93, 95,
211, 264, 273
vs. phoenix, 125, 173, 207,
269, 277
supporting, 61, 131, 140, 186
totem, defined, 38-41

jackal clan, 38, 39, 43, 186, 202, 270, 272
diversification of, 91-92, 94-95, 112, 122
Janoff-Bulman, Ronnie, 136
Jefferson, Thomas, 276
Jerusalem, Israel, 259
Johnson, Nadine, 118-20, 124
Johnson, Sally, 80-81
Jones, Jim, 141
Jones, Stephen, 60, 281, 288
Jones, Steven, 92-93
Junta, Thomas, 275

K Street, 169
Kaczynski, David, 71, 98, 161
Kaczynski, Ted (*see also* Unabomber), 161, 183, 186, 222, 224, 233, 271-72, 277
and anthropology, 77-78
and experts, 76-77, 79, 81
as icon of terror, 90, 91, 96, 97, 99, 125, 142
and McVeigh, 86-90
and mental health, 79-80, 82, 87-88
delusions, paranoid schizophrenia, 80, 93, 282
depression, 65, 72, 81-82, 84-85, 123
and society, 83, 90, 125
suicide, 82, 87-88
and other terrorists, 94, 99-102, 109-10, 112-13
and personal disenfranchisement, 84, 99, 203
profile, 15-16, 64, 70-72, 78, 100, 107-08
publication, 73, 90
and social isolation, 61, 65, 79, 85

at Supermax, 38, 49, 86-90, 137
and technology, 65, 73-76, 149
as terrorist, 22, 130
trial/retrial, 64, 86-88
Kagan, Daryn, 119
Kanemeyer, Sally, 189
Kansas, state of, 91-92
King, Stephen, 95
Kirn, Walter, 110
Kissinger, Henry, 173
Klebold, Dylan, 76, 83, 91, 95, 122, 193
Kleinman, Arthur, 131
Knoblauch, Chuck, 171, 173
Krugman, Paul, 150-51
Ku Klux Klan, 280
Kushner, Harvey W., 282

Lance, Peter, 226-28, 281
Larry King Live, 166
Las Vegas, Nevada, 157, 249, 250
Laverne and Shirley, 165
Leahy, Patrick, 230
Lee, Wen Ho, 224
Libeskind, Daniel, 143, 159
Lindh, Frank, 94, 186
Lindh, John Walker, 94-95, 248
Linenthal, Edward T., 142
Little League, 174
Logan airport, 259
lone, 22, 91, 218, 233-34
terrorist, 22, 112, 226, 233
"wolf", 39, 232-33
loner, 101, 121, 233-36
Lopez, Jennifer, 164
Lovett, Matthew, 112-13, 140
Lucas, George (*Attack of the Clones*), 163

Malvo, Lee, 94, 103, 107, 110,
111, 113
Markle Foundation, 244, 252
Marquesas Islands, 146
Marxism, 78
Maryland, Rockville, 105
Massachusetts, state of, 274
Matrix, 113
McDonald's, 159
McLaughlin, John Jason, 114
McVeigh, Tim, 16, 27, 47, 59-
63, 85, 102, 145, 186, 190
and adversariality with
government, 49, 59-62, 89,
209, 277
apprehension, trial, and post-
trial, 48, 60, 224, 254
and collateral damage, 58
conspiracy, 233, 281
execution, 59, 62, 89, 108,
142, 193
as a "good boy," 94
as icon of terror, 45, 91, 96,
98, 125
mental health, 288
speeches, 264, 276
at Supermax, 86-90
as terrorist, 22, 38, 62, 99,
142, 276
as veteran, 12, 110
Mead, Margaret, 9, 15-16, 65,
277
Melville, Herman, 92
mental health, 79, 160, 284
in America, 16, 42, 73, 83-84,
88, 115-23, 128-29, 273
and Kaczynski (*see also*
Kaczynski, Ted and mental
health), 65, 72-73, 79-82, 84,
87-90, 98, 117
and McVeigh, 288

mental illness, 80-83, 90, 118
Mercer, Heather, 161
Miami, Florida, 25, 95, 121
Michel, Lou, 288
militia groups, 91, 112, 193,
243
Minnesota, state of, 66, 95, 101
Missouri, state of, 149
Montana, state of, 64, 130, 193,
233
Montgomery County, Maryland,
105
Moore Michael (*Bowling for
Columbine*), 165, 280
Moose, Charles, 105, 109, 167
Morgan, Lewis Henry, 77-78
Moussaoui, Zacarias, 179, 213
and Minneapolis FBI, 177,
227, 236, 246-47
Mueller, Robert, 219, 279
on FBI reorganization and
culture change, 240-42
and letters from Coleen
Rowley, 224, 227, 235, 236,
239, 240
negative public response to,
231
post-9/11 speeches, 214, 228,
229-31, 240, 241
Muhammad, John, 12, 23-24,
45, 103-10
and media, 94, 108-09
phone calls, 67, 105-06
as terrorist, 103, 104, 106, 214
Murrah Federal Building, 45, 58
Mussina, Mike, 173
myth, 39-40, 257, 277
and baseball, 170-72, 175
cultural, 35, 52, 74, 241-42,
245, 257, 259
and culture change, 145, 147,
246, 248, 250
as story, 241

National Advertising Council, 166
national character (*see* American national character)
National Mall, 111
National Press Club, 166
national psyche (*see* American national psyche)
Native Americans (*see also* Dakota culture), 204
neo-Nazis, 280
New Bedford, Massachusetts, 92
New Golden Rule, 220
new normal, 30, 52, 94, 115, 168, 203-06, 207, 275
    as uncertain, 126-27
    and violence, 207
New York City, 40, 95, 146, 195, 282
    fire fighters, 133, 136, 148, 151, 187, 203, 274
    post-9/11, 119-20, 145-46, 148, 156, 158, 180, 184, 188, 267
    in post-9/11 national community, 58, 138, 156, 178, 202
    and 2001 World Series, 170-73
New York, state of, 62, 64, 189, 204
    governor of, 151, 180, 189
New York Times, 68, 110, 111, 127, 276
Newsday, 11-14
Newsweek, 66, 119, 148, 189, 203, 253
NFL (National Football League), 174
Nichols, Terry, 281
Nobel laureates, 273
NORC (National Opinion Research Center), 128
North Carolina, state of, 124
NRO (National Reconnaissance Office), 289
NSA (National Security Agency), 19, 250, 261, 289
Nutcracker Uncle Sam, 53

Oakland, California, 175
Oaklyn, New Jersey, 112
Ohio, state of, 113
Oklahoma City, 16, 145, 188
Oklahoma City bombing, 42, 45, 59-63, 67, 86, 124, 200, 281
    and mass trauma, 120-21, 123, 139
    and symbolic transformation, 142
Oklahoma, state of, 62, 110
Oldsmobile, 152
Olson, Sara Jane, 180, 222
Olympic Park, 112
Olympics, Winter, 169, 174
O'Neill, Paul, 243
orange alerts, 255-56
    and anxiety, 11, 131, 188, 207
Organized Crime/Terrorism 101, 240

Padilla, José, 208, 213, 289
panic, 11, 12, 171, 215
Pashtun, 244, 252, 276
Pataki, George, 151, 180, 189
Patriot Act, 187, 212, 214, 225, 273
Patriots (New England), 174
Paxil, 85
Pearl Harbor, 180, 196, 201
Pennsylvania, state of, 94, 114, 189
Pentagon, 30, 41, 141, 158, 267

pheasant, 40
Philippines, 281
phoenix
    authentic and fake, 270-27
    and baseball, 170-73
    clan, 140, 191
    and new normal, 127, 207
    and post-9/11 America, 46,
        49, 92, 103, 125, 143, 185,
        267, 269
    and post-traumatic stress, 135
    totem, defined, 39-43
    and whistle blowers, 155
Phoenix, Arizona, 170-72, 256
Phoenix Fire Department, 41,
    171
Phoenix memo, 41, 89, 177,
    235, 236, 240, 247, 268
Phoenix Project, 41
Phone Booth, 163
pipe bomb, 24-25, 95, 137
Pitt, Brad, 206
plumbing
    bathroom, 56-57, 199, 226,
        249
    bureaucratic, 249-51
Pogo, 45
police (*see also* Hurtt, Harold,
    and Moose, Charles), 196,
    235, 254, 256, 259
    New York, 148, 243
Pontiac, 153
Poppins, Mary, 163
post-traumatic growth, 135-39
post-traumatic stress (PTSD),
    136, 139, 284
    cultural, 37, 110, 113, 120-21,
        135, 147
    individual, 78, 120-21, 124,
        172
Potter, Harry, 163, 174
Pottery Barn, 158

Powell, Colin, 183, 243
Preger, Yaakov, 259
profile
    of anthrax perpetrator, 63-64,
        100, 230, 232-35
    of Helder, 95, 99-102, 104,
        107, 233
    of Kaczynski, 15-16, 64, 70-
        72, 78, 100, 107-08
    of Muhammad, 104-05, 107-
        08
profiling
    American culture, 116, 118,
        129, 269
    American terrorists, 47, 82-85
    the FBI, 225
    improving, 101, 107-08, 234-
        35
Prozac, 85, 121
psychological warfare, 43, 129,
    132, 209
Putnam, Robert, 192-97, 201,
    219-20, 288
Pyszczynski, Tom, 286

rage, 232, 275
    cell phone, 200
    road, 62, 90, 117, 200, 275
    sports, 174, 200, 275
Rand Corporation, 132-33
random victims, 24, 99, 104,
    112
Rather, Dan, 40-41, 147, 148,
    173
reality TV, 108, 146-47, 162,
    164-65, 168-69, 276
reciprocity
    generalized, 288
    inverse, 200
    social, 194-95, 198-99, 203,
        211, 218, 277, 288
Red Cross, 154-56

Reeve, Simon, 38
Rehn, Trista, 168
Reid, Richard, 138, 213, 217, 240
Remedial Social Thinking 101,
    63, 199, 236, 239, 240
Ridge, Tom, 44, 230, 256-57
Rite of Spring, 267-68
ritual, 111, 179, 272
    combat (*see also* sports), 145,
    162, 169-76
    culture as ritual object, 261-62
    objects, 53, 75, 261-62
    and recovery/revival, 141-42,
    145-47, 162, 167-76, 274
    sacrifice, 77, 92, 100, 141-45,
    173
Roberts, Julia, 274
Rockville, Maryland, 105
Rockwell, Norman, 180, 230
Romero, Anthony, 210
Ron, Rafi, 259
Rosenberg, Barbara Hatch, 227,
    231
Rowley, Coleen, 89, 217, 235,
    236-41, 268, 271
    and FBI publicity, 236
    foreword by, 11-14
    as humanized image for FBI,
    224
    and integrity, 238-39
    as internal FBI critic, 226, 227
Ruby Ridge, 224
Rudolph, Eric, 112, 233, 254
Rumsfeld, Donald, 83, 243, 287
Ryder truck, 45

sacrifice (*see also* human
    sacrifice), 36, 49, 77, 142,
    173, 276
Salt Lake City, Utah, 174-75
San Diego, California, 113
Sandler O'Neill, 157

Savage, Michael, 280
scapegoat, 223-24
scapegoating, 97, 165, 223
Schilling, Curt, 172
schizophrenia, 80-82, 100
Schneier, Bruce, 210, 248, 259,
    279
Schoor, Daniel, 182
Schwarzenegger, Arnold, 163
self-esteem, 128, 281
    cultural, 31, 108, 127-28,
    130, 139, 143, 190, 210-11
    individual, 122-23, 128
self-interest, 27, 34-36, 46, 248
    cultural rule serving, 28, 34,
    69, 128, 152-55, 192, 198
    and FBI, 71, 221, 237
    and organizations, 35, 152-
    53, 222, 226-28, 246-47,
    251, 260, 263
Senate, U.S., 242
Silicon Valley, 157
Simon, Paul, 18
60 Minutes, 240
social capital, 193-95, 197, 201,
    203, 219, 288
Social Darwinism, 77
social psychology, 116, 118, 132
Soliyah, Kathleen (*see* Olson,
    Sara Jane)
Spears, Britney, 76, 165
Spiderman, 163-64
sports (*see also* baseball, football,
    hockey, Olympics), 34, 38,
    84, 101, 123, 145, 162,
    181, 199-200
    and cultural recovery from
    9/11, 163, 169-76
    post-9/11, 145, 160, 187
    youth, 16, 275
St. Hilaire, Susan, 92-94
St. Patrick's Day parade, 146

St. Paul Pioneer Press, 15
stereotypes
  of Americans, 63, 137
  of FBI, 225-26
  of racial/ethnic groups, 108,
    213
  of terrorists, 82, 84
Stern, Jessica, 57
stories, 16, 131, 162, 167, 204,
    228
  cultural, 144, 168, 194, 250,
    254, 268-69, 271
  post-9/11, 144-45, 147, 157,
    184, 204-05, 239, 254, 276
stovepipes, 215, 241-57, 277
  break down of, 213, 252,
    262-63
Stravinsky, Igor (*The Rite of
    Spring*), 267
subculture, 33, 101, 194, 207,
    280
  American bureaucratic, 35,
    56, 213, 242, 245-46, 262
  of Berkeley in 1970s, 16, 64,
    72
  of FBI, 221-28, 240
suicide, 92, 93
  and Bishop, 25, 95, 121-22
  bombing, 114, 186, 189, 259
  and Flores, 109
  and Harris, 83
  and Helder, 100
  and Kaczynski, 81, 87-89
Sullivan, Scott, 243
Sun Tzu, 42-43
Super Bowl, 145, 165, 169, 174-
    75
Supermax federal prison, 38, 49,
    78, 86-90,137, 277
Supreme Court, U.S., 88
Survivor, 146, 165, 168

Symbionese Liberation Army,
    180
symbolism, 30, 130, 185, 204,
    263
  and cultural identity, 104,
    133, 137, 139, 141-76, 258,
    260, 274
  and FBI, 224-25
  and flag, 204-05
  and humans, 77, 99, 148,
    156, 160, 230, 276
  and profiles, 107
  and terrorism, 24, 30, 77, 99,
    108, 189, 286
  and totems, 38-41, 267

taboo, 132, 143, 150, 151, 154,
    217
Taliban, 141-42, 161, 244
  Americans and the, 94, 122,
    190
technology, 23, 130, 185, 204,
    207
  and critique of Unabomber
    Manifesto, 73-78
  and culture, 65, 263, 270,
    277
  and culture change, 56, 65,
    68, 241, 245, 252, 258-60,
    262, 271
  and fear, 117
  and Helder, 102
  and post-9/11 symbol shift,
    142-44, 147-50, 274
  in Unabomber Manifesto, 65-
    68
Tel Aviv, Israel, 259
television (*see also* reality TV)
    15, 46, 130, 148-49, 200
  post-9/11, 151-52, 164-68,
    182, 197

and terrorism, 89, 101, 106, 129, 140
terror, 235
  in America, 16, 21-114, 186, 191, 213-14, 234, 246, 264, 267-77
  and psychology, 118, 126-31, 186, 266
  and responses by U.S. government, 209-10, 215-16, 227, 232, 236, 259
  and symbols, 142, 189
terrorism, 16, 281
  combating, 11-12, 41-50, 177-220, 266-77, 280
  defined, 21-26, 279, 280
  domestic, 59-114
  and 9/11, 51-53
  and psychology, 115-40
  and symbolism, 141-76, 286
  and terror in America, 26-38
  and totems, 38-41
  and U.S. government, 221-64
terrorists, 38, 186, 277, 279, 281-82
  American/domestic, 12-289
  confusion in post-9/11 America about "domestic" terrorists, 213-26
  foreign, 38, 44, 46, 51-53, 57, 62, 67, 104, 241
  mental profile, 82-85
  9/11, 11, 36-37, 51, 56, 142, 144, 179, 209, 243
  pursuing and preventing, 13, 27, 35, 147, 192, 247
  symbols for, 38-41
Texas, state of, 207
Thirteen, 164
Time, 12, 13, 82, 87-88, 148, 184, 207
Times Square, 218

TIPOFF, 216
Titanic, 249
Tocqueville, Alexis de, 190
trauma (*see also* post-traumatic stress), 120, 123, 129, 135, 139, 267-68, 284
  cultural, 59, 92, 224, 276
  denial of, 103, 119, 126
  and media, 110
  terrorism and, 24-25, 37, 121
  and violence, 25, 126
  individual, 11, 25, 100, 118-19, 124, 126, 140, 180, 212
tribal
  as concept in U.S. government, 243-44
  social structure and process, 44, 244-45, 252, 256, 290
True, Jeff (*see* Burt, Leo)
trust, 13, 43, 67, 71, 73, 196-97
  ambiguity in trust of American government, 45, 188, 196, 242
  between public and American government, 49, 183-84, 187, 196, 198, 211, 215, 264, 276
  and FBI, 224-28
  in post-9/11 America, 126, 155, 169, 194-97, 201, 204
  on 9/11, 243
  within American government, 250-51
  within American public, 124, 194, 257
TSA (Transportation Security Agency), 255
Twin Towers, 129, 143, 268, 282
  and baseball, 170-73
  and media, 155, 164-65
  reinterpreted, 148, 273

Unabomber (*see also* Kaczynski, Ted, and Unabomber Manifesto), 15-16, 38, 63-95, 236, 269-70
investigation, 65-72, 79, 105, 167
and media, 161
and mental health, 65, 72-73, 79-82, 84, 87-90, 98, 117
and other terrorists, 94, 96, 105, 229, 269
and personal disempowerment, 84-85, 182, 203
profile, 64, 72, 107
and technology, 65, 73-76, 149
as terrorist, 23, 269
Unabomber Manifesto, 86-88, 132
analysis of, 64-72
compared to Helder's writings, 99-100
critique of, 73-82
United Kingdom Special Branch, 259
United Nations (*see also* Annan, Kofi), 21
United States, 4, 12, 215, 238, 248
University of Arizona, 12, 109
University of California, 15, 68, 82
University of Michigan, 272
University of Pennsylvania, 281
USA Today, 107, 256

Valley Stream, New York, 195
Vietnam veterans, 124
Virginia, state of, 70
Visa, 175

Waagner, Clayton Lee, 55, 94
Waco, Texas, 86, 224
Walker, David, 248
Wal-Mart, 137, 158, 182
Washington, D.C., 161
and antiterrorism, 250, 252, 256
and 9/11, 57, 58, 161, 230, 237
Washington Post, 68
Washington, state of, 94
Watkins, Sherron, 12
Watson, Dwight, 111
Werling, Delores, 99
West Virginia, state of, 113, 214
whistle blowers, 151, 155, 242
Williams, Kenneth, 236
Workman, Chuck, 274
World Series
2001, 41, 63, 156, 170-73, 181, 267
2002, 175
World Trade Center, 281-82
aftermath of 2001 attack, 11, 41, 120, 133, 175, 179, 274-75
1993 bombing, 38, 40, 86
2001 bombing, 30, 45, 141, 156-57, 205, 243
world view, 26, 127-29, 190, 202, 266, 286
World War I, 120
World War II, 121, 136, 180
WorldCom, 12, 243

Yale University, 24
Yankee Stadium, 170
Yankees (New York), 170-73
Yousef, Ramzi, 38, 86, 281

Zoloft, 78